Q

...d much...

MOTHER

*To my wife Elizabeth and
our daughter Madeleine*

QUEEN MOTHER

A Biblical Theology of Mary's Queenship

EDWARD SRI

— General Editor —
SCOTT HAHN

EMMAUS ROAD
PUBLISHING

Steubenville, Ohio
A Division of Catholics United for the Faith

The Letter & Spirit Project

Emmaus Road Publishing
827 North Fourth Street
Steubenville, Ohio 43952

Reprinted from the doctoral dissertation *Queen Mother* by Edward Sri.
Defended and approved February 20, 2001 at the
Pontifical University of St. Thomas Aquinas, Rome.

Library of Congress Control Number: 2004117767
ISBN: 1-931018-24-3

Cover design and layout by
Beth Hart

Cover artwork:
Agnolo Gaddi, *Coronation of the Virgin* (detail)
Samuel H. Kress Collection, Image © Board of Trustees,
National Gallery of Art, Washington

Contents

INTRODUCTION

— 1 —

CHAPTER ONE

Toward a Biblical Theology of Mary's Queenship

— 5 —

CHAPTER TWO

The Queen Mother in the Old Testament

— 45 —

CHAPTER THREE
The Queen Mother and the
New Testament Portrayal of Mary
— 67 —

CHAPTER FOUR
Summary Conclusions
— 105 —

The Letter & Spirit Project

This publication appears as part of the Letter & Spirit Project, a series sponsored by the St. Paul Center for Biblical Theology. The Project aims to advance the work of biblical theology by publishing studies of important themes in Sacred Scripture from literary, historical, and theological perspectives. Biblical theology requires the integration of these various fields of research.

Of all the documents history has bequeathed to us, Scripture is unique. Only the Bible is "inspired by God" (2 Tim. 3:16). The Church has always held that God the Holy Spirit is the principal author of Scripture, though the human authors freely cooperated in this work. This mystery of dual authorship reflects the mystery of Jesus Christ. He is the Word Incarnate; the Bible is the Word inspired. Christ is without sin; the Bible is without error. Like Christ, the Scriptures are given "for the sake of our salvation,"[1] and both give us God's definitive self-revelation.

Understanding of the Bible, then, requires the study of both the divine and human elements, the theological and spiritual as well as the literary and historical. Biblical theology, in particular, requires an integrated study of these divine and human elements. For they are united in a way analogous to the union of the two natures of Christ—integrally united, though without confusion or division. If we distinguish between these elements, we distinguish not to separate, but to unite. Biblical theologians since Augustine (and even before) have operated according to these principles: we can only arrive at spiritual and theological truth by first determining the human author's intended meaning. Hugh of St. Victor expressed this in a compact way: *Historia fundamentum est* ("history is the foundation"). Thomas Aquinas developed this by saying: "All other senses of Sacred Scripture are based on the literal."[2]

We begin with the human because it is in the humanity of the Word that the full revelation of divinity has come to us. Again, since the Lord of History is the author of the sacred page, there is no confusion or division. A single divine economy (*oikonomia*) is at work both in salvation history and in its inspired record. Augustine said that ordinary human writers use words to signify things; but God uses even created things to signify things. So not only are the words of Scripture signs of things that happened in history, but the very events of sacred history were fashioned by God as material signs that show us immaterial realities—temporal events that disclose eternal truths.[3] Thus, the literary sense of the Bible conveys historical truth, which is itself the Scripture's divine meaning. As Augustine said: The literary sense is the sign (*signum*), of which the historical truth is the signified (*signatum*).

Christ is the meaning of all Scripture. The New Testament itself makes this abundantly clear. Yet it is equally clear that the fulfillment of the Old Covenant did not terminate with His death and Resurrection. The fulfillment continues in the church through the sacraments, by the power of the Holy Spirit. This fulfillment takes place especially in the liturgy, but never apart from Scripture. Scripture is what explicates the meaning of the sacraments; the sacraments actualize the truths and mysteries of salvation history.

This Project takes as its starting point articles 11 and 12 of *Dei Verbum*, the Second Vatican Council's dogmatic constitution on divine revelation. Beginning from the premise of dual authorship, the council encourages scholars in the careful and faithful employment of methods of literary study—analysis of form, genre, grammar, logic, rhetoric—and to do the same with historical analysis, examining events against their cultural background.

The council's guidance culminates in the establishment of three criteria for interpreting Scripture. The *Catechism of the Catholic Church* extracts those criteria and distills them into imperative statements:

> 1. "Be especially attentive to the 'content and unity of the whole Scripture'" (no. 112).
>
> 2. "Read the Scripture within 'the living Tradition of the whole Church'" (no. 113).
>
> 3. "Be attentive to the analogy of faith"—that is the "coherence of the truths of faith among themselves and within the whole of revelation" (no. 114).

The *Catechism* concludes: "It is the task of exegetes to work, according to these rules, towards a better understanding and explanation of the meaning of Sacred Scripture in order that their research may help the Church to form a firmer judgment" (no. 119).

These principles stand as a safeguard against academic, cultural, or temporal provincialism. They also protect scholars from the danger of falling into allegorism. The events and realities of the biblical record possess their own historical dignity and integrity, but they stand also as signs of divine mysteries. This is a profound consequence of the Incarnation: the eternal comes to us through the temporal.

No study in this series can accomplish all the goals of the Project. That is the work of several lifetimes. Each study focuses on particular elements—literary, historical, or theological—and each shows a boldness in breaking down the artificial barriers and barricades raised by recent generations in the academy.

Most of these works began as doctoral dissertations, which were completed over the last several decades. They stand as examples of the kind of scholarship that can and should be done in service to the Church. They have been chosen for the quality of their technical presentation, but we hope that interested lay readers will also find them accessible. We present the Letter & Spirit Project to all who are interested in the cultivation of a deep faith informed by reason.

SCOTT HAHN, PH.D.
Founder and President
St. Paul Center for Biblical Theology

Foreword

In the course of the last century, theology, like most academic disciplines, has fragmented into many sub-disciplines, each working in isolation from all the others. Dogmatic theologians sometimes assume they have little to learn from biblical scholars. Exegetes, for their part, often neglect the insights of systematic and dogmatic theologians. To many scholars, these disciplines are almost contradictory: exegesis is opposed to dogma, and vice-versa.

With this majestic study, Edward Sri shows all these diverse practitioners a way out into a wider world, a more "catholic" vision. In *Queen Mother*, he shows us Mariology's potential to gather the scattered disciplines by modeling an integrative, holistic approach—a *biblical theology* that integrates such seemingly diffuse and disparate fields as dogma, exegesis, and liturgy.

There are many misconceptions about biblical theology and how it differs from systematic theology. It is not as if a systematic theologian is bound by logic while a biblical theologian is free to be illogical and unsystematic. Rather, the ordering principle behind systematic theology is the logical progression of the doctrines of theology, whereas the biblical theologian recognizes an order, a plan in salvation history. It is a different systematic ordering principle, but it is no less systematic.

Biblical theology admits (broadly speaking) of two angles of approach, one deductive and one inductive. The former approach, favored by the Fathers, begins with the divine *oikonomia*, the economy, the metanarrative or overarching plot of the canonical Scriptures. The latter approach, favored by the French Catholic biblical scholars in the twentieth century, observes in Scripture certain dominant themes—creation, sin, redemption, sacrifice, covenant, kingdom, temple—and marks their development through salvation history.

The great virtue of Sri's study is that he faces the choice between two angles of approach, and he chooses both. He traces the "queen mother" motif in the literature of the ancient Near East in general and in the Davidic kingdom in particular, and he identifies it in key prophetic texts, such as Isaiah 7:14 and Genesis 3:15. As he moves from the Old Testament to the New, he shows how the typology of Matthew 1–2 is illuminated by the Davidic kingdom in general and specifically the figure of the *gebirah*, the queen mother. Proceeding through the New Testament, he takes his investigation to the outer limits of the canon—to Revelation 12, the vision of the woman clothed with the sun—to show the convergence of all that the biblical record contains of the *gebirah*.

The inductive study of Scripture's themes leads Sri to the recognition of its overarching unity, the divine economy. On that firm foundation he is able to build his typological study. Thus, the typology he discerns is not merely a construct of literary symbols or an allegoristic reinterpretation of an ancient text. True typology is rooted in the literary sense that gives us the historical truth of the canonical record of Scripture, and that overarching historical truth is the divine economy.

Sri's approach demands a serious engagement of the biblical canon, and that means both testaments. *Dei Verbum* instructed biblical interpreters to "be especially attentive 'to the content and unity of the whole Scripture,'" and this instruction was repeated verbatim in the *Catechism of the Catholic Church* (*DV* 12; *Catechism*, no. 112).

Our attention "to the content and unity of the whole Scripture" leads us logically to a typological reading. Typology is an essential element in our biblical theology of Mary, and we need not shrink from it. It is superfluous to say that typology was integral to the patristic and medieval methods of exegesis and theology. It is self-evident that typology is the natural mode of understanding for the New Testament authors (and Jesus Himself), all of whom understood the entire Old Testament as inseparable from the Gospel they proclaimed. Saint Paul described Adam as a "type" of Jesus Christ (Rom. 5:14). It is no news that typology is endorsed by the *Catechism of the Catholic Church.*

Indeed, a cursory reading of the Old Testament should show that typological method predates Christianity by many centuries. Jewish exegetes and historians—Michael Fishbane and Alan Segal, to name only two—see it as pervasive in the Torah and the Haftarot, as well as the intertestamental literature.

What has all this to do with dogma, much less dogmatic theology? Cardinal Ratzinger has put the matter succinctly. Dogma, he says, "is by definition nothing other than an interpretation of Scripture."[1] His insight has been confirmed by the most august group of his fellow theologians, the International Theological Commission, in its 1989 document *On the Interpretation of Dogmas*: "In the dogma of the Church, one is thus concerned with the correct interpretation of the Scriptures."[2] Dogma, then, is the Church's infallible exegesis, and dogmatic theology is a reflection upon that work.

This, then, is the genius of Sri's work. It shows us the profound theological relationship between the *gebirah* of ancient Israel and the dogma of Mary's queenship. Here as elsewhere, dogma is dependent on exegesis. Indeed, dogma is nothing less than exegesis, confirmed authoritatively by Tradition and the Church.

Sri's study is important for Mariology, but it is important, too, as a model for all biblical theology. An approach like his provides theologians with superior interpretive and explanatory power and has the potential to heal historic divisions between scholars and Church, between the academy and the seminary, and among the various separated Christian bodies. Read without preconceived bias or agenda, the Scriptures yield meanings that are not at all in conflict with the meanings and purpose claimed for these texts by the Church. When we read the Bible in this way, we find no tension between letter and spirit—between literary and historical study of Scripture and faithful contemplation of its religious and spiritual meaning.

SCOTT HAHN, PH.D.
Founder and President
St. Paul Center for Biblical Theology

Acknowledgments

I wish to express my gratitude to the faculty of the Pontifical University of St. Thomas Aquinas for their teaching and guidance during my years of study in Rome. In particular, I thank Fr. Joseph Agius, O.P., for playing an important part in this process, serving as dean of theology and as president of the doctoral board. I also thank Sr. Mary O'Driscoll, O.P., for taking on this project as the second reader. Her valuable insights and critiques have been deeply appreciated and have enhanced the overall development of the work. Others who offered helpful feedback at different stages of the work deserve to be mentioned with gratitude as well: Fr. Terence McGuckin, Fr. Robert Christian, O.P., Dr. Scott Hahn, and especially Fr. Paul Murray, O.P., Dr. Richard White, and Curtis Mitch, whose generosity, wisdom, and friendship were particularly instrumental in bringing this work to its successful completion.

I also am grateful for my classmates and friends at the Angelicum and the Convitto Internazionale San Tommaso D'Aquino in Rome, as well as my colleagues and students at Benedictine College in Atchison, Kansas, and in FOCUS. Their prayers and support have been greatly appreciated. Thanks also goes to the faculty and staff at the Marian Library/IMRI at the University of Dayton, where I studied one summer and later conducted much of the research for this dissertation. I especially thank Clare Jones for her gracious assistance in the library during many rushed visits to

Dayton and Fr. Luigi Gambero, S.M., Fr. Bertrand Buby, S.M., Fr. Fredrick Jelly, O.P., and Fr. Johann Roten, S.M., for their feedback and encouragement in pursuing this work in its early stages.

Most especially, I thank my moderator Fr. Joseph Henchey, C.S.S., for his guidance, prayers, and encouragement throughout the course of this project. His taking on the thesis midstream, directing it from "long distance" and offering to take care of various administrative tasks for me in Rome while I was in the States goes above and beyond the ordinary role of a moderator, and thus deserves a special note of thanksgiving. His generosity, perseverance and prayerful dedication to directing this thesis will always be remembered and be so greatly appreciated.

I also thank my parents, who have offered much love and support while I pursued graduate studies in theology beginning in 1993. Above all, I express heartfelt gratitude to my wife Elizabeth for her patience, encouragement, many sacrifices, and untiring love over the past four years of my working on the dissertation amidst our wedding, our teaching and missionary endeavors, and the birth of our first child. With love and thanksgiving, I dedicate this work to you and our daughter Madeleine, and I look forward to our life together "A.D."— After the Dissertation.

May the Lord Jesus bless all who have been a part of this work.

EDWARD SRI

February 21, 2001

Introduction

From the art, liturgy, and patristic writings of the early Church to modern ecclesial teaching such as Pius XII's encyclical *Ad Caeli Reginam*, Vatican II, and the *Catechism of the Catholic Church*, the Church's Tradition and magisterial pronouncements bear strong witness to Mary's role as queen, sharing preeminently in Christ's reign in the kingdom of God. However, while there is much support for Mary's queenship in Tradition and magisterial teaching, the biblical basis for this doctrine has not been as clear.

Building on the insights of a number of contemporary biblical scholars and Mariologists, this study will attempt to unearth some of the scriptural roots of this doctrine by examining one biblical theme that is helpful for understanding Mary's queenship. This theme is the queen-mother tradition of the Old Testament. In the Davidic kingdom, it was the mother of the king who ruled as queen, not the king's wife. She shared in the king's rule over the kingdom and was, in fact, one of the most powerful persons in the kingdom. Within the biblical worldview of the Davidic kingdom, the mother of the king and queenship went hand-in-hand. It is this line of thought that we will explore in order to show how the queen-mother theme can serve as an important biblical basis for understanding why Mary, as mother of the new Davidic King, might be considered a queen in Christ's kingdom. While our aim is not to prove the queenship of Mary as a doctrine revealed explicitly in the Scriptures, we will demonstrate that the queen-mother theme can shed important biblical light on why Mary, the mother of the King, Jesus, would have a queenly office in the kingdom her royal Son established. We will conduct this study in four chapters.

In chapter one, we will first set the context for this discussion by briefly summarizing how Mary's queenship has been expressed in the Church's Tradition and magisterial pronouncements throughout the centuries. Then we will look at some common approaches taken to understanding the biblical foundations for this doctrine, including those that employ the Scriptures primarily as proof-texts for preconceived notions of the queenship, which are often based on secular-political models; those that arrive at the queenship by drawing secondary logical conclusions from other Marian truths revealed in the New Testament; and those that base the queenship on Old Testament typological figures (e.g., Esther, Wisdom), which are argued to be prefiguring Mary as queen even though such typological connections are not demonstrated to be found in the New Testament presentation of Mary. While some of these approaches can be helpful, we will see that they often have remained a step removed from the actual portrayal of Mary in the Scriptures, not taking advantage of the rich insights that can be gained from more fully allowing the Scriptures to shape one's view of the queenship and the kingdom. Our approach, however, will attempt to build more thoroughly upon a biblical study of Mary in the New Testament, and within the biblical view of the kingdom—in order to demonstrate more clearly how the Scriptures can lend support for the doctrine of Mary's queenship.

In chapter two, we will begin this biblical theology of Mary's queenship by examining the role of the queen mother in the Old Testament. First, we will consider the important position of the king's mother in the Davidic kingdom. We will see that she reigned as queen, serving as a high-ranking official in the royal court, as an advocate for the people, and as an influential counselor to her son. Then we will look at how the importance of the queen mother is reflected in Israel's prophetic tradition and how it became associated with Israel's messianic hopes.

In chapter three, we will examine how the queen-mother tradition can serve as a background for understanding Mary, mother of the new Davidic King, Jesus, in the New Testament. By studying the mother of the Messiah in Matthew 1–2, Luke 1:26–45, and Revelation 12 in light of the Davidic kingdom traditions those texts evoke, we will see that the Scriptures portray Mary, the mother of the King, in association with her royal Son in ways that recall the queen-mother figure of the Old Testament. We then will conclude that the Scriptures do lend support to an understanding of Mary as queen mother.

Finally, in the summary conclusions, we will offer some suggestions on how the biblical approach taken in this study can deepen our understanding of the Christological and ecclesial dimensions of Mary's queenship in ways that contribute to our understanding of the *meaning* of her royal office. In an era when most societies have moved away from the monarchical political structures of the past, referring to Mary as queen can appear anachronistic or triumphalistic to some, or as a symbol void of any real meaning to others. However, the biblical methodology this study employs can help underscore that her queenship must be understood in the context of *Christ's* kingdom—which is very different from the kingdoms of this world (cf. Jn. 18:36; Lk. 22:25–26). In the New Testament, Christ established His kingdom through humility, service, and obedience, even unto death, and He promised that those Christians who persevered with Him in such humble obedience would reign with Him over the powers of evil, sin, and death. As the obedient servant of the Lord and the first disciple of Christ, Mary has a unique share in Christ's reign and serves as a point of reference for all Christians who strive to realize their own royal vocation through the service and obedience to God's Word. By understanding Mary's queenship within this ecclesial and Christological context, such a biblical theology can help express this doctrine in a way that has more meaning and practical significance for Christians of all ages than approaches that begin *a priori* with secular-political views of queenship. Furthermore, we will see that by expressing Mary's royal office in light of the scriptural understanding of queenship and the kingdom, this biblical approach also will be more helpful for presenting this doctrine ecumenically, in a way that may be more congenial to other Christians than approaches that begin with Western political monarchies and abstract, logical deductions that are several steps removed from the biblical portrait of Mary.

Toward a Biblical Theology of Mary's Queenship

This chapter will set the context for our developing a biblical theology of Mary's queenship. First, we will provide a brief summary of the development of this doctrine by looking at liturgy, popular piety, magisterial teaching, and the writings of the Fathers of the Church throughout the centuries. Second, we will demonstrate how, although the Church's Tradition and Magisterium bear strong witness to this doctrine, the scriptural foundations have not always been as clear. This second section will evaluate the different ways scholarship has attempted to use the Scriptures in order to support Mary's queenship. Here, we will examine four common approaches: (1) some scholars have used the Scriptures as mere proof-texts for preconceived notions of Mary's royal office; (2) other scholars have begun with other truths revealed in the Scriptures (e.g., the divine maternity) and then have drawn out secondary logical conclusions based on those truths in order to arrive at the queenship; (3) some have viewed feminine royal figures in the Old Testament (such as Esther and Wisdom) as prefiguring Mary's queenship, but have not shown how such typological connections are grounded in the narrative presentation of Mary in the New Testament; and (4) some scholars have emphasized a salvation-historical approach, paying special attention to the presentation of Mary within the narrative context of the passages being considered. While the first three methods can be helpful, their conclusions could be strengthened if they were supplemented by the rich insights that can be gained from studying Mary in the context of salvation history and within a narrative analysis of pertinent Marian passages. Thus, we will distinguish these first three methods from the fourth approach. Following this fourth, more holistic approach, we will see later how the biblical queen-mother theme that emerges in salvation history can not only help shed important light on our understanding of Mary's queenship, but also can help supplement the other approaches that seek to clarify the biblical basis of this doctrine.

1.1 Doctrinal Development of Mary's Queenship

An extensive treatment of the doctrinal development of Mary's queenship throughout the centuries would be beyond the scope of this project. This has been thoroughly investigated already in a number of works.[1] Here, we will simply offer a brief overview of the doctrinal development in order to provide the context for the central purpose of this book: developing a biblical theology of Mary's queenship.

1.1.1 Church Fathers and Theologians in Later Centuries

In his article "La Regalità di Maria nel Pensiero dei Padri," Luigi Gambero offers a synthesis of patristic teaching on our topic. Gambero shows how some of the earliest Church Fathers, although not explicitly giving Mary the title "Queen," did implicitly express the reality of her queenship and attempt to offer some theological foundations for her royal character.[2] He notes two basic approaches to describing Mary's royalty in this early period: one based on the meaning of Mary's name, the other based on exegetical reasons.[3]

First, we will consider the etymological approach. Some Fathers saw royal significance in Mary's name. For example, according to Saint Jerome, "Mary" in Syriac can be translated as *domina*,[4] meaning "lady" or "sovereign," indicating her great dignity. Along a similar line, Peter Chrysologus said that Mary should be translated from the Hebrew as *domina* as well.[5] Although not emphasized as much in the East, this approach of stressing the etymology of Mary's name became a common way to demonstrate Mary's queenship in the West. Subsequent Western authors such as Eucher of Lyons, Isidore of Seville, and Venerable Bede would continue this line of approach when discussing Mary's royal position.[6]

On a more exegetical level, attention was drawn to Mary being called "the mother of my Lord" by Elizabeth in the Visitation scene (Lk. 1:43). For example, Clement of Alexandria, Jerome, Ambrose, and Augustine all emphasized Mary being the *mater domini*.[7] With deeper reflection on what it meant for Mary to be the mother of the Lord, there arose a deeper understanding of Mary being associated with Christ's royal lordship. It was Origen who made a significant "first step forward" along these lines by referring to Mary as "*kuria*" in his commentary on this passage.[8] Origen viewed Elizabeth's greeting Mary with the words "mother of my Lord" as honoring her with a royal dignity: σὺ μήτηρ τοῦ Κυρίου μου·σὺ ἐμὴ Κυρία.[9] Similarly, Saint Ephrem referred to Mary as "the Most Holy Sovereign Lady (*Domina*), Mother of God."[10] Jerome and Augustine also spoke of Mary's sovereignty.[11]

Another line of development might be seen in patristic references to Mary as the mother of the King.[12] With the New Testament bestowing on Jesus the title of king, it was easy for the early Fathers to describe the mother of Jesus as the mother of the King.[13] Although not a direct affirmation of her queenship, viewing Mary as *mater regis* linked her even more closely to her Son's royal status and helped set the stage for the title "queen" to be used explicitly by later Church Fathers. For example, one can see Chrysippus of Jerusalem making this very move from "*mater regis*" to "*regina*" in his homily on Psalm 44.

There, he says that Mary is the mother of the King and will be changed into a heavenly queen.[14] Kirwin shows the line of progression: "It was in this way that the implicit became explicit. Mary was honored as 'Mother of Christ who is King,' then as 'Mother of the King,' finally as 'Queen.'"[15]

As the early Church developed its understanding of basic Marian truths (especially after the Council of Ephesus), there was greater reflection on the meaning and extent of Mary's queenship.[16] For example, Idelfonse of Toledo discussed Mary's royalty in a way that surpassed anything that had come before him. Not only did he view Mary as a royal figure, but he even placed himself as a servant of the queenly mother of Jesus: "I am your servant, for your Son is my Lord. You are my Queen because you have become the handmaid of my King."[17] Andrew of Crete described Mary as a queen in Old Testament prophecy, in her birth, in her entering the Temple, and in her being crowned in heaven.[18] He honored her as queen, calling her "*O ter regina*," and described the great extent of her reign as the "*Regina universorum hominum*."[19] In the eighth century, Saint Germain of Constantinople called Mary "Queen," "Sovereign Lady," and "Queen of the Universe."[20] And John Damascene taught that Mary reigns with her Son and that she is queen because she is the mother of the Creator.[21] He even went on to ask Mary to rule over his entire life.[22]

Moving into the medieval period, Mary's queenship was frequently mentioned by writers such as Peter Damian, Anselm, Eadmerus, and Bernard of Clairvaux.[23] The queenship was generally taken for granted and simply highlighted in sermons, prayers, and hymns. With little mention of it in strictly theological treatises, however, there seemed to be little speculative reflection on the nature and extent of her queenship. Nevertheless, a deeper understanding of its theological foundations did begin to emerge in the writings of Bernard and Eadmerus, who grounded Mary's royalty in her divine maternity and in her unique cooperation in Christ's work of redemption.[24]

This two-fold foundation was increasingly discussed in subsequent centuries. In particular, a famous medieval work, the *Mariale super missus est*, explained how Mary's queenship is based not only on her divine maternity, but also on her cooperation in Christ's redemptive work. Since she was uniquely associated with Christ's suffering on the Cross, she was uniquely associated with His triumph and royal reign in the kingdom.[25] In the fifteenth century, Saint Bernardine of Siena and Denis the Carthusian made similar points.[26]

The nature and function of Mary's queenship also was discussed in more detail in this period. Bernardine of Siena, for example, taught that Mary has royal dominion over all creatures—not only over souls on earth but even over all devils, souls in purgatory, and souls in heaven.[27] The function of her royal office is to direct, protect, and intercede.[28] A popular title for Mary in this period was "Queen of Mercy," which described her royal position in terms of her intercessory role.[29] At the same time, there were some suggestions that Mary is queen not only because of her intercessory influence at her Son's throne, but also in a formal and proper sense. This can be seen, for example, in the writings of Peter Canisius and the *Mariale*.[30]

In the seventeenth century, there was increased emphasis on Mary's queenship in the strict, formal sense. The Jesuit Scripture commentator Ferdinand de Salazar and Christopher de Vega described Mary's queenship not only as a metaphor, but also in a formal sense, with real power and a real reign over her subjects. Although subordinate to her Son, Mary truly rules with Christ the King. Both theologians also raised a key question: how does the mother of the king receive a share in his royal dignity? They offered similar answers: if a king receives his reign by natural right or by right of conquest, the parents participate in that reign. They concluded that since Mary was mother of the King and shared in her Son's victorious work of redemption, she is queen by natural right and right of conquest, and therefore gains a share in her Son's royalty.[31]

Bartholomew de los Rios is another theologian of the period who stressed Mary's queenship as more than an honorary title of excellence, as having a real dominion. In scholastic fashion, he outlined the different kinds of royal authority and showed how all apply to Mary.[32] These notions were particularly developed in eighteenth-century reflections on the spiritual dimension of Mary's queenship, as seen in Saint Alphonsus Ligouri's *The Glories of Mary* and Saint Louis Marie de Montfort's *True Devotion to Mary*.[33]

1.1.2 Liturgy, Art, and Popular Piety

Liturgical worship in both the East and the West attests to the queenship of Mary. For example, the non-Byzantine liturgies of the East mention Mary's queenship implicitly in texts referring to her as "Lady" or "Our Lady." The Ethiopian rite expresses the universal nature of Mary's reign, calling her "The Lady of us all."[34] The Byzantine liturgy often calls Mary "Queen." In fact, Kirwin notes how she is given the royal title *Despoina* as often as she is called "Virgin" or "Mother."[35] She is called "Queen of the world" and "Queen of us all."[36] For the Feast of the Dormition, Mary is honored as being set upon a throne reigning with her Son.[37]

In the West, the Roman liturgy before the eighth century often alluded to Mary's royalty in prayers and antiphons for the Feast of the Assumption, but without giving her the explicit title of queen.[38] Since the eleventh century, however, the West has honored Mary as queen quite explicitly in sacred songs. The great Marian hymns *Salve Regina* and *Ave, Regina Caelorum* (eleventh century) as well as the *Regina Caeli* (twelfth–thirteenth century) all express her queenly status and have come to be part of the Church's liturgical worship.[39] The clearest affirmation of Mary's queenship in the Church's liturgy came in 1954, when Pius XII instituted the Feast of the Blessed Virgin Mary the Queen in his encyclical *Ad Caeli Reginam*.[40] Originally celebrated on May 31, Mary's queenship is celebrated in the revised liturgical calendar as a memorial on August 22, the octave day of the Assumption.[41]

Further witness to Mary's queenship is found in popular devotions such as the Rosary (the Fifth Glorious Mystery) and the Litany of Our Lady, which invokes Mary as "Queen" (Litany of Loreto).[42] Also, sacred art has commonly depicted Mary with queenly imagery (seated on a throne, crowned, wearing royal clothes, surrounded by angels and saints venerating her, and even being crowned by her Son).[43] Such evidence from popular piety and sacred art reflects an understanding of Mary's royal status in the believing Church.

1.1.3 Magisterial Teaching

Although Mary's queenship was not itself a topic of discussion in early papal teachings, a number of popes referred to Mary as a queenly figure in passing. For example, Kirwin notes how Pope Leo the Great called Mary "*Virgo Regia davidicae*" in a sermon.[44] The Third Council of Constantinople described Mary as Lady (*despoina*)—a queenly title. In a letter to Saint Germain, the patriarch of Constantinople, Pope Gregory II expressed the universality of Mary's queenship, calling her the ruler of all Christians who will triumph over enemies of the faith.[45]

One early Church council mentioned Mary's royal office in its official decrees. While defending the legitimacy of sacred images, the Second Council of Nicea referred to images of "our undefiled Lady (*dominae*), or holy Mother of God."[46] Although not the object of definition, this mention of Mary's royal position is significant. As Kirwin notes: "Certainly the term '*domina*' was not defined but it is equally certain that the term was used purposely. The Fathers in the council intended not only to define the legitimacy of the cult of images but also to pay tribute to Mary's queenly status."[47]

In his constitution on the Immaculate Conception (*Cum Praecelsa*), Pope Sixtus IV in 1477 referred to Mary as "the Queen of Heaven, the glorious Virgin Mother of God, raised upon her heavenly throne."[48] Further, we should note the importance of Pope Benedict XIV's (1740–1758) papal bull *Gloriosae Dominae* (1748).[49] This bull not only spoke of Mary as "Queen of heaven and earth," but also discussed how Christ grants to her "nearly all his empire and power."[50] As Carroll explains, "Much more than a mere title of excellence is involved by the name 'Queen of heaven and earth,' which the Church has always given to the Mother of the Redeemer; for her Son, the King of Kings, has in some way communicated to her His own empire and power."[51]

In addition to papal teachings, a number of papal actions throughout these centuries are worth noting. For example, in the eighth and ninth centuries, popes such as John VII (705–707), Adrian I (772–795) and Saint Leo IV (847–855) commissioned frescoes and inscriptions depicting Mary as queen. Gregory IX in 1239 ordered Roman churches to recite the *Salve Regina* every Friday after compline, in order to prepare for Saturday. Sixtus V in 1587 approved the Litany of Loreto, which includes several queenly Marian titles. In the early 1800s, Pope Pius VII crowned several Marian statues.[52] Although not papal teachings in the form of bulls or constitutions, each of these actions at least express some degree of papal promotion of Mary's queenship.

Turning to the nineteenth century, Pius IX's 1854 definition of Mary's Immaculate Conception (*Ineffabilis Deus*) described the universal extent of her queenship ("Queen of heaven and earth") and directly linked Mary's royal office with her intercessory power:

> And since she has been appointed by God to be the Queen of heaven and earth, and is exalted above all the choirs of angels and saints, and even stands at the right hand of her only-begotten Son, Jesus Christ our Lord, she presents our petitions in a most efficacious manner. What she asks she obtains. Her pleas can never be unheard.[53]

Popes from the time of Leo XIII to John Paul II have continued to teach of Mary's queenship with increased frequency and precision. Leo XIII (1878–1903) referred to Mary as queen in several encyclicals and other teachings.[54] Pope St. Pius X (1903–1914), in his encyclical *Ad Diem Illum* (1904), based Mary's queenship on her unique participation in Christ's redemptive work.[55] Writing during World War I, Pope Benedict XV (1914–1922) often entrusted the world to the protection of Mary, "Queen of Peace."[56] Pope Pius XI (1922–1939) entrusted the Church's missionary efforts to Mary, "Queen of Apostles," and the unity of the Church was entrusted to Mary "the heavenly Queen."[57] This brings us to Pope Pius XII (1939–1958), who was described by one theologian as making the queenship the Marian doctrine most illumined by all his papal teachings.[58] In a radio address to Fatima called "Mais de uma vez," Pius XII referred to Mary as "Queen," "Queen of Peace," and "Queen of the Most Holy Rosary." He then consecrated the entire human race to the Immaculate Heart of Mary, "Our Mother and Our Queen."[59] Kirwin notes the importance this consecration has for affirming Mary's queenship:

> The consecration of the world to Mary's heart implies Mary's dominion over the world. Theologians speak of a strict dominion exercised by Mary by reason of her queenship. An act of consecration is an explicit recognition of real depen-

dence upon the person towards whom such an act is made. We recognize that we are really, though analogously, dependent upon Mary as our Queen, just as we are really dependent upon Christ as our King.[60]

In his encyclical *Mystici Corporis*, Pius XII speaks of Mary as the "true Queen of Martyrs" and as reigning with her Son in heaven.[61] In the apostolic constitution *Munificentissimus Deus*, which defines the Assumption, Pius XII mentions how preachers and theologians have followed the patristic theme of describing Mary as queen, entering the royal court of heaven to sit at the right hand of her Son.[62] He also notes one argument for the Assumption from Bernardine of Siena, who drew attention to the "likeness between God's Mother and her divine Son, in the way of nobility and dignity of body and of soul—a likeness that forbids us to think of the heavenly Queen as being separated from the heavenly king."[63] Finally, Pius XII turns to Mary's cooperation with Christ's work of redemption as support for the Assumption and mentions the queenship in this context. As the new Eve sharing in the suffering and victory of the new Adam, she "finally obtained, as the supreme culmination of her privileges that she should be preserved free from the corruption of the tomb and that, like her own Son, having overcome death, she might be taken up body and soul to the glory of heaven where, as Queen, she sits in splendor at the right hand of her Son, the immortal King of Ages."[64]

The Magisterium's most extensive treatment on Mary's royal office came in 1954, when Pope Pius XII instituted the Feast of the Queenship of Mary in the encyclical *Ad Caeli Reginam*. Near the beginning of this document, the pope explains that he does not intend to propose Mary's royal status as a *new* doctrine, but that he is reaffirming a truth held by the faithful for centuries and instituting a liturgical feast to promote that truth.[65] He proceeds to show how Mary's queenship is expressed in the Fathers and saints of the Church as well as in liturgical writings and popular devotions from Eastern and Western traditions.[66] The encyclical then discusses two theological foundations for Mary's royal office: her divine motherhood and her unique cooperation in her Son's work of salvation. The divine maternity is "the main principle" on which Mary's queenship rests (*AC* 34).[67] Pius XII writes, "It is easily concluded that she is a Queen, since she bore a son who, at the very moment of His conception, because of the hypostatic union of the human nature with the Word, was also as man King and Lord of all things (*AC* 34)."[68] However, since Christ is king not only by natural right, but also by His salvific work, in a similar way Mary is queen not only by her divine motherhood, but also by her unique cooperation in Christ's work of redemption. Describing her cooperation in redemption as a second basis for Mary's queenship, Pius XII, quoting Suárez, teaches:

> For "just as Christ, because He redeemed us, is our Lord and king by a special title, so the Blessed Virgin also (is our Queen), on account of the unique manner in which she assisted in our redemption, by giving of her own substance, by freely offering Him for us, by her singular desire and petition for, and active interest in, our salvation." (*AC* 36)[69]

The encyclical then expounds on the two-fold meaning of Mary's queenship. First, Pius XII says it is a "Queenship of Excellence": "Hence, it cannot be doubted that Mary most Holy is far above all other creatures in dignity, and after her Son possesses primacy over all" (*AC* 40).[70] This unique dignity flows from Mary's Immaculate Conception. Citing Pope Pius IX's *Ineffabilis Deus,* Pius XII notes how Mary, from the first moment of her conception, was filled with every heavenly grace, and thus possessed a fullness of innocence and holiness to be found nowhere outside of God (*AC* 42).[71]

Second, her queenship is one of "efficacy." This refers to Mary's real share in Christ's influence over humanity. As queen, Mary has "a share in that influence by which He, her Son and our Redeemer, is rightly said to reign over the minds and wills of men" (*AC* 42).[72] The encyclical explains this royal power of Mary in the context of her role in the "distribution of graces" through her motherly intercession (*AC* 42).[73]

> With a heart that is truly a mother's . . . does she approach the problem of our salvation, and is solicitous for the whole human race; made Queen of heaven and earth by the Lord, exalted above all choirs of angels and saints, and standing at the right hand of her only Son, Jesus Christ, our Lord, she intercedes powerfully for us with a mother's prayers, obtains what she seeks, and cannot be refused. (*AC* 42)[74]

In later papal pronouncements, Pius XII continued to reaffirm some of the basic themes treated in *Ad Caeli Reginam*.[75]

While preparing for the Second Vatican Council, Pope John XXIII referred to Mary as Queen of the Church in an allocution given on December 8, 1960, in which he quoted Pius IX's prayer during the opening of Vatican I.[76] Further, Vatican II itself, in its dogmatic constitution *Lumen Gentium*, explicitly refers to Mary's queenship, linking it to her Immaculate Conception and Assumption:

> Finally the Immaculate Virgin preserved free from all stain of original sin, was taken up body and soul into heavenly glory when her earthly life was over, and exalted by the Lord as Queen over all things, that she might be the more fully conformed to her Son, the Lord of lords (cf. Apoc. 19:16) and conqueror of sin and death. (*LG* 59)[77]

Later, the document alludes to Mary's royal status by speaking of her being "exalted above all angels and men to a place second only to her Son, as the most holy Mother of God who was involved in the mysteries of Christ: she is rightly honored by a special cult in the Church" (*LG* 66). Peña notes how this article alludes to the two-fold basis for the queenship (divine maternity and cooperation in redemption) as described in *Ad Caeli Reginam*.[78]

Pope Paul VI described Mary as the "heavenly Queen" and as "Queen of heaven" in his encyclical *Mense Maio*.[79] In his most extensive Mariological work, the apostolic exhortation *Marialis Cultus,* Paul VI first alludes to Mary's royal status when speaking about the restored Solemnity of Mary the Holy Mother of God (January 1). He explains how this solemnity within the Christmas season is meant "to commemorate the part played by Mary in this mystery of salvation" and "to exalt the singular dignity which this mystery brings to the 'holy Mother'" (*MC* 5).[80] He then discusses how this is a fitting occasion to implore from God "through the Queen of Peace, the supreme gift of peace" (*MC* 5).[81]

In article 6, Paul VI explicitly treats the Feast of Mary's queenship, showing its link with the Solemnity of the Assumption of Mary. Here, the pope explains how in the revised liturgical calendar, the Solemnity of the Assumption is prolonged in the celebration of Mary's queenship, which occurs seven days later: "On this occasion we contemplate her who, seated beside the King of ages, shines forth as Queen and intercedes as Mother" (*MC* 6).[82] Article 22 mentions Mary's queenship when discussing how the Church's various attitudes of devotion express the relationships that unite the Church with Mary (*MC* 22).[83]

A significant development of thought on Mary's queenship can be seen in Pope John Paul II's *Redemptoris Mater.* While reaffirming the teaching of Pius XII and Vatican II and associating Mary's queenly position with her Assumption, the pope then expounds upon a new emphasis: he places Mary's exalted queenship in the context of her humble service in the kingdom. Peña notes three principle ideas set forth by John

Paul II along these lines: First, the pope shows how Mary's exalted royal office must be understood in relation to Christ's *kenosis* and royal exaltation. Christ himself humbly served even to the point of death, and was therefore raised and entered into the glory of His kingdom, exalted as Lord over all (see Phil. 2:8–9). The pope discusses the Gospels' portrayal of the true disciple, who will reign in the kingdom as the one who follows Christ's example through service: "To serve means to reign!"[84] In this regard, the pope notes how Mary is the model disciple. At the Annunciation, she called herself the "handmaid of the Lord," and she lived out this title throughout her life. She is the first disciple who served Christ in others and led them to Him. This is the basis of her queenship: "Mary, the handmaid of the Lord, has a share in this Kingdom of the Son" (*RM* 41).[85]

Second, the pope shows how Mary's queenship continues to be based on her servanthood, even in heaven: "The *glory of serving* does not cease to be her royal exaltation: assumed into heaven, she does not cease her saving service, which expresses her maternal mediation 'until the eternal fulfillment of all the elect'" (*RM* 41).[86]

Third, John Paul II also shows the ecclesial dimension of Mary's unique royal privilege, placing it in the context of the communion of saints, who all participate in Christ's reign: "Thus in her Assumption into heaven, Mary is as it were clothed by the whole reality of the Communion of Saints, and her very union with the Son in glory is wholly oriented towards the definitive fullness of the Kingdom, *when 'God will be all in all'*" (*RM* 41).[87]

Finally, one of the most significant magisterial affirmations of Mary's queenship in recent years is found in the *Catechism of the Catholic Church.* Article 966 of the *Catechism* reaffirms Mary's royal status and quotes the very text from *Lumen Gentium* 59 that we just cited above.[88]

1.2 The Biblical Foundations of Mary's Queenship

We have seen how Mary's queenship has been expressed by the Church Fathers and other theologians throughout the centuries and how it has been elaborated upon by magisterial teachings. While the Church's Tradition and Magisterium bear witness to Mary's royal office, the biblical foundations for this doctrine have remained somewhat obscure. In this next section, we will briefly examine four common ways scholars in this century have used Scripture to demonstrate the queenship. One approach builds a theology of Mary's queenship *detached from the Scriptures.* Here, biblical texts are not truly used as a guide for understanding the queenship, but are employed simply to confirm preconceived ideas about Mary's royal office. A second approach may be called *theological deduction.* Here, scholars begin with certain truths revealed in Scripture and then draw secondary logical conclusions based on those truths in order to arrive at the queenship. A third way scholars use Scripture to demonstrate Mary's queenship is to make arguments based on *"extra-biblical" typology.* This approach views Old Testament royal women, such as Esther or Lady Wisdom, as prefigurings of Mary and her queenly status, even though such typological connections are not demonstrated to be found in the actual New Testament portrayal of Mary (and thus can be called "extra-biblical"). Finally, a *salvation-historical* approach (the approach this study will take) more fully allows the Scriptures to animate our theology of Mary's royal office. Scholars following this line examine Mary in the context of salvation history, paying close attention to the narrative framework of Marian passages and often showing how the queen-mother tradition in the Davidic kingdom may help illuminate our understanding of Mary's royal role in the kingdom of her Son. While not intending to prove Mary's queenship explicitly in the Scriptures, this salvation-historical approach, which builds upon the biblical queen-mother theme, can offer important scriptural support for Mary's royal office and can help shed some light on this doctrine.

1.2.1 A Theology Detached from the Scriptures

Before Vatican II, many scholarly treatments of the queenship failed to examine thoroughly the biblical foundations of this doctrine. For example, at the 1938 Marian congress in Boulogne-sur-Mer, which focused specifically on Mary's queenly role, no single paper was devoted to the biblical foundations of her royal office. Even more alarming, every presentation drew only from the Church's Tradition (Church Fathers, liturgy, etc.) to support the queenship. The Scriptures simply were not seriously treated.[89]

The problem is quite evident in the two dominant approaches to Mary's queenship found in scholarship this century before Vatican II.[90] One school of thought patterned Mary's queenship on the kingship of Christ, while the other school emphasized the feminine character of Mary's queenship, rooted in her unique intercessory power. According to George Kirwin and Stefano De Fiores, both approaches were inadequate because they failed to give sufficient attention to what Scripture has to say about Mary's royal office.[91]

Let us briefly consider the first of these schools, represented by the Dutch theologian L. De Gruyter, who in his 1934 work *De Beata Maria Regina* offered a speculative treatment on Mary's queenship. De Gruyter devoted only four pages of his 176-page work to arguments from Scripture.[92] He concluded that only one text (Genesis 3:15) offers some scriptural support for the queenship, and that this text in itself does not enjoy a probative sense.[93] For De Gruyter, Scripture itself cannot demonstrate Mary's queenship. He instead depends on Tradition with Scripture in order to make his argument for Mary's queenship.[94]

De Gruyter went on to offer a speculative treatment on how Mary is queen in three senses. First, she is a queen in an "improper" and "analogous" sense because she is united to God more intimately than all other creatures. Due to her divine maternity and her exceeding all others in grace and holiness, Mary is in a sense greater than all others and holds a primacy over them.[95] Second, she is a queen in the sense that she is the mother of the King. Because God made Mary His mother, and because she responded to this high calling, Mary is loved more than any creature and given more gifts than anyone else.[96] Third, Mary is a queen in the "proper" and "formal" sense, given the task of ordering all people to their common end.[97] This is where De Gruyter primarily bases Mary's queenship, deducing it from her cooperation in Christ's redemptive work and placing it in likeness to Christ's kingship, but to a lesser degree. Just as Christ's kingship functions in people's interior lives by revealing truths and conferring grace, so does Mary as queen in a sense "reveal" truths by her work (as a model of holiness) and by her words (revealing to the Apostles and Gospel writers certain mysteries and incidents of Christ's life which they would not otherwise know). She also helps spread the faith by distributing graces as Mediatrix.[98] This latter function is the primary role of Mary's royal office: she governs all people by distributing the graces they need.[99]

According to De Gruyter, Mary exercises a power that is specifically Christ's, yet her royal office is subordinate to His. Christ's royal power is superior to Mary's: First, in the sense that Christ as man is a "cojoined" instrument of grace, while Mary is an instrument of grace which is separated from divinity. Second, Christ as a divine Person is a king with infinite dignity and a cult of "*latria*," while Mary is a human person with finite dignity and a cult of "*hyperdulia*." Third, Christ's merit is "*condigno*," while Mary's is "*congruo*." Christ is king by nature and conquest, while Mary is queen by grace. Thus, Mary's queenly mission completely depends on Christ's kingly mission.[100]

While De Gruyter's approach likens Mary's queenship to Christ's kingship, the second dominant school of thought on this topic emphasizes the distinctively feminine character of Mary's queenship. This school is often represented by the Dominican theologian M. Nicolas, who stressed that Mary is not a king "*au feminine.*"[101] Rather, her royal office is specifically different from Christ's.

Nicolas argues that, since royal power essentially involves the power to command, it cannot be said that Mary has royal power in a strict sense. Although she intercedes for us, she does not command us.[102] Only the king exercises the *imperium*—the act by which a sovereign directs his subjects to their common end. This act is proper only to the king because a true sovereignty demands that it be exercised by one person alone; otherwise, it would cease to be a monarchy.[103]

Thus, for Nicolas, Mary's queenship is specifically different from Christ's kingship and must be understood in its distinctively feminine character. He situates the queenship not in the "*imperium*" but in the "*consilium,*" in the sense that Mary exercises her royal office through prayerful intercession as Christ's intimate companion and associate.[104] Although she is not the spouse of Christ in a strict sense, no other woman was so intimately associated with His royal destiny than she was.[105] As the "new Eve," Mary is the woman linked with the sovereignty of the "new Adam." She becomes the new Eve at the beginning of her divine maternity when Christ becomes the new Adam,[106] and she remains the King's companion—His "helpmate"—throughout His work on earth, culminating in His redemptive work on the Cross.[107]

As mother-associate, Mary reigns by exercising influence over the King's heart, interceding on our behalf. Thus, strictly speaking, Mary does not have a governmental power, but an intercessory power. Her royal authority is found in her uniquely powerful, prayerful intervention.[108] She is united to the intentions of the King and embraces His royal mission,[109] and her prayers obtain graces for humanity.[110] In fact, Nicolas concludes that the unity forged between Mary and Jesus at the Incarnation and at the Cross is so great that no grace is given without the expressed will of Christ and the prayer of Mary.[111]

Nicolas does not even attempt to treat the biblical foundations of Mary's queenship. Instead, he builds his notion of the queenship primarily from earthly rulers and from considering the essence of royalty philosophically. In fact, in his two-part, fifty-three-page article, "La Vierge-Reine," Nicolas cites only two biblical texts.[112]

George Kirwin has directly critiqued these two approaches to Mary's royal office as not giving attention to the notion of queenship developed in the Sacred Scriptures. According to Kirwin, the heart of the problem with De Gruyter's work is his methodological starting points:

> The ultimate root of De Gruyter's approach is the method employed—a deductive method which tends at times to become rationalistic and which does not pay sufficient attention to the fonts of revelation. Instead of allowing himself to be guided by the scriptures, he uses them as a proof or confirmation of his own thesis.[113]

Kirwin also notes how Nicolas, although differing from De Gruyter in that he does not look for the essence of Mary's queenship in Christ's kingship, still falls into the same methodological problem: he uses "a rather abstract, deductive approach which does not sufficiently take into account the concrete facts of revelation proposed to us in scripture and developed within the living Tradition of the Church."[114]

Kirwin sums up the fundamental problem in these approaches to Mary's queenship: they start *a priori* with a secular-political or philosophical concept of royalty that guides their interpretation of biblical sources—sources whose notion of Christ's kingdom, while certainly having some points in common with earthly monarchies, is ultimately quite different. "But my kingship is not of this world" (Jn. 18:36); "The kings of the Gentiles exercise lordship over them. . . . But not so with you; rather let the greatest among you become as the youngest and the leader as one who serves" (Lk. 22:25–26).[115]

> The fundamental difficulty encountered with the . . . more deductive approach is the fact that the a-priori concept of queen dominated the interpretation of the sources in such a way that certain elements which seemed to pertain to revelation were at times neglected while other elements were over-emphasized. At times the facts seem to have been forced to fit the concept.[116]

1.2.2 Theological Deductions Drawn from Scripture

The method of theological deduction is another way some scholars have used the Scriptures for demonstrating Mary's queenship. This approach proceeds by way of logical deductions based on other truths revealed in the Scriptures, in order to demonstrate how one might systematically arrive at the queenship. While we affirm that such theological deductions can offer (and indeed have offered) important insights into Mary's royal office, we simply wish to distinguish it from other approaches, which draw more fully on the rich insights that can be gained from a study of Mary in the context of salvation history within the narrative framework of related New Testament texts, and in light of the Old Testament background those texts evoke.

We can find an example of this deductive approach to the scriptural basis for Mary's queenship in Pius XII's encyclical *Ad Caeli Reginam*. The encyclical notes how the Church Fathers drew from the angel's words at the Annunciation and

Elizabeth's greeting at the Visitation to expound upon Mary's royal status.[117] Then, at the beginning of the theological treatment of Mary's queenship, Pius XII again returns to these two passages to demonstrate the royal dignity of her divine maternity:

> In Holy Writ, concerning the Son whom Mary will conceive, We read this sentence: 'He shall be called the Son of the most High, and the Lord God shall give unto him the throne of David his father, and he shall reign in the house of Jacob forever, and of his kingdom there will be no end,' and in addition Mary is called 'Mother of the Lord'; *from this it is easily concluded* that she is a Queen since she bore a son who, at the very moment of His conception . . . was also as man King and Lord of all things. (*AC* 34, emphasis added)[118]

Although he does not expound upon these passages, Pius XII does offer these texts as scriptural foundations for Mary's queenship. Yet Kirwin is careful to note that *Ad Caeli Reginam* teaches only that Mary's queenship can be *deduced* from the biblical accounts of the Annunciation and Visitation. In other words, Pius XII does not affirm (or deny) that Luke explicitly portrays Mary as queen. What he does say is that since Luke portrays Mary as giving birth to the eternal, messianic King and Lord, we can deduce from these texts that Mary's unique association with such a royal Son implies that she, too, possesses a royal status. As Kirwin explains,

> The most we can say with certainty regarding the encyclical's approach to the scriptural foundation for the queenship is that there is a basis in scripture for this doctrine, particularly in the texts from Luke of the Annunciation and Visitation. . . . The Pope is not speaking of an explicit, formal revelation of queenship; he is speaking rather of a *deduction*."[119]

Similarly, Peña notes how the encyclical does not offer an argument from Scripture in a strict sense. Rather, Pius XII includes the biblical foundations within the argument from Tradition, showing how the Church Fathers and popular piety deduced Mary's queenship from certain biblical texts: "This already leaves a glimpse that the biblical proof is not explicit, but that tradition and the piety of the faithful have deduced certain logical consequences from some biblical facts read and understood in a comprehensive manner and in their full sense."[120]

We will now look at scholars who especially in the 1940s and 1950s have used the method of theological deduction in their treatment of the biblical foundations for Mary's royal office. For example, in his 1942 book on the queenship, A. Luis argues that the Annunciation scene offered support for Mary's queenship. First, he points out that Mary is clearly revealed as mother of the messianic King. This, he argues, makes her queen, exalted above all other creatures. Second, since this scene shows Mary as the spouse of the Holy Spirit, a divine Person, this also links Mary in a unique way with the royal concept.[121] Here we can see that Luis attempts to employ the method of theological deduction as he deduces the queenship from the two other truths that he finds revealed in the Annunciation scene: the divine maternity and bridal-like relationship with the Holy Spirit.

J. Fenton, in an article presented at the 1950 Mariological Congress in Rome, investigated the scriptural foundations for Mary's queenship as expressed in the liturgy.[122] Fenton first considers the Annunciation scene, in which Mary is presented as the mother of the eternal King of Israel and as one who is uniquely associated with Him and His work. Building on these related truths, Fenton goes on to deduce the queenship:

> And, since the office of a queen, in the proper sense of the term, is precisely that of the woman most intimately associated with the king in the government and the direction of

his own realm, Mary's position with reference to Our Lord constitutes her as a true and perfect queen in the kingdom of her Son.[123]

Fenton takes a similar approach when considering how Mary's queenship was won by her sharing in Christ's sufferings throughout her life and, in particular, at the Cross.[124] Since the Scriptures, as Fenton argues, show us that Christ merited His kingship through suffering and that Mary participated in those sufferings, she must have some type of share in Christ's royalty herself. He concludes:

> It was precisely in the function of that suffering with and for Our Lord that she may be said to have earned or merited her titles as queen and coredemptrix, in the same way that Our Lord accomplished His work of redemption and merited His kingship by means of His own sufferings.[125]

Thus, like Luis, we see that Fenton approaches the scriptural basis for Mary's queenship by making systematic theological deductions from other truths revealed in the New Testament. Fenton begins with the divine maternity, the fact of Mary's sufferings, and the way Christ merited His royal office through suffering on the Cross, and then draws the conclusion that Mary must be queen.

In a paper presented at the 1953 National Convention of the Mariological Society of America, F. Vandry stated in the first sentence that Mary's queenly role is not attested to in the Scriptures: "Although the Scriptures afford our faith no clear testimony of Mary's Queenship, nor of its universal nature, that dignity of the Mother of God is nevertheless acknowledged unanimously by the Christian Tradition."[126] Vandry rightly goes on to stress the need for the Church Fathers, liturgy, and magisterial teaching to shed light on Mary's royal office.

Still, Vandry does turn to the Scriptures—not to engage in exegesis, but to derive the queenship from other important themes found in the account of the Annunciation.[127] He argues that the Annunciation reveals that Mary not only consented to be the mother of Jesus, but also to share in His redemptive work. For Vandry, Luke's Annunciation scene presents Mary as accepting her Son precisely in His role as Savior and King. From this truth, he then derives the queenship:[128]

> *Fiat mihi secundum verbum tuum.* It is in this consent . . . that the Virgin first appears as the Queen of the Kingdom of Christ. In consenting to become the Mother of the Savior-King, she has thereby accepted to share in the work of man's salvation as God has willed it, and in the eternal reign of Him who was to save the world. Again, it is not so much because of her consent to become the Mother of the divine Son that Mary is so intimately associated with the work of Redemption as such; more pertinently it is by reason of her acceptance of her Son in His role of Savior and of King. She has shared in His life of Savior and of King, so much so that it is no longer possible to conceive the Kingdom of Christ without seeing Mary by the side of her Son, the Queen seated at the right hand of the King.[129]

Here we can see rather clearly that Vandry is employing theological deduction. He deduces the queenship from other truths revealed in this passage (Mary's consent to become mother of the Savior and King)—truths which he argues associate Mary with her royal Son's redemptive work in such a way that she must have a share in His reign and, thus, must be queen.

At the same 1953 National Convention for the Mariological Society of America, E. Smith presented an entire paper specifically devoted to the biblical foundations for Mary's queenship. He primarily considers three passages: the protoevangelium, the woman in Revelation 12, and the Annunciation.

First, Smith supports a Marian interpretation of Genesis 3:15. He notes how the close union between "the woman" and "her seed" suggests that she will be given preeminence among women, with a possible hint of royal lineage. He also highlights how the victory of the woman and her seed "not only intimates dominative power over the devil and his seed, but implies a consequent dominion over those freed from the slavery of Satan."[130] Smith concludes: "In Gen. 3:15, Our Blessed Lady is formally introduced as Christ's intimate associate in the work of Redemption. Since it was precisely the redemptive task that won for Christ the title of King by right of conquest, it follows that Mary, too, [in] her capacity as Coredemptrix, shares Christ's Kingship also by the right of conquest."[131]

Considering the woman in Revelation 12, Smith mentions the debate among scholars as to whether the woman should be interpreted only in an ecclesial sense or whether the woman admits a Marian interpretation as well. He seems favorable to a Mariological interpretation, which would view the passage in parallel to Genesis 3:15. With the stars and moon surrounding this woman, Smith sees clear queenly prerogatives given to this woman in Revelation 12.[132]

As for the Annunciation account, Smith notes how Luke presents Mary's consent as bringing about the Son whose kingdom will have no end. He concludes that Mary is made queen due to her union with the Word, who assumes the royalty of David's throne at the moment of conception.

> There is more than a theological inference here, inasmuch as the context provides a graphic picture of the intimate espousal of Our Lady with the Holy Spirit (Lk. 1:35), expressed in terminology too closely identified in Mother and Son not to have royal prerogatives correspondingly, as well as actually, present and communicated.[133]

During the discussion period at the convention, Smith was asked whether the queenship is formally contained in the

Annunciation account; Smith responded that it was.[134] He then summed up his paper by saying that the queenship is literally expressed in Genesis 3:15 and Revelation 12, and that her dominative power comes into existence at the Incarnation.[135]

Once again, we turn our attention to the approach taken by this scholar. Along these lines, we simply note that Smith also proceeds primarily by way of theological deduction. For example, we can see that his arguments from Genesis 3:15 (because Mary is linked to her Son's victory in this passage, she must have a share in His reign as queen) and the Annunciation (because of Mary's spousal-like relationship with the Holy Spirit and because of her intimate union with her Davidic Son, she must have a share in Christ's royal privileges) are secondary logical conclusions which remain a step removed from the actual biblical narratives that are referenced. This observation is not meant to diminish the contributions such theological deductions can offer; rather, it is meant simply to *distinguish* this method from other approaches, which will draw more fully on a consideration of Mary in the context of salvation history and remain closer to the narrative presentation of Mary in the New Testament.

In 1956, R. Peinador wrote an article specifically on the scriptural foundations for Mary's queenship.[136] In the beginning of this work, he argued that just because the queenship cannot be demonstrated by Scripture alone (apart from using sacred Tradition or making theological deductions), that does not mean the doctrine is not biblical. Tradition has the important role of transmitting truths revealed in Scripture and serves as an exegetical-theological criterion. Tradition does not impose an exterior meaning onto the biblical text, but can guarantee our subjective certitude of what is contained objectively in the text.[137] Peinador then sets out to show how the Scriptures in the literal sense offer at least some indications ("impressions") of Mary's queenship.[138]

After examining the Annunciation and Visitation scenes, Peinador argues that, by accepting the message of the angel, Mary enters into the promises and reign of the new kingdom. Exegetically, one cannot say anything more than this. Still, he thinks these passages do provide some foundation for establishing the queenship. If Scripture says anything about her royal office, it will be in these texts primarily.[139] Since Luke 1 clearly demonstrates Christ's kingship, it is given for us to see the royalty of the woman by whom Christ became the royal Son of David and received human nature. Furthermore, since some Lukan texts also insinuate that Christ will reign as the Son of God, one can arrive at a deeper appreciation of Mary's queenship by seeing her as the mother of Him whose human kingship is rooted in divine kingship.[140] At the end of the article, Peinador admits that the Lukan texts do not directly express the fact of the queenship but that they do present her as the mother of Him who has come as the Messiah-King.[141] Thus, these texts do offer some indication of and foundation for Mary's royal office.

Considering the protoevangelium, Peinador argues that, since the woman of Genesis 3:15 appears with her seed victorious over the serpent, this victory constitutes her as a ruler in the new kingdom that has eliminated the serpent's reign.[142] Mary's reign can be supported by the proto-gospel if the victory over the serpent (and thus sin and death) is seen as bringing about the kingdom by Christ and Mary, and if Mary's queenship is viewed in light of her coredemptive and maternal mission.[143] Yet Peinador does not claim that the queenship is formally expressed in this text itself.[144]

As for the scene in Revelation 12, Peinador says if there is any support for Mary's queenship in this text, it depends on its relationship with the woman in Genesis 3:15.[145]

Peinador engages the biblical text more thoroughly than the other scholars we have examined so far. He shows how

Luke 1, Genesis 3:15, and Revelation 12 together offer some "impressions" of Mary's queenship and some firm foundations upon which the queenship can be based.[146] Yet, like his predecessors who wrote on this topic, Peinador's line of reasoning (e.g., Mary is the mother of the King; therefore, she is queen) on its own remains a step removed from what we find in the narrative presentation of Mary in the New Testament. Certainly, systematic logical deductions such as Peinador's are valid and can be helpful for our understanding the queenship, especially in light of the subsequent tradition regarding Mary's royal office, which has emerged over the centuries in the Church's liturgical worship, theological reflection, and magisterial teaching. However, for the purposes of this study, we distinguish this method of theological deduction from other approaches that build their arguments even more fully from within the biblical worldview. As we will see, we can find further support for the jump from Mary as the mother of the Messiah-King to Mary as *queen* (which Peinador and others have made through a secondary theological deduction) if we consider her in light of the queen-mother theme that we find in salvation history.

In summary, we have examined a number of scholars who have approached the biblical foundations for Mary's queenship by using secondary theological deduction. This method seeks to establish the biblical basis for the queenship first by beginning with important Mariological truths found in the Scriptures (e.g., the divine maternity, participation in Christ's sufferings, etc.) and then by making systematic logical deductions based upon those truths which would lead to Mary's royal office. While valid and often insightful, we simply note that this approach primarily applies logic *to* the sacred texts, instead of building more closely upon the logic found *in* the texts. In other words, it does not take advantage of the important insights that can be gained from a more thorough investigation of Mary—both within the context of salvation history and within the narrative structures and inter-textual relationships found in the Marian passages of the New Testament. We will later see that such an investigation could in fact have the additional benefit of supplementing and strengthening some of the conclusions made through theological deduction. In particular, we will see that understanding Mary in light of the queen-mother tradition in salvation history can help shed even more light from a biblical perspective on the connection between the related Marian truths in Scripture (e.g., the fact that Mary is mother of the Messiah) and the theological conclusion that the method of theological deduction seeks to offer (i.e., that Mary has some queenly role, sharing in her royal Son's reign).

1.2.3 "Extra-Biblical" Typology

Now we will examine a third way the Scriptures have been used to support Mary's queenship: the use of what one scholar has called "extra scriptural" typology. This approach views certain feminine royal figures of the Old Testament as prefiguring Mary in her queenship in a typological sense. For example, some have considered how people such as Andrew of Crete, Pope Benedict XIV, Conrad of Saxony, Saint Thomas Aquinas, Richard of St. Lawrence, Bernardino of Busti, Gabriel Biel, and Saint Peter Canisius have viewed Esther as a figure of Mary.[147] Similarly, the royal woman in Psalm 44:10 has been considered a prefiguring of Mary in her queenship by Athanasius, Aquinas, Bonaventure, and in the ancient liturgy of Saint John Chrysostom.[148] It has also been pointed out that the royal Wisdom figure of the Sapiential Books has been used in the liturgy in reference to Mary in her queenship.[149]

After evaluating these possible typologies, however, scholars such as Luis, Iglesias, and Peinador conclude that these Old Testament figures cannot be used as direct theological arguments in favor of Mary's queenship. These scholars argue that, for these Old Testament figures to be considered with certitude types of Mary, such a connection must be established within the Sacred Scriptures or in the Tradition of the Church.[150] Until such a connection is clearly shown to exist, these texts on their own cannot be given probative value for establishing the biblical foundations of Mary's queenship.

Eustice Smith seems to go even a step further. He argues that to build the strongest case for a Marian typology the connection must be made by the New Testament writers themselves. Considering Mary's queenship, Smith mentions how tradition has applied Psalm 44:10 to Mary and how the liturgy has used Wisdom texts (Wis. 8:22–36 and Sirach 24:11–25) in reference to Mary. He concludes, however, that these "types" have been established by "extra scriptural agents" (by the liturgy, the saints, and theologians in the Catholic tradition) and are not developed within the Scriptures themselves. Thus, for Smith, while these texts might be used collaboratively to support the queenship of Mary, they do not have the same force as those typologies that are actually drawn out in the New Testament.[151]

> Types or figures foreshadowing the Blessed Virgin undoubtedly exist in the Old Testament. Difficulty with the typical sense in this regard is had in the fact that persons, events, and things have been employed as symbols by *extra scriptural agents*. . . . A mariological type must conform to all the requirements of a messianic type and above all, that *it be revealed as such in Scripture.*[152]

This raises an important issue. There seems to be a distinction between (1) types and figures that are developed by "extra scriptural agents," such as the Church Fathers, the liturgy, or conciliar teaching, and (2) those that are developed in the New Testament.

The Pontifical Biblical Commission (PBC), in its 1993 document *The Interpretation of the Bible in the Church*, seems to make a similar distinction. This can be seen in the document's discussion of the "*sensus plenior*," which the commission defines as "a deeper meaning of the text, intended by God but not clearly expressed by the human author."[153] The PBC sets forth two different ways that the fuller sense of a biblical text can be known. First, there is a level of *sensus plenior*, which comes to be known when the Scriptures are read in the light of "authentic doctrinal tradition or a conciliar definition."[154] For example, the PBC mentions how patristic teaching about the Trinity "expresses the fuller sense of the teaching of the New Testament regarding God the Father, the Son and Holy Spirit."[155] In this case, the fuller sense of the Scriptures is known by an extra-biblical source, the teaching of the Church Fathers.

This is distinguished from an inter-biblical level of *sensus plenior*, which is found in "the meaning that a subsequent biblical author attributes to an earlier biblical text, taking it up in a context which *confers upon it a new literal sense*."[156] Here, the fuller sense is found not in a post-biblical agent but in the literal sense of the New Testament itself.[157]

The PBC document makes a similar point when discussing typology.[158] The document states that an authentic typological sense of Scripture is found in the connections made by the New Testament writers: "The connection involved in typology is ordinarily based on the way in which *Scripture* describes the ancient reality (cf. the voice of Abel: Gen 4:10; Heb 11:4; 12:24) and not simply on the reality itself. Consequently, in such a case one can speak of *a meaning that is truly scriptural*."[159] Note how the document describes this typology as "truly scriptural." It is not based on the way extra-biblical sources—such as the Church Fathers, the liturgy, or Church councils—reflect on Old Testament people, places, events, and institutions. Rather, it is based on the way subsequent *scriptural* texts describe those ancient realities. Here again, the PBC gives special attention to Scripture as the criterion for determining an authentic typological sense.[160]

In summary, the key difference between the two kinds of typology is this: *Extra-biblical typology* involves the creative discernment of the theologian, who perceives connections between the Old Testament, the New Testament, and the Christian faith; *inter-biblical typology* can be observed in the New Testament writer's interpretation of the Old Testament. In this later case, it is the New Testament itself that points out how a particular Old Testament figure foreshadows a reality in the New. Both approaches have value, but extra-biblical typology remains a step removed from the Scriptures themselves, and therefore seems secondary to the inter-biblical typology found in the literal sense of the New Testament itself. As Raymond Brown has noted, "Advocates of typical exegesis have been more persuasive when the types they proposed could be related to patterns already supported *in the Scriptures*, e.g., Davidic typology for Jesus, exodus typology for elements of the Christian salvific mysteries."[161]

All of this background is helpful for a balanced consideration of the extent to which Old Testament figures such as Esther, Judith, the woman of Psalm 44, or "Lady Wisdom" may serve as biblical foundations for Mary's queenship. We would conclude that unless it can be demonstrated that the New Testament portrays Mary as the fulfillment of these figures, these typologies should be considered "extra-biblical" as opposed to "inter-biblical," since the connections do not seem to be found in the actual portrayal of Mary in the New Testament itself. This should in no way downplay the important contributions these extra-biblical typologies can make toward understanding Mary's queenship.[162] Rather, it is simply meant to draw attention to the fact that these typologies are not made by the New Testament writers and thus are one step removed from the New Testament presentation of Mary.

1.2.4 Salvation-Historical Approach: Mary as the New Queen Mother

We will now consider one final approach for demonstrating the biblical foundations of Mary's queenship. Especially since Vatican II, many scholars addressing this topic have taken a salvation-historical approach, using the Old Testament queen-mother tradition as the primary backdrop for understanding Mary's queenship. In the late 1950s and 1960s, scholars such as H. Cazelles,[163] A. Del Moral,[164] D. Stanley,[165] B. Ahern,[166] C. Stuhlmueller[167] and R. Laurentin[168] specifically used this theme in order to explain Mary's royal office. A number of them discussed how in several ancient Near Eastern kingdoms the queen-mother figure was given a special place ruling in the royal court.[169] They also examined how various biblical texts in 1 and 2 Kings and in the Book of Jeremiah show that, in the kingdom of Judah, the queen mother held an official position as queen, participating in her son's reign by serving as an advocate for the people and as a counselor to her son.[170] It is commonly noted how Bathsheba gained considerable power when she became queen mother after her son Solomon assumed the throne. Pointing to a scene in 1 Kings 2, many have shown how King Solomon honors his queen mother by bowing before her, having her sit at his right hand, and saying he will grant her any request she makes. Some scholars also demonstrate how the queen-mother figure plays an important role in two passages from Israel's tradition, which eventually became associated to some extent with the Messiah: Isaiah 7:14 and Genesis 3:15 closely associate a royal mother with her royal son and his work.[171] These scholars conclude that, with this Old Testament background in mind, Mary should be understood as the queen mother in the new kingdom of her Son.[172] For example, in the New Testament, Mary and Jesus are shown as fulfilling Isaiah 7:14 (Mt. 1:22–3; Lk. 1:26–31), thus connecting Mary with the queen-mother concept.[173] Most of these scholars also point out how Mary is queen mother by turning to the Visitation scene, where Elizabeth calls Mary "the mother of my Lord"—words probably used in reference to the queen mother in the Old Testament.[174]

All these themes (and more) will be treated much more extensively in chapters two and three, in which I will draw upon the insights of these and other scholars. At this point, I only intend to underscore *the approach* taken by these scholars. Note how they do not arrive at the queenship by making abstract correlations from certain truths found in the Scriptures (theological deduction). Nor do they seek to base Mary's queenship primarily on a typology that has not been clearly demonstrated to be found in the New Testament itself (extra-biblical typology). Rather, they place Mary in the context of salvation history, in which we find a pattern of a queenly mother being intimately associated in the reign of her royal Son. With this background in mind, they then proceed to show how the New Testament portrays Mary in ways that recall this queen-mother tradition of ancient Israel. They conclude that, because she is the mother of the messianic Davidic King, Mary can be seen as the queen mother in the kingdom of her Son. Therefore, by presenting Mary's royal office in terms of the biblical view of queenship in the Davidic kingdom, this approach more deeply allows the Scriptures to guide our understanding of the queenship, and thus has much to offer in terms of biblical support for this doctrine.

The most extensive treatment to date on this subject has been George Kirwin's 1973 doctoral dissertation, *The Nature of the Queenship of Mary*. Kirwin does excellent work summarizing the development of this doctrine—highlighting attestations of Mary's queenship in the Church Fathers, magisterial teachings, and liturgy, as well as in theological writings, sacred art, and popular piety throughout the centuries.[175] He also provides an excellent overview and critique of the more rationalistic, deductive approaches of the two major schools of thought on Mary's queenship from earlier this century, represented by De Gruyter and Nicolas (which we briefly looked at above).[176] Following the call of Vatican II, Kirwin rightly emphasized the need for a biblical salvation-historical methodology for approaching Marian doctrine.[177] This is the method he seeks to employ in treating Mary's queenship. Building on the insights of some scholars before him, Kirwin attempts to trace the queen-mother tradition throughout salvation history, placing this theme at the heart of his presentation on Mary's queenship.[178]

In his fourth chapter (entitled "Mary: Queen Mother in Salvation History"), Kirwin summarizes the role of the queen mother in the ancient Near East[179] and in the monarchies of ancient Israel.[180] He then argues that some of Israel's key messianic prophecies (Gen. 3:15; Is. 7:14; Mic. 5:2) place the queen mother in an important role, linked with her royal son's messianic work.[181] However, although he gives a good treatment of the queen-mother theme throughout the Old Testament, Kirwin does not go on to demonstrate adequately the New Testament presentation of Mary in light of this background. After completing his examination of the queen-mother theme in the Davidic monarchy (by evaluating 1 and 2 Kings and Jeremiah 13 and 22) and the importance of the queen mother in key Old Testament messianic prophecies (by examining Genesis 3:15, Isaiah 7:14, and Micah 5:2), the reader would expect Kirwin to go on and evaluate specific New Testament texts, in order to show how this queen-mother background can illuminate Mary's role in the kingdom of her messianic Son. Rather surprisingly, however, it is just at this point that he ends his study of the queen-mother theme in the Scriptures.[182] He does not carry it into the New Testament; instead, he simply states: "It is probable that this queen-mother [of Gen. 3:15, Is. 7:14 and Mic. 5:2] is Mary and that to appreciate her significance in salvation history one must look to the Gebirah tradition since this is the setting in which the Messiah and His Mother have been placed by God."[183]

Although Kirwin thoroughly demonstrated the importance of the queen mother in the Old Testament, he did not examine New Testament texts in any extensive way in order to show how Mary should be understood in light of that background. While pertinent New Testament passages are mentioned briefly at different points throughout his thesis,[184] his treatment of New Testament texts is sparse and unsystematic. For example, Kirwin devotes only five pages to a specific treatment of Revelation 12.[185] Furthermore, pertinent Lukan,[186] Matthean,[187] and other Johannine passages[188] are nowhere treated on their own in order to support the queenship. These relevant New Testament texts are sometimes mentioned either in passing or in the context of reporting a history of modern scholarship on this topic. Yet this is ironic. Although Kirwin's work calls for a biblical salvation-historical approach to Mary's queenship, his thesis seems to give much more attention to reporting what scholars say about Mary's queenship in the New Testament than it does to examining what the New Testament texts themselves say about this topic. This is most apparent in the first chapter, which devotes thirty-two pages to the scriptural basis of Mary's queenship.[189] One would expect to find an evaluation of particular *biblical texts* (with insights from scholarship used to shed light on the meaning of those texts). Instead, it reports what *recent scholarship* has said about the scriptural foundations for the queenship, evaluating one theologian after another. Unlike Kirwin's more thorough treatment of the Old Testament, in which he studied how various biblical texts present the queen mother in the life of the Davidic monarchy and in Israel's prophecies, his approach to the New Testament seems to use contemporary scholarship as the primary point of departure, not the Scriptures themselves.

Over the twenty-five years since Kirwin's thesis, biblical and Mariological studies have provided a number of insights that strengthen the queen-mother theme as a primary biblical lens for viewing Mary's queenship.

For example, some scholars have contributed to a deeper understanding of the role of the queen mother in ancient Israel.[190] There also has been a greater appreciation for the Davidic kingdom themes in Matthew 1–2, which have led some to argue more clearly that Mary is being presented as the new queen mother in these passages.[191] Some works have helped strengthen positions that see queen-mother allusions in the Lukan Annunciation and Visitation scenes.[192] Other studies in Johannine theology have helped strengthen the Marian sense of Revelation 12, which is important for demonstrating Mary's queenship in this passage, especially in light of the queen mother.[193] Also, having firmly grounded Mary's royal office in the Scriptures with the queen-mother theme, a number of scholars have gone on to elaborate on the nature of the queenship[194] and to shed light on other Marian doctrines,[195] as well as other areas of theology.[196] These and other themes will be treated more extensively in the next three chapters. However, at this point, we simply wish to highlight that with all these new insights into our topic, there certainly is a need to synthesize the significant contributions made by scholarship in the past twenty-five years. Such an endeavor would deeply enrich our understanding of the biblical foundations of Mary's queenship.

In summary, although a number of scholars have recognized the Old Testament queen mother as a backdrop for understanding Mary,[197] few have attempted to develop these insights fully into a biblical theology of Mary's royal office.[198] Kirwin's work surely stands out among the rest as the project that has offered the most extensive treatment. Yet, as we have seen, there have been many important scholarly insights since the time of Kirwin's thesis that need to be incorporated into the development of the queen-mother theme; also, Kirwin's very effort to present the biblical foundations of this doctrine in light of this theme could be significantly strengthened by a more thorough treatment of New Testament texts and by systematically demonstrating the implications of such an approach for understanding the significance of Mary's royal office.

That is why in this study, while we certainly will build upon the important work of Kirwin, we will go beyond him in three ways. First, and most significantly, this project will offer a more thorough treatment of the pertinent Lukan, Matthean, and Johannine texts, in order to clearly demonstrate how the queen-mother tradition can help illuminate the New Testament presentation of Mary. As we saw above, this was something Kirwin did not adequately demonstrate or even attempt to treat in any extensive manner. Second, we will incorporate a number of insights from recent biblical studies and Mariology that have significant bearing on our topic— insights that came after the time Kirwin's thesis was written. And thirdly, we will show how the biblical methodology employed in our treatment of Mary's queenship can help make significant contributions to our communicating the meaning of Mary's queenship in the modern world.

In closing, we have seen in this chapter how Mary's queenship is firmly rooted in the Church's Tradition and magisterial teachings, although the biblical foundations for her royal office have not always been as clear. While evaluating the common ways scholars have used Scripture to demonstrate this doctrine, we saw that many approach the scriptural basis of Mary's queenship in terms of proof-texts, theological deduction, and extra-biblical typology. Whatever light these approaches may shed on Mary's queenship, we noted that they do not take advantage of the valuable insights that can be gained from a deeper investigation of Mary within the context of salvation history, and within the narrative structures and intertextual relationships found in the Marian passages of the New Testament. Thus, while often valid and insightful, these approaches should be distinguished from those that build their theology on a more holistic narrative reading of Marian passages in the context of salvation-history. This is the approach we will take, giving special attention to the biblical queen-mother theme, which can serve as an important backdrop for understanding Mary in the New Testament.

Our salvation-historical approach to Mary's queenship will take on the following shape: First (in chapter two), we will examine the role of the queen mother in the Davidic kingdom and then show how the queen-mother theme sheds light on the mother-son prophecies of Isaiah 7:14 and Genesis 3:15. With this background, we will then examine (in chapter three) how the New Testament portrays Mary, the mother of the Messiah-King, in ways that recall the queen-mother figure of the Old Testament. Finally (in chapter four), we will provide some summary conclusions and offer a few brief suggestions on how the biblical theological approach taken in this book can enhance our understanding of the *meaning* of Mary's queenship (highlighting the Christological and ecclesiological dimensions of this doctrine) and have some value for ecumenical dialogue as well.

This approach truly allows the Scriptures to guide our views of the queenship—not the other way around. De Fiores argues that such a biblical theology not only will help preserve the traditional content of Mary's royal title but also will enrich it with a broader, non-culturally bound meaning that will have more significance for Christians of our time. He proposes a two-fold approach: "Return to the Bible in order to understand the queenship of Mary in the context of Christ and the people of God, and give attention to the culture of our time in order to translate in more simple terms the content and significance of Queen Mary."[199]

One last note: while this study focuses on a biblical theology of Mary's queenship, it is my hope that the methodology employed here will have contributions not only for Mariology, but also for systematic theology as a whole. We have seen (above) some of the problems that can arise when theology remains detached from the Scriptures, when *a priori* notions are imposed upon the biblical texts, or when the Scriptures are used more as proofs than as actual sources of revelation. Yet Vatican II has insisted that Scripture be the very soul of sacred theology.[200] Hence, in an age of specialization when the distance between biblical scholarship and dogmatic theology has greatly widened,[201] I hope the results of this study will implicitly show the profound rewards of building a dogmatic theology that gives primacy to the referential language of the Bible,[202] which uses salvation history to guide its systematization of doctrine,[203] and which allows itself to be truly animated by the Sacred Scriptures.[204]

CHAPTER TWO

The Queen Mother in the Old Testament

In this chapter, we will study the position of the queen mother in the Old Testament. First, we will briefly consider how the mother of the king played an important role in the monarchies of the ancient Near East in general. Then, we will examine the queen mother's office in the Davidic monarchy in particular and see how she had great influence in the kingdom—holding one of the most powerful positions in the royal court, serving as an advocate for the people, and offering counsel to her royal son. Finally, we will consider how the queen mother may be in the background of some of Israel's messianic hopes. All this will serve as an important foundation for our examination of how the queen-mother theme can shed important light on Mary's queenship.

2.1 The Queen Mother in the Ancient Near East

The mother of a ruling monarch held a powerful position in many ancient Near Eastern kingdoms. She often influenced political, military, economic, and cultic affairs in the royal court and played a key part in the process of dynastic succession.[1] In fact, the *mother* of the king often was more important than the king's *wife*! Indeed, it was generally the king's mother who ruled as queen, not his wife.[2]

The great preeminence of the king's mother may seem odd until we recall that most ancient Near Eastern kings practiced polygamy.[3] Think of King Solomon, who is reported to have had seven hundred wives (1 Kings 11:3). Imagine the chaos in the royal court if all seven hundred wives were awarded the queenship! One can see the practical wisdom in bestowing the queenship on the royal heir's mother. As David Stanley explains, "The existence of the [king's] harem made the position of the king's wives or concubines an anomalous one. Accordingly, it was *the mother of that royal son* who succeeded his father who, as dowager queen, enjoyed a position of preeminence surpassed only by her son."[4]

Further, the mother of the king received a special place in the royal court because of her role in securing the kingship for her son. Since the kings practiced polygamy, the resulting situation inevitably led to rivalries among wives, each vying for their son to become heir to the throne. Thus, the son who eventually became king often owed his kingship to the influence of his mother. As Barnabas Ahern explains,

> [In ancient Near Eastern kingdoms] monarchs practiced polygamy, a social anomaly which often resulted in the conflicting claims of rival wives. Accordingly, when a favorite royal son succeeded to the throne, he frequently owed his kingship to the influence of his mother, so that the dowager queen was wont to occupy a position of preeminence at court, sharing the glory and prerogatives of her son's rule.[5]

Let us now consider the prominent role given to the mother of the sovereign in a few, specific ancient Near Eastern kingdoms. It has been pointed out that in Hittite and Ugaritic texts, the mother of the heir-apparent ruled as queen, participating in political, military, economic, and religious affairs. In fact, during a king's extended absences or upon a king's death, the queen mother served as regent.[6] Holding an office independent of the king's, she retained her position even after the death of her son. Although she could be removed from her office for serious crimes against the state, this was a rarity.[7] Her preeminent position is seen in a tale of a Ugaritic king who himself even honors his mother by calling her "the Queen, my Mother" and then falling at her feet as a sign of respect.[8]

In Egypt, too, the queen mother was greatly revered. The Egyptians viewed the birth of a Pharaoh as resulting from a sexual union between the Pharaoh's mother and a deity. The queen mother held great importance because it was therefore believed that she was the instrument for bestowing divine status from the deity to her royal son. Thus, she was honored with titles of dignity, was mentioned with Pharaoh, and participated in the affairs of the state.[9]

In Assyria, the king's mother was an important lady in the royal court. Called "the mother of the king, my lord," the queen mother received official letters from servants of the state about sacrifices and military operations.[10] The Assyrian version of the Gligamesh epic portrays the queen mother as "versed in all knowledge," a wise counselor and a powerful intercessor for her royal son.[11]

Finally, some suggest that Daniel 5:10–12 offers a glimpse of the queen mother's prestigious role in the Persian Empire.[12] The scene following the mysterious hand writing on the wall during King Belshazzar's feast shows the queen mother's dignity and influence in the kingdom: "The queen, because of the words of the king and his lords, came into the banqueting hall; and the queen said, 'O king, live forever! Let not your thoughts alarm you or your colour change. There is in your kingdom a man in whom is the spirit of the holy gods. . . . Now let Daniel be called, and he will show the interpretation'" (Dan. 5:10–12). Ahern concludes, "It is noteworthy that the queen mother dominates the whole scene. She it is who takes charge of the critical situation and gives the counsel which is immediately carried out."[13]

2.2 The Queen Mother in the Davidic Kingdom

We will find great importance given to the mother of the king in the monarchies of ancient Israel as well. To that topic we now turn our attention.

2.2.1 Queen Mother: An Official Position in the Royal Court

Just like her Near Eastern neighbors, Israel bestowed great honor upon the mother of the ruling king. Roland De Vaux notes how the queen mother was given a special preeminence over all the women in the kingdom of Judah, even the king's wife. He highlights the fact that although one particular woman from the royal harem usually held the king's preference, "the king's favor was not enough to give this wife official title and rank."[14] This is seen in the fact that throughout the entire Old Testament, the word *queen* (feminine form of *melek*, or "king") is used only once in association with Israel, and even there it is used primarily poetically, not politically.[15] On the other hand, the prestigious title *gebirah* was used often in the Old Testament to describe the mother of the king. Meaning "mistress," "great lady," or "queen," *gebirah* is the feminine form of *gebhir* ("lord" or "master").[16] De Vaux notes how the term corresponds to *adon* (Lord), the feminine of which is not used in Hebrew.[17] In the Old Testament, *gebirah* is often used as a title for the mother of the king, but it is never used to describe the wife of an Israelite king.[18]

By examining various Old Testament passages involving the mother of the Davidic king, we can see that the queen mother held an official position in the royal court of Judah.[19] Her power in the kingdom was not based simply on a mother's influence over a son; the queen mother actually "held a significant official political position superseded only by that of the king himself."[20]

The importance of her office can be seen in a number of Old Testament texts. First, the narrative of 1 and 2 Kings views the king's mother as having such an important role that it mentions her name while introducing almost every new monarch in Judah (all except three).[21] Miguens notes how the narrator employs a stereotyped formula for introducing each king of Judah alongside his mother.[22] An example can be found in 1 Kings 15:1: "Now in the eighteenth year of King Jeroboam the son of Nebat, Abijam began to reign over Judah. He reigned for three years in Jerusalem. *His mother's name was Maacah, the daughter of Abishalom.*" This typical formula is never used to introduce the king and his wife, but it is consistently used to introduce the king and his mother. Furthermore, all but one queen mother is introduced with her family name (e.g., 2 Kings 15:33: "His mother's name was Jerusha *the daughter of Zadok*") or geographic origins (e.g., 2 Kings 15:2: "His mother's name was Jecoliah *of Jerusalem*").[23] Thus, at the crucial transition points of dynastic succession, we see the narrative of 1 and 2 Kings consistently highlighting the queen mother's important place alongside the new king: "On the throne the queen mother represented the king's continuity with the past, the visible affirmation of God's ongoing plan for his people, the channel through which the Lord's dynastic promise to David was fulfilled."[24]

It is also significant that 2 Kings 24 mentions the queen mother among the members of the royal court whom King Jehoiachin surrenders to the king of Babylon: "Jehoiachin the king of Judah gave himself up to the king of Babylon, himself, and *his mother*, and his servants, and his princes, and his palace officials" (v. 12). As Gray observes, "The fact that his mother is listed but not his wives is noteworthy. Since the queen mother is listed with the officials in describing the political fall, the author of 2 Kings recognizes that the mother of the king holds an important office that is worthy of note."[25] Father Manuel Miguens goes a step further, highlighting how the queen mother is listed before the king's wives and the other royal officials in 2 Kings 24:12–15:

. . . she is mentioned *before* the 'wives of the king' (2 Kings 24:15) and before the ministers, dignitaries and officers (2 Kings 24:12, 15; Jer. 29:2). Significantly these biblical passages say that the *gevirah* is the second, only to the king, in the list of prominent official persons brought into captivity. The detail speaks very highly of the political significance of "the mother of the king."[26]

Finally, the official character of the queen mother's role also can be seen in 1 Kings 15, in which King Asa actually deposes the queen mother from her position. "He also removed Maacah his mother from being queen mother because she had an abominable image made for Asherah" (1 Kings 15:13). This shows that the king could not change the blood relationship between him and his queen mother, but he could depose her from her *office* in the royal court.[27]

2.2.2 The Queen Mother's Influence in the Kingdom

How much influence did the queen mother wield in the kingdom? In this section, we will examine three ways she exercised power in the kingdom. First, we will see that the queen mother held a position of great authority in the royal court, in which she shared in her son's rule of the kingdom. Second, we will consider her role as an advocate for the people. Third, we will look at how she served as an important counselor to the king.

Royal Authority. Probably the best example of the queen mother's display of royal authority would be found in Bathsheba. A number of scholars have noted the excellence of Bathsheba's position in the kingdom once she became queen mother during Solomon's rule. Compare, on one hand, the humble attitude of Bathsheba as spouse of King David (1 Kings 1:16–17, 31) with, on the other hand, her majestic dignity as mother of the next king, her son Solomon (1 Kings 2:19–20).[28] As spouse of the king, Bathsheba bows with her face to the ground and does obeisance to her husband David upon entering his royal chamber. In a striking contrast, after her son Solomon assumes the throne and she becomes the queen mother, Bathsheba receives a glorious reception upon meeting with her royal son.

> So Bathsheba went to King Solomon, to speak to him on behalf of Adonijah. And the king rose to meet her, and bowed down to her; then he sat on his throne and had a seat brought for the king's mother; and she sat on his right. Then she said, "I have one small request to make of you; do not refuse me." And the king said to her, "Make your request, my mother; for I will not refuse you." (1 Kings 2:19–20)

This account reveals the sovereign prerogatives of the queen mother. As one scholar points out, "Nowhere else in the Bible does the king honor someone as Solomon does the Gebirah."[29] Note how the king rises and bows as the queen mother enters, and note his commitment to her petitions. Most of all, Bathsheba's seat at the king's right hand has the greatest significance. In the Bible, to sit at the right is to be given the place of ultimate honor.[30] "She was seated at his right, the place offered to the king by God (Ps 110:1), i.e., *she took precedence above all others.*"[31] Thus, the queen mother sitting at the king's right hand symbolizes her sharing in the king's royal authority and illustrates how she holds the most important position in the kingdom, second only to the king.[32]

Another example of the queen mother's power is found in Athaliah, after her son, King Ahaziah, died (2 Kings 11:1–3). Ahaziah's sudden death after a short one-year reign left the kingdom with sons who were too young to begin to rule. This power vacuum left the door open for Athaliah, who used her influence in the kingdom to secure full dynastic authority for herself. She massacred the royal family and proceeded to rule the kingdom for seven years (while Jehosheba kept one royal son in hiding). The fact that Athaliah was able to get away with this and continue to rule the kingdom in the absence of a king points to her strong power base and demonstrates the high ranking of the queen mother's office.[33]

Finally, the Prophet Jeremiah tells how the queen mother possessed a throne and a crown—symbols of her position of authority in the kingdom (Jer. 13:18).[34] In the oracle about the upcoming fall of Judah to the Babylonians, it is important to note that God instructs Jeremiah to address this oracle to both the king *and his mother*: "Say to the king and the queen mother: 'Take a lowly seat, for your beautiful crown has come down from your head. . . . Lift up your eyes and see those who come from the north. Where is the flock that was given you, your beautiful flock?" (Jer. 13:18, 20).

Why would the queen mother be addressed in this oracle? Again, this points to her preeminent position in the kingdom. By addressing both the king and his mother, this passage seems to recognize the queen mother's important role in the royal court. First, in ominous royal imagery pointing to their downfall, the king and queen mother are told to "take a lowly seat"— symbolizing how they *both* will soon lose their thrones. Second, *both* are told that they will lose their crowns—again foreshadowing their imminent fall from authority (Jer. 13:18; cf. Jer. 22:26, 29:2). Third, it is interesting to note how this oracle portrays the people of Judah as being shepherded by *both* the king and queen mother. "Where is the flock that was given you, your beautiful flock?" Thus, the prophet seems to understand that the queen mother had a shared role in ruling the kingdom.[35]

Advocate. A second form of the queen mother's influence in the kingdom can be seen in her role as advocate to the king. The passage about Bathsheba's petition to Solomon (discussed above) exhibits her intercessory role in the royal court.[36] In this context, Adonijah asks Bathsheba to take a petition for him to the king. He says to her: "Pray ask King Solomon—he will not refuse you—to give me Abishag the Shunammite as my wife" (1 Kings 2:17). It is clear that Adonijah recognizes the queen mother's position of great influence over the king ("he will not refuse you"); thus, he confidently turns to Bathsheba as an intercessor for his request. As we saw above, Bathsheba brings this petition to King Solomon with great confidence ("Do not refuse me"), and the king, after going through the ritual of bowing down before her and seating her at his right hand, replies: "Make your request, my mother; for *I will not refuse you*" (1 Kings 2:20).[37] Indeed, Solomon's words reveal the king's commitment to the queen mother's petitions.[38]

Counselor. The queen mother also served as a counselor to the king in the royal court.[39] In Proverbs 31, a queen mother gives wise counsel to her son, warning him against the dangers of women and wine. Andreasen writes, "Little doubt surrounds the fact that, whoever the king was, he is here being instructed by his mother. She warns him against women and wine and instructs him to comfort the distressed (with wine) and to secure justice for the oppressed."[40] Although not always positive, the queen mother's counsel had great influence in the kingdom. For example, 2 Chronicles 22:3 tells how King Ahaziah "walked in the ways of the house of Ahab [an evil king], for his mother was his counselor in doing wickedly." This shows how the queen mother's counsel was influential in leading Ahaziah's reign into wickedness.[41]

In sum, we have seen how the queen mother held an important office in the kingdom due to her unique relationship with the king and her role in dynastic succession. This position seems to have been second only to the king himself in the royal court. In her office, the queen mother served as an intercessor for the people and a counselor to her royal son. All this serves as background for understanding two key Old Testament texts that took on messianic significance, and that involve a royal mother figure and her son.

2.3 Queen-Mother Themes in Israel's Messianic Hopes

In this section, we turn our attention to two Old Testament passages which bear witness to the importance of the *gebirah* in Israel's traditions: Isaiah 7:14 and Genesis 3:15. Here, we will consider how Mariologists and biblical scholars alike have pointed out the importance of seeing the queen-mother tradition as a background to these texts. Whatever view one may hold about the development of messianism in ancient Israel,[42] the important point for our purposes is to note how these passages involve a mother figure intimately linked with a royal son who at least to some extent became associated with Israel's messianic hopes.[43]

2.3.1 Isaiah 7:14

The famous prophecy of Isaiah 7:14 must be read in its original context—a time of dynastic crisis in the kingdom of Judah. Troops from Syria and Israel were threatening Jerusalem and plotting to replace Judah's King Ahaz with "the son of Tabeel." The Davidic dynasty was in great danger (Is. 7:1–6).

In Isaiah 7, the prophet assured Ahaz that this plan would not come to pass (7:4–9) and challenged him to entrust his throne to the Lord with the warning: "If you will not believe, surely you shall not be established" (Is. 7:9).[44] Then Isaiah even offered Ahaz the opportunity to ask for any sign from the Lord in order to help give the faithless king cause for resting the security of his dynasty in Yahweh. But Ahaz refused, replying, "I will not put the Lord to the test" (Is. 7:12). Nevertheless, Isaiah goes on to give a sign that will serve as a confirmation of Yahweh's words to Ahaz:

> Hear then, O house of David! Is it too little for you to weary men, that you weary my God also? Therefore the Lord himself will give you a sign. Behold, a young woman [*almah*] shall conceive and bear a son, and shall call his name Immanuel. (Is. 7:14)

Identifying the young woman (*almah*) and the Immanuel child in this prophecy has been a topic of great debate through-out the centuries.[45] Scholars who have attempted to address this question have offered a number of common interpretive options. For example, following the New Testament interpre-tation of Isaiah 7:14 in Matthew 1:23, some scholars defend the traditional view of this prophecy, which understands it as a direct prediction of the virginal conception of Christ, with the *almah* referring to the virgin mother Mary and the Immanuel child referring to Jesus.[46] In addition to the fact that *almah* is not a technical term for a virgin,[47] understanding this prophecy in its historical context makes it difficult to accept this traditional view as the exclusive meaning of the text. Since the prophets of the Old Testament were primarily interested in addressing God's challenge to Israel in their own immediate historical setting,[48] one would expect the sign Isaiah offered Ahaz to have bearing on the particular situation the kingdom was facing at the time.[49] In this light, it is difficult to see how an event occurring hundreds of years later (the virginal con-ception of Christ) could be a sign for Ahaz and the House of David during the Syro-Ephraimitic crisis. The sign makes most sense if it has meaning within a relatively short period of time, especially since Isaiah 7:15–16 links the maturity of the Immanuel child with the land of the two threatening powers (Syria and Israel) being devastated.[50]

Others have offered a collective interpretation, suggesting that the *almah* does not refer to a particular individual woman, but represents the many women in the kingdom who would bear forth children that year and give them the name "Immanuel" to celebrate the imminent withdrawal of Syria and Israel.[51] However, the presence of the definite article (*the* young woman, or *ha almah*) in Isaiah 7:14 suggests that the prophet was referring to a particular woman whom the king would have known.[52] Furthermore, ordinary women giving birth to male children and naming their sons Immanuel was unlikely to be a meaningful sign for Ahaz.[53]

Still others contend that the *almah* is to be identified as Isaiah's wife and that the Immanuel child is Isaiah's son Maher-shalal-hash-baz, mentioned in 8:3.[54] Yet, since Isaiah's wife already bore him a son who was old enough to walk with him (Is. 7:3), it is highly unlikely that she would be designated an *almah*—a young woman of marriageable age—in 7:14.[55]

Most convincing is a fourth view, which interprets the *almah* as a wife of King Ahaz and "Immanuel" as an heir to the Davidic throne. This approach best shows how this sign for the House of David relates to the immediate context of the dynastic crisis at hand. We first note how the passage resounds with several dynastic overtones, as the oracle is situated within the context of the kingdom of Judah being threatened by foreign invaders. Not only was the Davidic line in danger of expiring (Is. 7:6), but, as a result, God's faithfulness to the Davidic dynasty was placed in question (2 Sam. 7:11–14).[56] It is within this setting that Isaiah specifically addressed "the house of David"[57] with this oracle announcing the Immanuel child in 7:14. Given this context, it is likely that the child represents some type of dynastic sign guaranteeing the succession of the endangered Davidic line. This view finds further support in the fact that the child's name ("God with us") is itself bound up with the idea of the preservation of the Davidic tradition. Since God promised to be "with" the sons of David in a special way (2 Sam. 7:9; 1 Kings 1:37; Ps. 89:22, 25; 1 Kings 11:38), the sign of a child named Immanuel gives assurance that God will remain faithful to his promise to the Davidic dynasty: God will still be with His people even through this crisis in which the House of David appears to be crumbling.[58] All this strongly supports an understanding of the child as a successor to the Davidic throne—an heir to King Ahaz who would continue the dynasty.[59] As Wildberger explains,

> If the sign in 7:14 is in any way connected with the oracle of salvation in 7:4-9, with its prominent conclusion in v. 9b, then the name . . . (Immanuel) must also be interpreted according to its connection with the Davidic traditions. But if that is the case, it is the unavoidable conclusion that Immanuel is the son of the king and the . . . (almah) is the wife or at least one of the wives of Ahaz.[60]

We conclude that the prophet offers the House of David a sign of a Davidic son who would manifest God's faithfulness to the people of Judah in this time of dynastic crisis: "The child would help to preserve the House of David and would thus signify that God was still 'with us.'"[61]

Once we see the Immanuel child as a Davidic king, the *almah* would have been understood as a wife of King Ahaz.[62] Furthermore, in this oracle addressed specifically to the Davidic household (Is. 7:13), the young woman bearing forth the royal son, the heir to the throne, would have been understood as a queen mother.[63] Stuhlmueller points out that after Ahaz refused to ask for a sign, Isaiah turned away from the unfaithful king and looked to the future by focusing on the heir to the throne and his queen mother. In this prophecy, "the wife, who would bear the royal successor, seemed much more important than Achaz! She would also later stand beside the child as queen mother."[64] Similarly, Montague also notes how the attention is shifted from Ahaz to the queen mother in this oracle: "The spotlight fell upon the woman who would carry the future of Israel in her womb—the next queen mother."[65] He explains that the queen mother always played an important part in dynastic succession,[66] and that she continues to do so in this oracle of Isaiah 7:14.

> Ahaz' role in begetting his successor is, because of his lack of faith in the divine promise, passed over in favor of the instrumentality of the true queen mother. She, not Ahaz, will name the child Immanuel. . . . Because it is a future king that is

envisioned and the present king has been an unworthy transmitter of the promise, it is the *mother* of the future king who passes on the promise.[67]

With Isaiah's overriding concern for dynastic succession in the House of David, it is fitting that this prophecy links the royal son with his queen mother, who, as we have seen above, played an important role in dynastic succession and in the royal court.[68]

Finally, we note that the extent to which this passage can be viewed as messianic prophecy is still debated. Some place this prophecy at the stage of dynastic messianism,[69] while others see the Immanuel child as referring to the Messiah-King who would reign in the age to come.[70] Still others (including myself) see a double fulfillment, with the successor to Ahaz bringing the prophecy to a partial fulfillment and Christ giving it its ultimate fulfillment.[71] Whatever position one may hold regarding the messianic relevance of this prophecy in its original announcement, we simply wish to highlight the role of the queen-mother figure in this oracle. And for our purposes, this will be important because one thing that is *not* debated about this prophecy is that Matthew's Gospel will employ it in relation to Mary and her royal Davidic Son, Jesus, in the New Testament (Mt. 1:23).[72]

2.3.2 Genesis 3:15

At first glance, Genesis 3:15 may not appear to be relevant to our study of queen-mother themes in the Old Testament. However, by considering recent studies that have pointed out the rich kingdom imagery in Genesis 1–3 (and in Genesis 3:15 specifically), we will again find a woman intimately associated with a royal offspring in a way that may at least shed some light on our topic.

Here, we will build upon the insights of biblical scholars who have demonstrated the various ways in which the narrative of Genesis 1–3 portrays Adam and Eve as royal figures.[73] First, we begin in Genesis 1 and note how the creation story depicts man and woman as being given the mission to rule over all creation. As the creation drama reaches its climax in the creation of man and woman in Genesis 1:26–30, God gives them the vocation of having *dominion over* the fish, birds, cattle, and all the earth (v. 26)—all the life forms that had been created on the previous days.[74] The narrative further elaborates on their dominion as they are told to subdue the earth and rule over the rest of creation (v. 28)—a royal task.[75] And later, Adam is told to establish order among the animals and name them (Gen. 2:19–29), the latter (name-giving) being a function which Von Rad and others point out is a kingly prerogative related to Adam's dominion in 1:28.[76] Furthermore, this human share in God's rule over creation can be seen in the notion of the *imago Dei* (Gen. 1:26). While there are numerous views on what it means to be made in God's image and likeness,[77] one dimension of our understanding is that man and woman reflect the deity's sovereignty over the universe, and thus are called to serve as God's royal representatives.

> The text speaks less of the nature of God's image than of its purpose . . . domination in the world, especially over the animals. . . . Just as powerful earthly kings, to indicate their claim to dominion, erect an image of themselves in the provinces of their empire where they do not personally appear, so man is placed upon earth in God's image as God's sovereign emblem. He is really only God's representative, summoned to maintain and enforce God's claim to dominion over the earth.[78]

This perspective goes well with the description of humanity in Psalm 8—man is made a little lower than the angels, *crowned* with glory and honor, and made *to rule* over all of God's creation (vv. 5–8). It also fits into the ancient Near Eastern world-view, in which the divine image was used to describe the king ruling in God's behalf.[79] Gordon Wenham thus concludes:

> Another consideration suggesting that man [as depicted in Genesis 1] is a divine representative on earth arises from the very idea of an image. Images of gods or kings were viewed as representatives of the deity or king. . . . Whereas Egyptian writers often spoke of kings as being in God's image, they never referred to other people in this way. It appears that the OT [Old Testament] has democratized this old idea. It affirms that *not just a king, but every man and woman, bears God's image and is his representative on earth.*[80]

As we move into Genesis 2–3, we note that some biblical scholars have given good reason to believe that it can be helpful to read these passages with the Davidic kingdom in mind. Wolf and Clements, for example, have argued that many Yahwistic texts in Genesis 12–50 are framed against the background of the Davidic covenant.[81] This is significant for our chapters because Brueggemann, Witfall, and others have extended this demonstration of Davidic themes into Genesis 2–11 as well.[82] Along these lines, Brueggemann has argued that "in Gn 2–11, just below the surface of mythological materials and affirmations about 'the human predicament' lies the story of David's family and the God of the Davidic house."[83]

One example can be found in Genesis 2:7, where the creation of Adam is described in royal terms. In this verse, the imagery of Adam being taken from the dust of the earth (Gen. 2:7a) is something we find elsewhere in the Old Testament to describe how God establishes a man as king by lifting him up from the dust (1 Kings 16:2–3; 1 Samuel 2:6–8; Psalm 113:7).[84] In the process of examining various Old Testament texts that employ this imagery in relation to royal authority,[85] Brueggemann states that there are thus royal overtones in

Genesis 2:7: "Behind the creation formula lies a royal formula of enthronement. To be taken 'from the dust' means to be elevated from obscurity to royal office."[86] He concludes, "Adam, in Gen 2, is really being crowned king over the garden with all the power and authority which it implies. This is the fundamental statement about man made by J. He is willed by God to occupy a royal office. . . . *Thus creation of man is in fact enthronement of man.*"[87]

Witfall has gone on to show how the imagery of God breathing the breath of life "into his nostrils," found in the second half of Genesis 2:7, is also present later in the royal context of Lamentations 4:20, in which the author laments King Zedekiah being captured at the fall of the Davidic dynasty. In this passage, the author equates "the breath of our nostrils" with the anointed king: "The breath of our nostrils, the Lord's anointed, was taken in their pits" (Lam. 4:20).[88] Similarly, the "breath of life" (Gen. 2:7b) given to Adam by God might be linked with the divine gift given to the messianic king figure in Isaiah 11:1–2.[89] Witfall concludes that the Yahwist here is "portraying the relation of David to Israel as the prototype for the relation of Adam to mankind. According to this perspective, God's creative breath worked at the beginning through Adam to all of mankind just as it continued to work through the House of David to all of Israel and its empire."[90]

Thus, with all this rich kingdom imagery found in the opening chapters of Genesis, it is not surprising that we should continue to find royal themes in Genesis 3:14–15. In 3:14, the serpent is cursed to crawl on the earth and eat the dust. In the Old Testament, the imagery of eating the dust was a sign of royal defeat, loss of power, or being subjected to an elevated, triumphant king.[91] For example, Psalm 72 uses this image to describe how the king's enemies are to bow before the king and "eat the dust" (Ps. 72:9). As Brueggemann explains, "The well-being and elevation of the king . . . depends upon the subjugation of the opposition. The wish for the enemy to be in the dust is the counterpart of the enhancement of the king who moves from death to life in its rich, powerful royal form."[92] Thus, when the serpent figure is cursed to "eat the dust," it is depicted in a way similar to the enemies of the king, who were conquered in the times of the Davidic monarchy.

These kingly themes then continue into Genesis 3:15: "I will put enmity between you and the woman, and between your seed and her seed; he shall bruise your head, and you shall bruise his heel." Here, the seed of the woman will attack the head of the serpent.[93] A similar picture was used during monarchical times to describe how Davidic kings would crush their enemies in dust beneath their feet (Ps. 89:23; 2 Sam. 22:37–43).[94] And the Psalms use analogous under-the-feet imagery to portray the royal authority God gave to man (placing "all things under his feet" in Psalm 8:6) and the dominion He would give to the Davidic king (making "your enemies your footstool" in Psalm 110:1).[95] Thus, Genesis 3:15 presents the position of the woman's seed in ways similar to the royal position Davidic kings held over their foes.[96] As Kearney concludes, "The offspring of the woman in Gen. 3:15 will strike the head of the serpent's offspring, as kings do against their enemies (Num. 25:17; cf. Ps. 110:6)."[97]

Given the royal themes both in the wider context of Genesis 1–3 and in 3:15 itself, this passage points to a future kingly figure who will crush the head of the serpent in a way that Davidic kings would subdue their enemies. Therefore, it is important to note that in the midst of all these kingly images, we find a mother figure intimately linked with a royal "seed" who will bring about some type of future victory over the serpent.

This brings us to the question of the extent to which Genesis 3:15 can be considered a "protoevangelium"—the first prophetic announcement of the Messiah (cf. *Catechism*, no. 410). A few interpreters argue that this passage is a clear, direct prediction of the Messiah, Jesus, and His victory over the devil.[98] The majority of critical scholars, however, point out that this first view reads too much into the text of Genesis 3:15. They instead hold a second view which denies any promise of the Messiah in this verse.[99] Many in this camp conclude that verses 14–15 involve simply an etiology that either explains why snakes crawl on the ground without legs or describes the never-ending strife between snakes and humans.[100] It is also argued that since the Hebrew word for the woman's seed (*zerah*) has a collective meaning, referring to the woman's descendants as a whole, it cannot refer to an individual Messiah and his mother.[101] Von Rad expresses this view in his commentary on Genesis: "The exegesis of the early church which found a messianic prophecy here, a reference to a final victory of the woman's seed (Protoevangelium), does not agree with the sense of the passage, quite apart from the fact that the word 'seed' may not be construed personally but only quite generally with the meaning 'posterity.'"[102]

There remains one more interpretive option, however, which stands as an alternative between these first two views. Scholars holding this third view do not claim Genesis 3:15 in its original context is an obvious, detailed messianic prophecy, but at the same time, they disagree with those who want to rid the association of "protoevangelium" with this passage altogether.[103] This third view recognizes that Genesis 3:15 does not offer a detailed portrait of the Messiah, but nevertheless maintains that the passage, while remaining obscure, at least seems to suggest some type of eventual victory of the woman's seed over the serpent.

This third approach seems to make the most sense out of the text, recognizing that there may be something more to Genesis 3:14–15 than simply an etiology about snakes and humans. Since symbolic imagery is employed throughout Genesis 1–3,[104] a strict literalistic view of the serpent in Genesis 3 seems unlikely.[105] As Wenham argues, many elements in the narrative "are highly symbolic, and the dialogue between snake and woman employs ambiguity and innuendo with great subtlety. If elsewhere in the narrative we have double-entendre and symbolic language, it would be strange for it to disappear here, so that the serpent is just a snake and not an anti-God symbol."[106]

Furthermore, there is good reason to interpret Genesis 3:15 as hinting at some type of eventual defeat of the serpent figure. First, when we read 3:15 in light of its previous verse, we see that the description of the strife between the two seeds is given to us in the context of the *serpent* being cursed (v. 14). Therefore, the strife between the seeds ultimately must be considered as part of the malediction on the serpent, suggesting that the serpent will in some way lose in the end.[107] Moreover, the humiliating, defeatist imagery of the serpent being cursed to crawl on his belly and lick the dust in 3:14 (as explored above) also points to a subjection of the serpent figure.[108] Finally, Genesis 3:15 portrays the serpent in a tactically weaker position (the serpent is only able to strike at the heel, while the woman's seed strikes at the serpent's head)—again hinting at some type of victory over the serpent.[109] This point is seen even more clearly when the royal image of crushing the head (discussed above) is considered.[110]

All these factors seem to suggest that the reader might expect an eventual defeat of the serpent.[111] This is why scholars such as Feuillet have concluded that, although the passage remains obscure, we can at least say that it "allows us to catch a glimpse of the moral victory of humanity which will crush the head of the tempting serpent, the cause of its initial ruin."[112] Following this perspective, while we would agree that the text does not offer an explicitly detailed portrait of the Messiah in this verse, we maintain that Genesis 3:15 does offer some future hope for the woman's seed to defeat the serpent—a hope which further revelation would later clarify and eventually associate with the victory of the Messiah in ways that make the traditional Christian designation of this passage as the "protoevangelium" seem fitting.[113]

For our purposes, after having highlighted the many royal overtones in Genesis 1–3 and in 3:15 itself, and after having established the woman's association with her royal offspring's triumph, we conclude that Genesis 3:15 presents a mother figure placed within a dynastic context and associated with her kingly offspring in bringing about some type of royal victory over the enemy. Such a mother sounds somewhat like the queen mother in the Davidic kingdom. In fact, it is also significant that the woman takes center stage in relation to the royal offspring—the man is left out. We found a similar scenario in the queen-mother-and-son prophecy of Isaiah 7:14.[114] With all this in mind, a number of scholars have suggested the possibility of seeing the woman in Genesis 3:15 as a prototypical queen-mother figure.[115] They would argue that, since the drama of Adam and Eve has been placed within the framework of the Davidic kingdom (as discussed in detail above), the woman of Genesis 3:15 should be understood within this Davidic context as well. If that is the case, then who would be the woman who was the wife to the king and who would give birth to a royal son? Within the Davidic context of these "Yahwistic" passages, the woman is viewed by some as a prototypical queen-mother figure.[116] This is, in fact, what Ahern has suggested: "It does not seem altogether unlikely that the [Yahwist] editor has seen the motherhood of the 'woman' in the light of the queen-mother tradition of Juda."[117] Cazelles, Robert, Feuillet, Laurentin, and Stuhlmueler have made similar observations in their discussion of the woman as a prototype of the queen mother.[118] Kearney sums up his royal perspective of the woman in Genesis 3:15, by saying: "No doubt [the queen mother] has her place in Gen 2–3. The 'woman' in these two chapters is queen as the wife of the royal figure Adam. . . . She is most clearly queen mother as the one whose royal offspring strike at the serpent's head."[119]

———•••———

In summary, we have seen how the queen-mother figure plays an important role in the Old Testament. In the Davidic kingdom, the mother of the king held an official position in the royal court, in which she shared in her son's reign and served as an advocate for the people and a counselor for her son. We have also seen how the queen mother was associated with two key Old Testament texts, bound up with Israel's messianic hopes. The prophecy of Isaiah 7:14 involves the sign of a queen mother who will conceive and bear the future Davidic King, Immanuel. The queen-mother figure also may appear prototypically in Genesis 3:15, which also associates a mother with her royal offspring in a context that has important Davidic kingdom overtones. With all this background in mind, we are now prepared to examine how Mary, the mother of the Davidic King *par excellence* in the New Testament, can be understood in light of this queen-mother tradition of the Old Testament.

CHAPTER THREE

The Queen Mother
and the New Testament
Portrayal of Mary

In chapter two, we examined the role of the queen mother in the Davidic kingdom and then looked at how that queen-mother tradition illuminates two Old Testament texts that eventually came to take on messianic significance: Isaiah 7:14 and Genesis 3:15. Now we turn our attention to the New Testament. With the importance given to the queen mother in the Davidic kingdom and in Israel's messianic hopes, one should not be surprised to find a royal mother figure intimately associated with the new Davidic King, Jesus Christ, in His establishment of the kingdom of God. Keeping the Old Testament background in mind, we will now look at how the queen-mother tradition can shed light on the New Testament portrait of Mary, the mother of the King, in ways that might lend some important biblical support for our understanding of Mary's queenly office.

3.1 Matthew 1–2

As we turn to Matthew's Gospel, we will first examine how the infancy narrative (Mt. 1–2) resounds with important Davidic overtones, placing the various scenes involving Jesus' origins, birth, and infancy in the context of the hopes surrounding the Davidic kingdom.[1] Secondly, by interpreting Mary's role in the infancy narrative in light of that Davidic kingdom context that Matthew evokes, we will consider how the queen-mother tradition might be helpful for understanding Mary, the mother of the newborn Davidic King, in Matthew 1–2.

3.1.1 Davidic Kingdom Themes in Matthew 1–2

Jesus is placed in a Davidic context in the very first verse of Matthew's Gospel. Right away he is called *christos* (1:1), meaning "anointed one." This term translated the Hebrew word *masiah* (also meaning "anointed one"), which often was used in the Old Testament to describe Israel's king as "the Lord's anointed" (e.g., 1 Sam. 24:6; 2 Sam. 1:14).[2] In post-exilic times, Jews came to use *masiah* (and *christos*) to designate the future Davidic King whom God would use to restore the kingdom and establish a perfect, everlasting reign.[3] Thus, when Matthew uses "Christ" in reference to Jesus five times in the first two chapters alone, he quickly draws attention to Jesus' Davidic heritage (Mt. 1:1, 16, 17, 18, 2:4). In using this word, Jesus is identified as the long-awaited anointed King who would restore the House of David to its former glory.[4]

This messianic portrait of Jesus is filled in more by a related title that immediately follows: "son of David" (1:1). It may be significant that this is one of the first titles Matthew bestows on Jesus. "Son of David," one of Matthew's favorite Christological titles, is used by him more frequently than any other Gospel writer.[5] By the first century, this title designated the messianic king who would fulfill the promises God made to David for the eternal reign of one of David's offspring (2 Sam. 7:10–16; cf. Ps. 89:1–4, 19–37, 132:11–12).[6] Thus, Matthew shows us that Jesus is not just any descendant of David, but *the* Son of David who would inaugurate the perfect kingdom and whose reign would have no end.[7]

Then the genealogy goes on to make the point that Jesus is a true Davidid. This is seen in a number of ways. First, in addition to the reference to the four women (1:3, 5, 6), the brothers of Jeconiah (1:11) and the Babylonian exile (1:12), the otherwise monotonous genealogy (the series of "and A was the father of B") is also broken up by explicit mention of David's title as "the king," which underscores that this genealogy is tracing a *royal* lineage (1:6).[8] Second, another link between David and Jesus can be seen in the fact that of all the names in the genealogy, only two are given a title: David and Jesus. David is described as "the king" (1:6) and Jesus is called "the Christ" (1:16).[9] Third, with the genealogy divided into the three sets of fourteen generations, Matthew sets forth the second section (the kings from David to the exile) to highlight Jesus' monarchical ancestry and the third set (vv. 12–16) to show that the Davidic line has continued up until Jesus' day despite its apparent disappearance after the Babylonian exile.[10] This last section, therefore, is important for connecting the end of the monarchy with the final anointed King, Jesus Christ.[11] Fourth, there also may be Davidic imagery in the concluding verse of the genealogy where Matthew draws attention to the *number* of generations listed from Abraham to Jesus:

> So all the generations from Abraham to David were *fourteen* generations, and from David to the deportation to Babylon *fourteen* generations, and from the deportation to Babylon to the Christ *fourteen* generations. (Mt. 1:17)

By highlighting three periods (Abraham to David; David to the Babylonian exile; and the exile to Christ) each consisting of fourteen generations, Matthew is drawing our attention to the number 14. This has royal significance because in Hebrew, the numerical value of the letters in David's name adds up to this very number. The three Hebrew consonants in David's name are *dwd* (d = 4, w = 6), giving a total of 14. Thus, some have concluded that the very structure of Matthew's genealogy being centered around three sets of fourteen generations rings out with Davidic overtones, subtly proclaiming Jesus as the "thrice-Davidic Son of David."[12]

After the genealogy, Matthew highlights Joseph's Davidic lineage with the angel addressing him as "Joseph, son of David" (1:20).[13] Then Matthew shows how Jesus can be a true son of David even though he is not a physical son of Joseph. In 1:25, the angel instructs Joseph to name the child Jesus. In Jewish circles, a man naming a child would have signified acknowledging the child as his own. Brown explains how Joseph naming the child shows him legally accepting Jesus as his own son: "Joseph, by exercising the father's right to name the child (cf. Luke 1:60–63), acknowledges Jesus and thus becomes the legal father of the child."[14] This is important because it shows how Joseph's Davidic descent is passed on to Jesus, not through physical fatherhood, but through "legal paternity."[15] Finally, in 1:22–23, Matthew uses his characteristic fulfillment formula to show Jesus is Immanuel, the royal Son fulfilling the prophecy of Isaiah 7:14.[16]

In chapter two, Jesus' kingship is highlighted in the story of the magi in many ways. Matthew links the child with David by noting that he was born in Bethlehem (2:1), the same place where David was born.[17] The magi call him "the king of the Jews" (2:2) and want to give royal homage to the newborn King (2:2).[18] A star often served as a sign of a king's arrival in ancient Roman culture,[19] as well as in the Old Testament.[20] Herod himself even refers to the newborn child as the Messiah (2:4).[21] The Gospel further highlights Jesus' Davidic character by portraying him as the fulfillment of the messianic prophecy of Micah 5:2:

> And you, O Bethlehem, in the land of Judah, are by no means least among the rulers of Judah; for from you shall come a ruler who will govern my people Israel. (Mt. 2:5–6)

The Davidic inference is made most explicit in verse 6b, where Matthew diverges a little from the Micah prophecy and inserts the words "you will shepherd my people Israel"—the same words spoken to David when the people asked him to become king over all twelve tribes of Israel (2 Sam. 5:2).[22] Further, the scene of the magi paying royal homage to the newborn child also reveals Jesus' kingship. This is especially seen in the gifts that the magi bring, for they are gifts fit for a king, as is seen in this passage's allusions to Isaiah 60:1, 5–6, Psalm 72:10–11, and 1 Kings 10:2, 10.[23] Moreover, non-Jewish magi from the East bringing these gifts and coming to pay homage to the newborn King shows the universal extent of Jesus' kingship.[24]

After the magi scene, we find another Davidic allusion at the end of chapter two. Matthew points out how Jesus' dwelling in Nazareth fulfills the mysterious words of the prophets, "He shall be called a Nazarene" (2:23).[25] Here, Matthew is probably associating Jesus in his hometown (Nazareth) with the Hebrew word for the messianic branch (*neser*) that shall grow out of the stump of Jesse (Is. 11:1).[26]

Finally, Nolan has argued that Matthew places special emphasis on Jesus as "the child" in a way that draws attention to Jesus being the dynastic successor. The royal son in the prophecy of Isaiah 7:14 is called "Immanuel" and then two verses later is referred to as "the child" (Is. 7:16). Similarly, Jesus is identified as Immanuel in Matthew 1:23, and then is referred to as "the child" often throughout the rest of the infancy narrative. In fact, τὸ παιδίον is used nine times in 2:8–21 alone. As Nolan explains, "The heavy emphasis on 'The Child' in Matthew 2 presents the heir to David who will rule the Gentiles and his people Israel."[27]

3.1.2 Queen-Mother Allusions in Matthew 1–2

Clearly, the portrait of Mary in the Gospel of Matthew is not as extensive as what we find in Luke.[28] Matthew 1–2 gives us only a few glimpses of Mary: her name appears in Jesus' genealogy (1:16), her extraordinary pregnancy is the subject of the first message of the angel appearing to Joseph in a dream (1:18–25), and she is mentioned frequently alongside her Son in Matthew 2 (Mt. 2:11, 13, 14, 20, 21). In Matthew's infancy narrative, Joseph seems to play a more prominent role.[29] And when it comes to his account of Jesus' public ministry, Matthew devotes little space to Mary, mentioning her only twice in passing (12:46–50; 13:53–58).[30]

Still, the few glimpses of Mary that Matthew 1–2 does offer are important ones: Matthew places her in the royal genealogy along with the other four women (Mt. 1:16).[31] He also shows Mary's role in fulfilling prophecy (Mt. 1:23; Is. 7:14)[32] and highlights her close association with her Son several times in chapter two (Mt. 2:11, 13, 14, 20, 21).[33] These are themes that we will now consider. After having demonstrated how Matthew 1–2 clearly places Jesus in the context of the Davidic kingdom, we will now note how within this royal framework, Matthew highlights Mary's role as the mother of this new Davidic King in ways that associate her with the queen-mother figure of the Davidic royal court.

First, some suggest that Matthew's genealogy may hint at Mary being associated with royal matriarchal figures of the past.[34] In addition to Mary, four other women are mentioned in the genealogy of Matthew 1: Tamar, Rahab, Ruth, and Bathsheba. Since it was rather unusual to list the name of a woman in a genealogy in first-century Judaism, the fact that Matthew lists five women (all of whom would have been considered scandalous to some extent) has led interpreters to consider what his purpose was in placing them in the genealogy.[35] While various theories have been offered,[36] one common thread uniting all five women is that they each gave birth to a child through irregular unions—which might be scandalous to some. Yet, nevertheless, God carried out His plan through these unusual relations.[37] By mentioning the first four women who had these "holy irregularities,"[38] Matthew's genealogy prepares the reader for understanding Mary's extraordinary motherhood, which is intimated at the end of the genealogy (Matthew is careful to note that Jesus is born of Mary, but not of Joseph in 1:16) and which is elaborated upon at the end of chapter one (Jesus is conceived of the Holy Spirit in 1:21).[39]

On another level, however, some have suggested that the genealogy also may be portraying Mary as standing in line with the queen-mother tradition by associating her with Bathsheba, the queen mother of Solomon and the first and most prominent queen mother in the history of the dynasty (Mt. 1:6). Thus, according to Branick, Mary appears as "the mother of the Messiah and is associated with the matriarchs and queen mothers of the Old Testament."[40] Susan Ackerman goes even further. She suggests that in addition to the irregular or extraordinary marital unions, another thing linking the four women with Mary is that they are all motherly predecessors to the Davidic kings in this royal lineage. Like Mary,

> they either are queen mothers (Bathsheba) or adumbrate that office in the premonarchic period: thus Tamar bears Perez through Judah, to whom is already assigned, in Gen 49:10, the 'scepter' and the 'ruler's staff' as emblems of monarchy; Rahab, through Salmon, is the mother of Boaz, and Ruth, through Boaz, is the mother of Obed, both of whom are important in biblical tradition because they are immediate ancestors of David, the founder of the Judean royal dynasty.[41]

Menninger makes a similar observation: "What connected each of these women to Mary is the thought that they all bore children of the line of David."[42] These hypotheses are interesting because they draw attention to the Davidic character these four women have within the genealogy of Matthew 1. This is seen clearly in three of the women: Tamar, Ruth, and Bathsheba. Tamar and Ruth stand out as important motherly ancestors of David. Tamar was the mother of Perez through Judah, with whom the monarchy was foreshadowed in the patriarchal times (Gen. 38:18; 49:8–12), while Ruth was the great-grandmother of King David (Ruth 4:13–22). Bathsheba not only was David's prized wife, but she also served as the foundational queen mother in the Davidic dynasty during Solomon's rule (2 Sam. 12:24; 1 Kings 1:13–20). However, a weakness with this perspective might be found when one considers the other woman in the genealogy, Rahab. Matthew lists Rahab as the mother of Boaz through Salmon (1:5), which would make her the great, great-grandmother of David. Yet, nowhere was this woman associated with Davidic ancestry either in the Old Testament or in Jewish tradition, and outside of Matthew 1, there is no mention of her as the wife of Salmon or mother of Boaz.[43] Thus, while this interpretation might be possible, it is not clear that Matthew would have included Rahab among the four women in the genealogy specifically because she was a royal maternal predecessor to David and a prefiguring of the queen mothers of the Davidic kingdom (and of the final queen mother, Mary).

There is a second approach to interpreting Mary in Matthew 1–2 in light of the queen-mother figure. This approach underscores how Matthew associates Mary and Jesus with the queen-mother-and-royal-son prophecy of Isaiah 7:14 (which we examined in chapter two). In 1:23, Matthew portrays Mary as the *parthenos* whom Isaiah prophesied would give birth to the Immanuel child in Isaiah 7:14 (LXX). Thus, "according to the fulfillment of the prophecy, Mary became queen-mother of the Messiah."[44] In the Isaian oracle, the queen mother of Immanuel brings forth a child who would ensure the perseverance of the Davidic dynasty.[45] Here in Matthew 1, Mary does the same, bringing forth the Davidic heir who would secure the true Davidic kingdom forever.[46] As Serra explains,

> Just as she [the queen mother in Isaiah 7:14] gave birth to a
> son who guaranteed the continuation of the House of David,

so Mary gives birth to a son who will reign forever on the throne of David, in the house of Jacob, in the 'Israel of God' (cf. Mt. 28:20; 16:18; Gal. 6:16; 2 Sam. 7:16). One notes the royalty of the two women.[47]

A third approach shows the significance of Matthew frequently placing the newborn King alongside His mother. In fact, some have pointed out how Matthew constantly mentioning the child and His mother together—five times in chapter two alone[48]—could draw attention to Mary's association with her royal Son in a way that recalls the Old Testament queen-mother tradition.[49] Matthew's recurring phrase "the child and his mother" has "a Davidic resonance"[50] that might bring to mind the way the Book of Kings repeatedly introduces each new Davidic king alongside the queen mother (as discussed in chapter two). As Branick argues:

> Matthew has the powerful figure of the Old Testament *gebirah* or queen-mother in mind as he repeatedly mentions Mary in this story of the birth and infancy of 'the newborn king of the Jews' (2:2). Just as the queen-mother was constantly mentioned in the summaries of the Judean and Israelite kings, so Matthew here repeatedly mentions Mary as Jesus' Mother (1:18; 2:11, 13, 14, 20, 21; 12:46, 47; 13:55).[51]

A fourth approach to viewing Mary in terms of the queen-mother tradition in Matthew 1–2 examines her position alongside her royal Son when the magi pay Him homage (Mt. 2:11). As mentioned above, this scene involves a number of Davidic kingdom themes: Jesus is called the "king of the Jews" (2:2). The star guiding the magi recalls the star in Balaam's oracle about the royal scepter rising out of Israel (Num. 24:17). The narrative centers on the city of Bethlehem,[52] where David was born (1 Sam 17:12) and out of which the future Davidic King would come (Micah 5:2). And the magi bringing gifts and paying the child Jesus homage recall the royal Psalm 72:10–11 (cf. Is. 60:6).[53]

Within this Davidic kingdom context, Matthew singles out Mary as being with the child when the three magi come to honor the newborn King. Notice how Joseph is conspicuously not even mentioned: ". . . going into the house, they [the three Magi] saw *the child with Mary his mother*, and they fell down and worshipped him" (Mt. 2:11).[54] Why does Matthew focus on Jesus and Mary, leaving Joseph out of the picture at this point? All throughout the narrative in Matthew 1–2, Joseph is much more prominent than Mary. Matthew traces Jesus' genealogy through Joseph. The angel appears to Joseph three times. It is Joseph who leads the Holy Family to Bethlehem, to Egypt, and back to Nazareth. However, in this particular scene of the magi coming to honor the newborn King, Mary takes center stage, and surprisingly, Joseph is not mentioned at all in the entire pericope. As Aragon notes, "Her mention in this moment, along with the omission of Joseph, underlines that Mary is a person especially important for the narrator, and that is why he puts her in this very high position."[55] This link between royal child and mother in such a regal context again may bring to mind the queen-mother tradition. Indeed, if Jesus is the newborn "king of the Jews" in this scene (2:2), then Mary, as the mother of this King (cf. 2:11), could be understood as a queen mother.[56] As Brown has observed, "Since the magi story puts so much emphasis on homage paid to a Davidic king in Bethlehem of Judah, 'the child with his mother' might evoke the peculiar importance given to the queen mother (*gebirah*, 'the Great Lady') of a newborn or newly installed king in the Davidic dynasty."[57] Branick notes how the queen-mother background "would explain the interest Matthew has in Mary being with the child as the nobles of the East reverence the new king, a scene where Joseph is not even mentioned."[58] This seems especially probable when we consider how Matthew has the Davidic kingdom traditions as a key context for understanding this infancy narrative. Bastero de Eleizalde thus concludes:

> In the act of adoration of the magi, St. Matthew, a good expert on the Davidic traditions, thinking of the readers of his gospel, does not omit the significant detail of showing 'the child with Mary, his mother.' In this way, he associates and confirms Mary as the *gebirah* of the messianic kingdom. Moreover, it is she who enthrones and presents the king-Messiah to the adoration of the magi, exercising one of the specific missions of the *gebirah*.[59]

In conclusion, we have seen how Matthew clearly places his infancy narrative in the context of the hopes surrounding the Davidic kingdom. Interpreting Mary with those Davidic traditions in mind, we can see that, as mother of the newborn Davidic heir, she could be understood as a queen mother. Indeed, we have seen how the queen-mother tradition can illuminate Matthew's narrative presentation of Mary, shedding light on her being linked with the queen mother and Immanuel prophecy of Isaiah 7:14, frequently associated with her royal Son in Matthew 2, and placed on the regal stage beside her royal child as the magi pay Him homage (while the generally more central Joseph is not even mentioned).[60] Thus, we conclude that the queen-mother tradition can be a helpful background for understanding Mary, the mother of the newborn Davidic King, in Matthew 1–2.

3.2 Luke 1:26–45

Now we turn to two passages from Luke's Gospel that may shed light on our topic: the Annunciation (Lk. 1:26–38) and the Visitation (Lk. 1:39–45). While it is often pointed out that Luke's overall portrait of Mary presents her as "a true disciple" of Jesus (Lk. 1:38, 42, 45, 2:18, 51, 8:19-21, 11:28;

Acts 1:14),[61] we will see that the Annunciation and Visitation scenes also present her as the mother of the Messiah-King (1:26–35, 43).[62] It is this latter theme that we will now explore in order to investigate how these passages may support an understanding of Mary as a queen-mother figure.

3.2.1 The Annunciation (Lk. 1:26–38)

In this section, we will first look at how Mary enters the stage of Luke's Gospel within an array of Davidic kingdom motifs in which she is presented as the mother of the Messiah-King. Secondly, we will consider how her royal maternal vocation in this scene can be understood in light of the queen-mother tradition of the Davidic kingdom.

3.2.1.1 Davidic Kingdom Themes in the Annunciation to Mary

In the Annunciation scene, Luke presents Mary's vocation as mother of the Messiah within a Davidic kingdom framework. At the very beginning of this account, Mary is introduced in the context of her betrothal to a descendant of David: "[T]he angel Gabriel was sent from God to a city of Galilee named Nazareth, to a virgin betrothed to a man whose name was Joseph, *of the house of David*" (1:27). This phrase, "House of David," was used in the Old Testament in reference to descendants of David (I Sam. 20:16; 1 Kings 12:19, 13:2; 2 Chron. 23:3).[63] Luke mentions this detail of Joseph's heritage in order to prepare the reader for understanding Jesus as a Davidic heir.[64]

Then, the angel's announcement itself presents Mary as the mother of the Davidic Messiah. Fitzmyer discusses how the angel made "a two-stage declaration" of the child's identity to Mary.[65] In the first stage (1:32–33), Gabriel described Mary's child as the royal Son of David. He is "Son of the Most High" by virtue of His role as the heir to the Davidic throne. In the second stage (1:34–35), Jesus is presented as "Son of God" by the power and Spirit of God, associating His sonship not just with His function as Davidic king, but with His divine origin.

Let us consider the first stage, which sets forth Jesus as the Davidic Messiah. This is first intimated when Gabriel tells Mary that her child will be called "Son of the Most High" (1:32). Since "Most High" was a title for God in the Old Testament and a common divine title in Luke as well,[66] the description of Jesus as "Son of the Most High" would refer to him as Son of God.[67] This expression could also be understood in light of the Old Testament designation of the Davidic king as God's son.[68] Thus, Jesus as "Son of the Most High" likely recalls Nathan's oracle (2 Sam. 7:14) and the royal Psalms (Ps. 2:7; Ps. 89:26–27; cf. Ps. 110:1)—both of which describe the Davidic king as having a special filial relationship with God.[69] That this is a primary understanding of the child's divine sonship in 1:32 is made clearer in the following verses, which include even more direct allusions to the Davidic covenant and thus bring Jesus' kingship into sharper focus:

> And the Lord will give to him the throne of his father David, and he will reign over the house of Jacob for ever and of his kingdom there will be no end. (Lk. 1:32–33)

Here, the child will be given "the throne of his father David" (1:32), showing Jesus as fulfilling Nathan's promise for the Davidic dynasty in which God would establish "the throne of his kingdom forever" (2 Sam. 7:13).[70] When the angel describes how the child will "reign over the house of Jacob forever" and says "of his kingdom there will be no end" (1:33),[71] these words further explicate Jesus' kingship in terms of the hopes surrounding the Davidic covenant (2 Sam. 7:13; Ps. 89:36–37; Is. 9:6–7).[72]

Furthermore, it has often been shown that there are clear parallels between Luke 1:32–33 and the Davidic covenant promises described in 2 Samuel 7:9–16 (great name, throne, divine sonship, house and kingdom).[73] Brown, for example, notes how Gabriel's words are a "free interpretation" of Nathan's oracle, which became the foundation for Jewish messianic hopes.[74] He nicely demonstrates these parallels in the following chart:

Luke 1:
32a: He will be great and will be called Son of the Most High.
32b: And the Lord God will give him the throne of his father David
33a: and he will be king over the House of Jacob forever,
33b: and there will be no end to his kingdom.

II Sam 7:
 9: I shall make for you a *great* name . . .
13: I shall establish *the throne of his kingdom forever.*
14: I shall be his father, and he will be *my* son . . .
16: And your *house* and your *kingdom* will be made sure *forever.*[75]

With these words of Gabriel, Jesus is clearly identified as the Davidic Messiah.[76] As Joel Green summarizes:

The connection of vv 32-33 with the expectation of a restored Davidic monarchy is unmistakable. See, for example, the reference to David's throne, 'his kingdom' (2 Sam 7:12, 13; cf. v 16), the perpetual character of this kingdom (2 Sam 7:13, 16), and the correlation of kingship and sonship (2 Sam 7:14). . . . Following such hints as those in Isa 9:7 and Dan 7:14, Luke has in mind a single ruler reigning forever as opposed to the dynasty ('house') envisioned by Nathan's prophecy to David. This reflects the eschatological correlation of David's reign with the greater emphasis on the definitive, everlasting dominion of Yahweh.[77]

Thus, in this first stage, it is significant that the first thing Luke tells the reader about Jesus is that the Davidic promises will be fulfilled through Him. From the beginning, the Davidic kingdom is a significant context for Luke's presentation of Jesus.[78]

In what Fitzmyer calls the second stage of Gabriel's declaration about the child's identity, Jesus is described as the Son of God through the power and Spirit of God.[79]

> And the angel said to her, 'The Holy Spirit will come upon you, and the power of the Most High will overshadow you; therefore the child to be born will be called holy, the Son of God.' (Lk. 1:35)

Brown notes how the words Luke uses in this verse relate to the picture drawn in 1:32–33 of Jesus as the Davidic Messiah.[80] First, Luke's description of the Spirit coming on Mary's womb might recall the Spirit descending on David (1 Sam. 16:13) and the future Davidic King described by the Prophet Isaiah (Is. 11:1–4).[81] Second, Luke describing Jesus as Son of God by the Spirit and power of God further develops the messianic sonship of verse 32. In 1:35, the child's divine sonship is based not simply on His role as Davidic king, but is grounded in His origin.[82] Whereas 1:32–33 associates Jesus' divine sonship with the special filial-like relationship the Davidic king had with God, Luke 1:35 shows that Jesus' divine sonship is the result of the divine intervention in His conception. Mary will conceive through God's intervention—"*therefore* the child to be born will be called . . . the Son of God" (Lk. 1:35).[83] As Fitzmyer explains, "The 'holy Spirit' coming upon her and the 'power of the Most High' overshadowing her are parallel expressions for God's intervention. The result of it will be that the child will not be merely the Davidic Messiah, but God's own Son."[84]

Nevertheless, any hints of Jesus' divine sonship being associated with His divine origins in 1:35 would not run counter to Jesus' divine filiation as the Davidic King in 1:32–33.[85] In fact, 1:35 could be seen as amplifying 1:32–33. Since the

Davidic king was considered to have a special filial relationship with God (2 Sam. 7:14), Jesus as *the* Son of God in 1:35 would fit well with His being the *true* Davidic King. As Son of God by origin, the Child Jesus is the Davidic King *par excellence*.[86] As Strauss explains,

> Though v. 35 exceeds traditional Jewish expectations, it does not leave the context of the Davidic promises. Rather the close contextual link between vv. 32 and 35 indicates that Jesus' divine sonship serves as proof that he is indeed the heir to the throne. Through his unique conception by the power and Spirit of God, Jesus is revealed to be the *Davidic Son of God* (cf 2 Sam. 7.14; Ps. 2.7).[87]

Finally, we also may find an allusion to the messianic prophecy of Isaiah 7:14 in Luke 1:31, where the angel says to Mary, "And behold, you will conceive in your womb and bear a son, and you shall call his name Jesus." John McHugh notes how this verse is "a virtual citation of the Greek text of Is 7:14"[88]—only the child's name is substantially different (Immanuel vs. Jesus).[89]

Fitzmyer lists seven possible Lukan parallels to Isaiah 7:10–17. These include: "house of David" (Lk. 1:27; Is. 7:13), "the Lord" (Lk. 1:28; Is. 7:10), "virgin" (Lk. 1:27; Is. 7:14 LXX), "are going to conceive" (Lk. 1:31; Is. 7:14 LXX), "will bear a son" (Lk. 1:31; Is. 7:14), "you will name him (Lk. 1:31; Is. 7:14), and "over the house" (Lk. 1:31; Is. 7:17).[90] To this list, Joel Green adds the angel's greeting Mary with the words "the Lord is with you," which may echo the name of the prophesied child in Isaiah 7:14, "Immanuel."[91]

Despite these numerous parallels, Fitzmyer does not think that Luke 1:31 is drawing specifically on Isaiah 7:14. Instead, it is pointed out that these phrases in Luke's Annunciation account, which correspond to Isaiah 7:10–17, also find parallels with a number of other Old Testament passages and fit into the pattern of the stereotypical annunciation scene in the Old Testament.[92] He concludes that we cannot know whether Luke was drawing either upon Isaiah 7:14 specifically or on those common themes found in other birth-annunciation narratives of the Old Testament.[93]

Others, however, note that both scenarios seem likely, arguing that, although Luke may indeed be alluding to a variety of Old Testament passages and placing Mary within the typical Old Testament annunciation pattern, there is no reason to exclude the importance of Isaiah 7:14 for Luke 1:31.[94] Especially since there is no single text in the Old Testament that has more verbal similarities to Luke 1:31 *and* brings together the various Davidic themes that the Lukan Annunciation account emphasizes, an allusion to Isaiah 7:14 seems even more probable.[95] As Green observes, "The conjunction of so many points of correspondence between the Gabriel-Mary encounter and Isa 7:10-17 cannot help but produce an echo effect."[96] Similarly, Strauss explains,

> . . . the description of Mary as παρθένος (Lk. 1.27, 34; cf. Isa. 7.14 LXX), the reference to the οἶκος Δαυίδ (Lk. 1.27; Isa. 7.13 LXX), and the greeting 'the Lord is *with you*' [sic] (Lk. 1.28; cf. Isa. 7.14, 'Immanuel')—all in the context of Davidic expectations—suggest that Luke indeed had Isa. 7.14 in mind.[97]

Such a view of Luke alluding to the prophecy of Isaiah 7:14, as well as the Old Testament annunciation pattern in general, thus seems most probable and fits in well with the royal messianic themes we have seen throughout Luke 1:26–35.

In summary, Luke's Annunciation scene clearly presents Jesus as the Davidic Messiah-King. This is seen especially in the allusions to two key Davidic texts from the Old Testament. Verse 31 seems to tie Jesus with the Immanuel prophecy of

Isaiah 7:14, which became associated with hopes for the future Davidic King who would restore the kingdom. Luke 1:32–35 associates the child of Mary with the foundation of the Davidic covenant, when God promised that one of David's sons would receive a great name, sit on a throne in an everlasting kingdom, and be called God's son (2 Sam. 7:9–16).

3.2.1.2 Mary as Mother of the Messiah-King in the Annunciation

The extensive Davidic kingdom context we have examined so far is crucial for understanding Mary's royal vocation in this passage. With this background, we are now ready to see how the queen-mother theme of the Old Testament might be helpful for shedding some light on Mary's calling in Luke 1:26–38. First, if Luke is showing us that the child she will bear is to be the Messiah-King from the House of David, then Mary is being given the vocation to become the mother of the Davidic King. As McHugh explains: "These verses recapitulate the promises about the Messianic king: he will be of the line of David, a savior to his people ('Jesus' means 'savior'), and of his kingdom there will be no end. Gabriel's message here is that *Mary is to be the mother of the Messianic king.*"[98]

This is why some have suggested that there may be hints of the queen-mother tradition in the background of Luke's Annunciation scene.[99] Indeed, in this passage, we find Mary portrayed as a mother linked with the House of David and giving birth to a Davidic heir. Especially since Luke places this scene in the context of the Davidic kingdom, it seems that Mary's role should be understood in light of that Davidic tradition as well. In that context, Mary, as mother of the Davidic King, could be seen as queen mother of her royal Son.[100] Ackerman concludes, "If Jesus is characterized as the royal Messiah, Israel's new king, then Mary, at least figuratively, is depicted as queen-mother."[101]

Valentini also sees Mary as a queen mother in this passage: "Mother of the Davidic Messiah, Mary is the *gebirah*, the glorious queen mother to whom goes the homage and the veneration of the whole messianic people."[102] He explains that since the interweaving of Isaiah 7:14 and 2 Samuel 7:10–14 in Luke 1:31–33 presents Jesus as the Davidic King, Mary as His mother is being given the role as queen mother of this royal child:

> Thanks to the intertwining of these prophecies [Isaiah 7:14 and 2 Sam 7], the Lucan text looks also at the mother of the Messiah. She is the mother of the king, the *gebirah*, the queen-mother, with all the dignity that this figure was honored with in the culture of the Middle East and in the tradition of Israel.[103]

Furthermore, the allusion in verse 31 to Isaiah 7:14 would strengthen this view, since the woman giving birth to the Immanuel child in Isaiah was a queen-mother figure (as we saw in chapter two). If Mary and Jesus are associated with the queen mother and royal Immanuel child in Isaiah 7:14, Mary could be understood as the queen mother who gave birth to the ideal Davidic King, foretold in the oracle of Isaiah.[104]

In conclusion, the presentation of Mary as the mother of the Messiah in this passage may offer some biblical support for the Church's doctrine regarding Mary's royal office. Understanding Mary in light of the Davidic kingdom tradition, which Luke clearly evokes throughout this scene, would suggest that as mother of the messianic King in the Davidic kingdom, she could be seen as a queen mother. Thus, while the angel's words speak of Jesus as the Messiah-King, they also provide a basis for Mary's royal maternity. As Cazelles explains:

> One could not more explicitly announce the birth of the Messiah who was waited for and announced by the prophets. However, by speaking directly to the mother of the Messiah,

the angel implicitly evoked the woman who was the mother of the king, linked to her son. It is thus that these words contain a theology of the queenship of Mary.[105]

Similarly, Montague concludes, "Though it is only implied in the text, any Jew hearing this would understand that Mary is here being given the vocation of queen-mother."[106]

3.2.2 The Visitation (Lk. 1:39–45)

Now we turn to Luke's account of the Visitation. Here we will see how Elizabeth's greeting Mary with the title "the mother of my Lord" (Lk. 1:43) is charged with great royal significance that is helpful for our topic.

This is the first time Jesus is called "Lord" in Luke–Acts. While *kurios* (LXX translation of the Hebrew *adonai*) was used often in the Old Testament as a circumlocution for avoiding the Tetrogrammaton (*Yahweh*),[107] it also referred to the Davidic King (2 Sam. 24:21; 1 Kings 1:13–47) and the royal Messiah (Ps. 110:1).[108] Within the Lukan narrative, the title "Lord" later came to refer to Jesus' total authority and placed him on par with Yahweh (Acts 2 and 10).[109] However, at this point in the narrative, its use is not as clear. Bock explains that its use by Elizabeth is "a prophetic foreshadowing" of Jesus' full identity to be revealed later in the narrative.[110] But in this first use of the title "Lord," "it could be seen to signify simply the Lordship of the Messiah (Luke 20.41-44)."[111]

Furthermore, Elizabeth's words to Mary, "And why is this granted me, that the mother of my Lord should come to me?" (Lk. 1:43), echo 2 Samuel 24:21, where the phrase "my Lord" is used as a royal title honoring the king. In that text, Araunah greets King David, saying, "Why has my lord the king come to his servant?" (2 Sam. 24:21).[112] With this in the background, Elizabeth's words here in 1:43 would have regal connotations that further present Jesus as a Davidic king.[113]

It is also significant that the title in 1:43 is not used in an absolute sense, but stands alongside the first person possessive, "*my* Lord." This may further signify its royal messianic meaning, since this expression was used in the Old Testament to denote the king and the future Messiah.[114] As Brown has observed, "Both in the Gospel (20:41–44) and in Acts (2:34) Luke uses Ps 110:1, "the Lord said to *my Lord*," to show that Jesus is the Messiah and Son of God; and Elizabeth is recognizing Mary as the mother of 'my Lord' i.e., of the Messiah."[115]

Thus, when Elizabeth calls Mary "the mother of my Lord," these words not only point to Jesus as the Messiah, but they also tell us something important about Mary.[116] While recognizing the messianic lordship of Mary's child, Elizabeth, at the same time, acknowledges Mary as the mother of her King. Here it should be pointed out that in the New Testament, Mary often is referred to as the "mother of Jesus" or "his mother," but nowhere is she called the "mother of my Lord" except here in 1:43.[117] Thus, this unique title for Mary seems to draw attention to her role not just as mother of Jesus in general, but as mother of Jesus specifically in His role as messianic Lord. In other words, Elizabeth greeting Mary as "the mother of my Lord" refers to her as *mother of the Messiah-King.*[118]

This is why a number of scholars have seen the words "the mother of my Lord" as pointing to Mary as a queen-mother figure.[119] It has been pointed out that in royal court language of the ancient Near East, the title "Mother of my Lord" would have been used to address the queen mother of the reigning king (who himself was addressed as "my Lord," cf. 2 Sam. 24:21).[120] Thus, within the strong Davidic context of Luke's infancy narrative, Elizabeth addressing Mary with this royal title provides a basis for viewing her in light of the queen-mother tradition of the Old Testament.[121] As Perez explains: "Certainly, Mary is there recognized and proclaimed by Elizabeth—and by the evangelist—in her dignity as mother of the Messiah, implying her participation in the royalty of her son, in the way it was done by the mother of the king in the Old Testament."[122]

Similarly, Kirwin concludes:

> When Elizabeth greets Mary with this title she is recognizing in Mary a singular excellence and dignity. She is the Mother of the Savior whom the Jews were awaiting. Mother of my Lord, Mother of my Sovereign, is equivalent to 'my Lady', 'my Queen.' Elizabeth's words are the formal recognition of the royal dignity of Mary objectively revealed in the words of the Archangel Gabriel.[123]

In summary, we have seen how Luke's Annunciation account presents Mary as being given the vocation to be the mother of a Davidic king. As mother of a king in the House of David, she could be understood as a queen mother. Allusions in this passage to the prophecy of Isaiah 7:14, which describes a queen mother conceiving and bearing a royal son, would strengthen this view even more. The queen-mother tradition also can illuminate the visitation scene in which Elizabeth gives Mary the royal greeting "Mother of my Lord," recognizing her as the mother of the Messiah-King. Thus, in these two scenes, Luke's infancy narrative provides further New Testament support for understanding Mary's role as the queen mother of the newborn messianic King.

3.3 Revelation 12

Before discussing how Revelation 12 may shed light on Mary's queenship, we must first look at the complex issue concerning the identity of the "woman clothed with the sun": to what extent, if at all, can we find Marian significance in this figure? We will see that while the majority of scholars argue that the woman in Revelation 12 refers to the people of God (either of the Old Testament, of the New Testament, or both), some Protestant and Catholic scholars alike have recognized the possibility that the woman in Revelation 12 may also refer to the mother of Jesus, Mary. This discussion will be important before we can consider how this passage may lend some support for our understanding Mary as a queenly mother.

3.3.1 Interpreting the "Woman Clothed with the Sun"

The vision in Revelation 12 describes a "woman" in heaven giving birth in great pain to a child who will "rule the nations with a rod of iron" (12:1–2, 5). A great red dragon, identified as "that ancient serpent" (12:9), seeks to attack the offspring (12:3–4), but the child is swept up to God (12:5). The woman flees into the wilderness (12:6), and the dragon is conquered and thrown down to the earth by Michael and his angels (12:7–12). Then verses 13–16 describe how the dragon pursues the woman, who is given eagle's wings to fly to a place in the wilderness where she will be nourished, and verse 17 tells how the serpent goes on to focus his attacks on the rest of the woman's offspring who are described as "those who keep the commandments of God and bear testimony to Jesus."

Two of the three main characters in this vision are easily identifiable. First, verse 9 tells us explicitly that the great dragon is "that ancient serpent, who is called the Devil and Satan."[124] Second, since the male child is described as the one who will "rule the nations with a rod of iron" (a direct reference to the messianic Psalm 2) and as being taken up to the throne of God in heaven, the narrative is clearly pointing to his identity as Christ.[125]

However, the identity of the third character, the "woman clothed with the sun," has been debated throughout the centuries.[126] Basically, there have been three general views: (1) an exclusively Marian interpretation: the woman refers only to the individual woman, Mary; (2) an exclusively corporate interpretation: the woman is a symbol for the collective people of God (either of the old covenant, the new covenant or both); and (3) a corporate and Marian interpretation: the woman refers both to God's covenant people and to the individual mother of Jesus, Mary.[127]

3.3.1.1 Background to the Woman in Revelation 12

Before we interpret the "woman clothed with the sun," it will be important to discuss some of the Old Testament themes that serve as a background to the drama in Revelation 12.

(a) Conflict with the ancient serpent. With the dragon identified as "the ancient serpent" (Rev. 12:9), his battle with the "woman" and her messianic male child evokes the strife described in Genesis 3:15.[128] Christian awareness of the serpent-Eve conflict can be found in other New Testament texts (2 Corinthians 11:3 and probably Romans 16:20).[129] Here in Revelation 12, we find clear points of contact with Genesis 3:15–16 in the fact that both passages involve the ancient serpent in conflict with a woman figure and her offspring, who eventually will overcome the serpent. Moreover, the reference to the woman crying out "in her pangs of birth and in anguish for delivery" (Rev. 12:2) might also echo the first woman's childbearing pains in Genesis 3:16.[130] Furthermore, the reference in Revelation 12:17 to the dragon attacking the woman's other offspring (σπέρματος αὐτῆς) may add additional confirmation that Revelation 12 is alluding to the strife between the serpent's seed and the woman's seed (σπέρματος αὐτῆς) in Genesis 3:15 (LXX).[131] As Brown observes, the author of Revelation 12 portrays this drama as the climactic fulfillment of Genesis 3's description of the serpent's war with the "woman" and her royal messianic offspring. "There can be no doubt that Revelation is giving the Christian enactment of the drama foreshadowed in Gen iii 15 where enmity is placed between the serpent and *the woman*, between the serpent's seed and her seed, and the seed of the woman enters into conflict with the serpent."[132]

(b) The woman's birth pangs. Another background to the woman in Revelation 12 is the woman Zion figure of the Old Testament. There are significant parallels between the woman who gives birth to the messianic child in travail in Revelation 12:1–5 and the Old Testament prophetic image of Zion's metaphorical birth pains symbolizing remnant Israel, the faithful people of God, in the troubled times they would endure before the arrival of the messianic era.[133] For example, Revelation 12 may draw, at least in part, from Isaiah 26:17 which describes the inhabitants of Jerusalem like "a woman with child, who writhes and cries out in her pangs when she is near her time."[134] With the images of a woman figure, a pregnancy, labor pains and an imminent birth, this Isaian passage is likely in the background of Revelation 12.[135] There also may be an allusion to Isaiah 66:7–8, which similarly describes Zion as a mother figure giving birth in pain to the messianic people: "Before she was in labour she gave birth; before her pain came upon her she was delivered of a son. . . . For as soon as Zion was in labour she brought forth sons."[136] This image is especially significant because it describes Zion giving birth to an individual son and to a plurality of sons—a two-fold maternity that would fit well with the picture of the woman in Revelation 12, who gives birth to the individual Messiah (12:5) and is the mother of a multitude of children (12:17).[137]

(c) Clothed with the sun, moon under her feet, crowned with twelve stars. Since Canticles 6:10 describes Solomon's bride as "fair as the moon, bright as the sun," some have suggested that this passage may be behind the images used to portray the woman in Revelation 12:1.[138] Some also have argued that the Lady Zion figure in Isaiah 60 is an important backdrop for the description of the woman in 12:1.[139] This Isaian passage describes Zion as a mother of God's people (v. 4) filled with the radiant splendor of Yahweh's light, no longer needing the sun or moon: "Arise, shine; for your light has come and the

glory of the Lord has risen upon you . . . the sun shall be no more your light by day, nor the moon give light to you by night but the Lord will be your everlasting light" (Is. 60:1, 19–20).[140] While it is possible that these passages from Canticles and Isaiah may be in the background, Revelation 12:1 even more clearly alludes to images in the dream of the patriarch Joseph in Genesis 37:9–11.[141] In fact, whereas Canticles 6:10 and Isaiah 60:1 make no reference to stars, the number 12, or a crown, Joseph's dream contains more parallels with the woman's description in Revelation 12:1, including sun, moon, stars, and a reference to the number 12 (with eleven stars representing Joseph's eleven brothers bowing to Joseph, the *twelfth* son).[142] Although no crown is mentioned explicitly, the dream certainly involves the theme of royal authority, which the crown symbolizes. In the dream, the images of the sun, moon, and stars were used in a way that showed how Joseph would obtain a preeminent share in Pharaoh's rule over all of Egypt and an ironic position of authority over his family. There, Joseph came to hold the most powerful position in all the land—second only to the king (Gen. 41:40, 57).

(d) The woman's flight to the desert. In Revelation 12, the woman is described as being given two wings of a great eagle so that she might fly into the desert to be protected from the dragon/serpent (12:6, 14). Many of these images in the woman's flight to the desert recall the Exodus story.[143] For example, the pursuit of the woman is similar to Pharaoh's pursuit of Israel as they fled Egypt (Ex. 14:8),[144] and the eagle's wings, which enable the woman to flee to the wilderness, likely reflect the Old Testament portrayal of God as an eagle protecting the people of Israel in the desert (Ex. 19:4).[145] The woman being nourished in the wilderness (12:14) may bring to mind God's provision for his people, nourishing them with the manna.[146]

(e) The woman's maternity. In Revelation 12:5, the woman gives birth to a "male child" who is "to rule all the nations with a rod of iron" and who is "caught up to God and to his throne." As discussed above, the child is portrayed in light of the messianic Psalm 2, suggesting that the woman figure in some sense brings forth the Messiah. Later in the narrative, however, the woman is said to have a plurality of offspring. Revelation 12:17 tells how the dragon attacks "the rest of her offspring," who are described as "those who keep the commandments of God and bear testimony to Jesus"—referring to the Christians who strive to follow Christ in the face of trials and persecutions.[147] Thus, the narrative portrays the woman as having not only an individual male child, but also, in some sense, other offspring who represent the Church in its ongoing struggle against the forces of evil.[148]

3.3.1.2 Various Interpretations of the Woman

With this background, we are now prepared to discuss the identity of the woman in Revelation 12. Few argue that the woman refers to Mary in any exclusive sense.[149] Her portrayal in Revelation 12 indicates that the woman has the role of representing the community of faith out of which the Messiah was born. For example, as discussed above, the woman is described in many ways that recall Zion giving birth to the new covenant people. Since the prophetic image of Daughter Zion represented the people of God, such imagery describing the woman of Revelation 12 would lead the reader to conclude that she has a symbolic meaning, referring to the community of faith.[150] Thus, Feuillet concludes:

> The Woman whom John contemplates is first and foremost the ideal Sion of the prophets, who, by bearing (metaphorically) the Messiah, becomes the Church. This is the undeniable meaning of the Old Testament passages which the author of Apocalypse 12:1-6 has used, especially Is. 26:17; 60:19-20; 66:7, and doubtless also Cant. 6:10.[151]

Furthermore, the woman fleeing to the desert for divine protection from the dragon (12:6, 13–16) has important ecclesial significance describing how the Church, like Israel during the Exodus, will be protected from her enemies and nourished by God.[152] Along these lines, Beale argues that the woman has a referent that extends beyond the individual mother of Jesus: "The woman is persecuted, flees into the desert, and has other children, who are described as faithful Christians. . . . This goes beyond anything that could have been said about Mary and her children."[153]

This is why most interpreters recognize that the woman represents God's people, either of the Old Testament, or of the New, or of both. Here, let us briefly consider these three common views.

First, some hold that the woman clothed with the sun is a figure for the Christian Church.[154] This view has the strength of fitting into the Apocalypse's portrayal of the new covenant people of God as the woman-bride.[155] It also may help explain how the woman can be the mother of Christ's followers (12:17). As a symbol for the Church, the woman metaphorically gives birth to the Christian community and nurtures it. While this view is helpful, some emphasize that the woman should not be understood as referring *only* to the Church since such a view would not provide a coherent reading of Revelation 12 as it fails to explain the woman giving birth to the messianic child in 12:5.[156] As McHugh asks, "How can the Christian Church of the New Testament be called the mother of its Lord?"[157]

A second view interprets the woman of Revelation 12 as a symbol for Old Testament Israel or the faithful remnant who gives birth to the Messiah.[158] First, as discussed above, the imagery of the twelve stars recalls the twelve tribes of Israel, and when standing alongside the sun and the moon imagery, 12:1 recalls the dream of Joseph in which these celestial symbols were associated with the patriarchal family of Jacob-Israel himself. Second, as we saw above, the prophets used the imagery of painful childbirth to describe the trials the remnant of Israel would endure in the period leading up to the messianic age (Is. 26:17, 60:19–20, 66:7–8). Thus, viewing the woman as that remnant people of the old covenant would fit well with the description in Revelation 12:2–5 of the woman crying out in the pains of labor before the birth of the messianic child. Furthermore, the lady Zion image in Isaiah 66 may help shed light on the dual-maternity of the woman figure in Revelation 12. Since Zion would give birth to the messianic people (sons), this image would shed light on the woman being the mother of a collective offspring in Revelation 12:17—those who bear testimony to Jesus and keep his commandments. And since Isaiah 66:7–8 speaks of Zion as the community of faith also bearing forth a singular male (which the targumic tradition equates with the messianic king),[159] this view can help make sense out of the woman bearing forth the male child (Messiah) in Revelation 12:5 as well.[160] However, some have suggested that the woman should not be understood as referring *only* to Israel since such a view would not account for the woman fleeing to the desert, being protected from the attacks of the devil and being nourished by God after the male child's birth and rising to a heavenly throne (which was a New Testament event).[161] For example, Beale argues: "It is too limiting to view the woman as representing only a remnant of Israelites living in trial at the last stage of history, since the following verses show that the woman symbolizes a believing community extending from before the time of Christ's birth to at least the latter part of the first century A.D."[162] He concludes that though there are significant points of contact between Old Testament Zion imagery and Revelation 12, a view of the woman as referring *only* to remnant Israel fails to explain the latter part of Revelation 12 (12:6, 13–17).

Others favor a third interpretive option, which views the woman as a symbol of God's people—both of the new old and new covenants.[163] In this perspective, the woman in Revelation 12 is understood as Israel, or more specifically as the remnant of faithful Israelites in the Old Testament, who then became the community of Christian believers in the new covenant and who suffer persecution. "It is most likely that the woman is a personification of Israel, the people of God of the OT, and that the Christian adaptation of the symbolism involves having the woman, after the birth of the messianic child, become the Church, the people of the NT."[164] This view of the woman representing both the old and new covenant people should not be troublesome if we keep in mind that apocalyptic writings often include symbols with mutliple layers of meaning.[165] While discussing the figurative language of apocalyptic literature, Brown explains that "sometimes the symbols are polyvalent,"[166] and he uses our very passage as an example, saying: "The woman in Rev 12 may symbolize Israel giving birth to the Messiah as well as the church and her children in the wilderness under Satanic attack after the Messiah has been taken up to heaven."[167] Furthermore, Mounce stresses that such a view is quite sound especially if we keep in mind that the woman represents the one, continuous people of God spanning both the Old and New covenants. "It is out of faithful Israel that the Messiah will come. It should cause no trouble that within the same chapter the woman comes to signify the church (v. 17). The people of God are one throughout all redemptive history. The early church did not view itself as discontinuous with faithful Israel."[168]

In sum, we conclude with the majority of interpreters that the woman refers to the community of believers—and it seems likely that this collective body is best understood as God's people of both the old and new covenants. Now we must consider if there is any basis for interpreting the woman as Mary as well. In doing so, we will explore the possibilities of interpreting the woman in Revelation 12 in light of the Gospel of John.

The authors of *Mary in the New Testament* have discussed the possibility of seeing in the woman a secondary reference to Mary if Revelation is read in light of the Fourth Gospel (Jn. 19:25–27).[169] Such a view presupposes that the Book of Revelation has some significant relationship with the Gospel of John—a supposition that continues to be debated in modern scholarship.[170] Few today would conclude that Revelation and the Fourth Gospel were written by the same author.[171] In fact, many deny any significant link between the two books, not only in terms of authorship, but even in terms of circle of influence.[172] At the same time, however, another widely held position in scholarship maintains that, while the Book of Revelation and the Gospel of John may not have been written by the same author, the two books at least flow from some significant common sphere of influence.[173] It is this latter view which the authors of *Mary in the New Testament* have suggested as a possibility, and it is this line of thought which we now will consider in order to explore the potential fruit which reading Revelation 12 in light of a particular passage from the Johannine tradition (Jn. 19:25–27) may have for our interpretation of the woman of the apocalypse.

It is often pointed out that John 19:25–27 has numerous elements in common with Revelation 12.[174] First, like Revelation 12, John 19:25–27 involves a "woman" (γύναι) figure who is portrayed as the mother of the Messiah.[175] Second, while Revelation 12 portrays the woman in anguish as she bears forth the Messiah, we also can find birth pain imagery in the background of John 19:25–27 when the passage is read in light of John 16:20–21. Within the context of discussing His Passion, Jesus in 16:20–21 uses the childbirth image to describe how the disciples will experience suffering during Christ's death, but great joy in His Resurrection—like a woman (γυνὴ) who is in pain during childbirth, but who rejoices after delivery. Since the allegory of the woman in 16:20–21 foreshadows Calvary, this parable of the woman's labor pains can shed light on the scene of the "*woman*," the *mother* of Jesus, witnessing her son's death in John 19. The thematic similarities (maternity, Christ's death) and the verbal correspondences ("woman," "hour") between these two passages show even more clearly that John 19:25–27 is meant to be read in light of the birth allegory in John 16:20–21.[176] Thus, with this birth-pain imagery in the background of John 19:25–27, we find further support for viewing this scene at the Cross in relationship with Revelation 12's imagery of the woman clothed with the sun giving birth in anguish to the Messiah-child.[177]

Third, the metaphorical labor pains and birth (which in John, as we have seen, symbolize Christ's death and resurrection) are portrayed in John's Gospel as Christ's "hour" of victory in which the devil is cast out of this world (12:27–31).[178] This again is similar to Revelation 12, in which the woman in anguish gives birth to a male child who is taken to his victorious throne in heaven while the devil is conquered and thrown out (Rev. 12:7–9). [179]

Fourth, the woman's maternity in John 19 is portrayed not only in terms of her being "the mother of Jesus," but also in terms of her being given some type of maternal relationship with the beloved disciple[180]—a figure who in John's Gospel symbolizes the ideal disciple.[181] Similarly, Revelation 12 depicts the "woman clothed with the sun" not only as the mother of the Messiah (Rev. 12:5), but also as the mother of "those who keep the commandments of God and bear testimony to Jesus" (Rev. 12:17). Brown has noted how the woman's "other offspring" in Revelation 12:17 are depicted in a way which could bring to mind the beloved disciple in the Fourth Gospel, which would strengthen the link between these two passages even more.

> The symbolism of the Fourth Gospel has a certain resemblance to that of Rev xii 5, 17 where a woman gives birth to the Messiah in the presence of the Satanic dragon or ancient serpent of Genesis, and yet also has other offspring who are the targets of Satan's wrath after the Messiah has been taken to heaven. It is interesting that the offspring of the woman of Revelation are described as 'those who keep the commandments of God'; for in John xiv 21-23 we are told that those who keep the commandments are loved by Father and Son, so that a beloved disciple is one who keeps the commandments.[182]

All these parallels between the woman in John 19 and the woman in Revelation 12 have led a number of scholars to conclude that since the former is understood as "the mother of Jesus" (Mary), the woman in Revelation 12 can be understood as having a reference to Mary.[183] Indeed, if Revelation and the Fourth Gospel do at least spring from a common circle of influence, these parallels point to some common thought in the Johannine tradition concerning the "woman" figure who is the mother of the Messiah, and this in turn would lead to a Marian interpretation of the woman in Revelation 12.

Therefore, if Revelation is read in light of the Gospel of John, we can conclude that while the "woman clothed with the sun" refers to God's people, it also may have a reference to Mary, the mother of Jesus. As discussed above, however, not everyone is convinced that these two writings have a common influence that would warrant reading Revelation 12 in light of John 19. Nevertheless, regardless of what position one may hold about the relationship between Revelation and the Fourth Gospel, these parallels between the "woman clothed with the sun" and the "woman" at the Cross remain significant because a canonical interpretation of these texts would lend support to a Marian view of the woman in Revelation 12.[184] As the authors of *Mary in the New Testament* explain, one thing that is certain about the "woman clothed with the sun" is that when the Book of Revelation "was taken into the canon of Scripture, the possibility was opened of interpreting its imagery of the woman in terms of the mariology of the other canonical books."[185] Furthermore, Revelation 12's symbol "of the woman who is the mother of the Messiah might well lend itself to Marian interpretation, once Marian interest developed in the later Christian community. And eventually when Revelation was placed in the same canon of Scripture with the Gospel of Luke and the Fourth Gospel, the various images of the virgin, the woman at the Cross, and the woman who gave birth to the Messiah would reinforce each other."[186] Thus, in conclusion, while the woman in Revelation 12 refers to the people of God, there is a basis for seeing a reference to Mary as well when the passage is read in light of John 19—whether such a reading is based on belief in a common Johannine influence or on a canonical interpretation of Revelation 12.

3.3.2 Queenship Themes in Revelation 12

After having discussed a certain Marian interpretation of the woman in Revelation 12, we now can consider how this passage might contribute to our understanding of Mary's queenship.

Like the other Marian passages we have studied, Revelation 12 is filled with royal themes. On one level, this is seen in the woman's son, who is described as the messianic King exercising his universal dominion. The author of Revelation chose the messianic Psalm 2 to describe how this child will "rule all the nations with a rod of iron" (12:5). He is taken up to heaven to sit on a throne (12:5). This son ushers in the kingdom of God as the enemy is defeated: "[N]ow the kingdom of our God has come, for the accuser has been thrown down" (12:10).

On another level, royal images are also associated with the woman herself, who as the mother of this king, is portrayed as a majestic queenly figure: "And a great sign appeared in heaven, a woman clothed with the sun, with the moon under her feet and on her head a crown of twelve stars" (Rev. 12:1).[187] First, the woman's crown is a symbol of royal authority and victory.[188] In the Book of Revelation, the symbol of the crown is never a superfluous decoration, but connotes a real reign.[189] It often refers to the share the saints have in Christ's kingship and the reward they receive for victorious perseverance during times of persecutions and temptations (Rev. 2:10, 3:11, 4:4, 10, 6:2, 14:14).[190] Thus, the woman having a crown of her own shows that she, too, has a royal status.[191] The twelve stars point to her relationship with the twelve tribes of Israel (Rev. 21:12) or the Church, founded on the twelve apostles (Rev. 21:14).[192] Second, the woman described as having the moon *under her feet* also may point to her royal authority. We saw in chapter two how in the Bible, under-the-feet imagery often was used to denote royal dominion and subjugation of enemies, especially within a Davidic kingdom context. "To have someone or something under the feet signifies having power." [193] Thus, the woman depicted as subjugating the moon under her feet suggests that she, too, has some type of royal position.[194]

Further, the images of the sun, moon and twelve stars portray the woman in light of an Old Testament passage that may highlight the woman's royal authority. It is sometimes proposed that Isaiah's depiction of the new Jerusalem's splendor in 60:19–20 (illumined by God's glory, no longer in need of the sun or moon) and Song of Songs 6:10 (the bride described as beautiful as the moon and resplendent as the sun) have influenced the woman's radiant description in Revelation 12:1.[195] As discussed above, while these texts may be in the background, Joseph's dream in Genesis 37:9–11 seems to be more central because it has even stronger parallels with Revelation

12:1–2.[196] In this famous dream, the sun, moon, and stars bow down before Joseph, symbolizing the royal authority he would have over his father, mother, and brothers when he would rise to a preeminent position ruling in Egypt as the most powerful person in Pharaoh's royal court. Thus, in light of the royal significance of the sun, moon, and stars in Genesis 37:9–11, the woman in Revelation 12:1 being depicted with these celestial images may add further color to her royalty.

Therefore, the woman in Revelation 12, portrayed alongside her kingly son and depicted with all these royal images, clearly would be seen as some type of queenly figure.[197] As Luis explains,

> In the Apocalypse she shines brilliantly with majesty and greatness, crowned with a royal diadem, and as the Mother of 'a royal son who has to rule all nations with an iron hand,' a son who is 'caught up to God and to His throne.' Once more the Mother of the King offers herself to our eyes showing forth the attributes of her exalted queenship.[198]

And once again, the Old Testament tradition of the *gebirah* could shed light on this queenly woman of Revelation 12, as a number of scholars have suggested.[199] Indeed, she is the mother of the Davidic King (Rev. 12:5; Ps. 2:7), and she wears a crown as did the queen mothers in the Davidic kingdom (Jer. 13:18). In his dissertation on the woman in Revelation 12, Farkas emphasizes that Revelation 12 presents a *royal* woman (12:1) giving birth to the Messiah-King (12:5). Although corporate interpretations often view the woman as a symbol for God's people, no Old Testament or Jewish text speaks of a *queenly* figure personifying the collective people of God and giving birth to *the Messiah*.[200] However, a close fit can indeed be found in the Old Testament tradition of the queen mother. The queen mother was a royal woman well known in the Scriptures for having given birth to the Davidic king and for being closely associated with his reign.[201] This is similar to the queenly figure in Revelation 12. As such, the queen mother may be in the background for understanding the royal woman who gave birth to the Davidic Messiah in Revelation 12. "The woman of Apocalypse 12 is the Mother of the Messiah-King who on the day of His birth, 'caught up to the throne of God' is ruler of the universe. . . . Here too, she is the Queen-Mother, Mother of Christ Head and Members, Mother of the Church."[202]

These insights would be strengthened by considering how Revelation 12 portrays the woman in light of the Immanuel prophecy of Isaiah 7:14,[203] which as we saw in chapter two involves a queen mother who will give birth to a Davidic son. The woman in Revelation 12:1 is introduced as "*a sign*" (σημεῖον) recalling the sign (σημεῖον) given to the House of David in this prophecy (Is. 7:10 LXX). This sign in Revelation is located in the heavens, like the sign as "high as heaven" that was offered to King Ahaz (Is. 7:10). The sign in Revelation involves a royal woman giving birth to a kingly son (12:1–2, 5) like the queen mother who would conceive and bear a Davidic heir in the Immanuel prophecy.[204]

In conclusion, we have seen in this section that while the woman in Revelation 12 refers to God's people, she also can be understood as the mother of Jesus, Mary, when the passage is read in light of the Gospel of John and the wider New Testament canon. Since the woman is portrayed with a number of royal images, she is presented to the reader as some type of queenly figure. And since she is presented as the mother of the Davidic Messiah (12:5), the queen-mother tradition of the Old Testament can shed light on the woman's queenly position in this passage. It is thus, as we have seen, that Revelation 12 lends biblical support for an understanding of Mary as a queen mother.

In summary, we have studied the New Testament portrayal of the mother of the Messiah in Matthew 1–2, Luke 1:26–45, and Revelation 12. By examining her in light of the Davidic kingdom traditions those passages evoke, we have seen how the queen mother can serve as a background for understanding Mary, the mother of the Messiah-King, in the New Testament. With this study in mind, we will consider in the closing chapter how the queen-mother theme can help offer biblical support for the Church's doctrine on Mary's queenship, and we will offer a few brief reflections on how this study might make some contributions to our understanding of the meaning of her royal office.

Summary Conclusions

We have examined how the *gebirah* tradition lends biblical support to the doctrine of Mary's queenship which has emerged over the centuries. While our goal has not been to prove the queenship as a truth revealed explicitly in Scripture, we have demonstrated how the queen-mother theme can shed important biblical light on why the mother of Jesus might be considered a queen in God's kingdom.[1] We have conducted our investigation in two parts. First, in chapter two, we studied the important role of the mother of the king in the Old Testament. In the Davidic kingdom, it was the king's mother who ruled as queen, not the king's wife. She held an official position in the royal court, serving as an advocate for the people and as an influential counselor to the king. She also shared in the king's rule over the kingdom and, in fact, was one of the most powerful persons in the kingdom under her royal son. We also considered the importance of the queen mother as reflected in Israel's prophetic traditions, seen clearly in Isaiah 7:14 and prototypically in Genesis 3:15—passages which eventually became associated with Israel's messianic hopes. Thus, in the biblical worldview of the kingdom—both in the structure of the Davidic kingdom in Judah and in Israel's later hopes for the kingdom's restoration—the mother of the king and queenship went hand-in-hand.

Second, with this Old Testament background in mind, we turned to the New Testament in chapter three, in order to consider how the queen-mother tradition can serve as a background to understanding the mother of the new Davidic King, Jesus. First, we examined how Matthew 1–2 is framed in large part around the hopes surrounding the Davidic dynasty. When Mary is considered with this background in mind, her role as mother of the Davidic heir can be seen in terms of the queen mother in the Davidic kingdom. Indeed, we saw how her association with the queen mother in the Immanuel prophecy of Isaiah 7:14, the frequent link between "the mother and child," and her being placed in the center of the regal scene of the magi paying homage to the newborn King of the Jews bring to mind the dynastic role of the *gebirah*. Similar themes are found in Luke's Annunciation scene, which introduces Mary in the context of the House of David as the mother of the ultimate Davidic heir, the Messiah. Viewing Mary in light of the many Davidic kingdom motifs Luke evokes throughout this scene suggests that she, in her role as the mother of the King, would be understood as a queen mother. And Elizabeth greeting Mary in the Visitation scene with the royal title "mother of my Lord" provides further basis for viewing her in light of the queenly mother of the Davidic royal court. Finally, we saw that in Revelation 12 the queenly woman clothed with the sun, crowned with twelve stars, and portrayed with the moon under her feet is presented as the mother of the Davidic Messiah, who will "rule all the nations with a rod of iron" (Rev. 12:5; cf. Ps. 2:9). If we interpret the royal mother figure with this Davidic context in mind, we see that the queen mother of old may shed light on the woman's royal maternity in Revelation 12. While this mysterious royal woman certainly represents the people of God, we saw that she also may be understood as having a reference to Mary when the passage is read in light of the Gospel of John and the wider New Testament canon. It is along these lines that Revelation 12 can lend further biblical support for understanding Mary as queen mother.

In conclusion, by studying the mother of the Messiah in Matthew 1–2, Luke 1:26–45 and Revelation 12 in light of the Davidic kingdom traditions those texts evoke, we can conclude that there is rich scriptural support for viewing Mary, the mother of the Messiah-child, as a queen-mother figure.

Viewing Mary in light of the biblical queen-mother background offers a unique contribution to our understanding the scriptural basis of Mary's queenship. In chapter one, we saw that while previous attempts to treat the biblical foundations of this doctrine through theological deduction or extra-biblical typology can shed light on Mary's royal office, they at the same time should be distinguished from those which build more fully upon a biblical study of Mary within the context of salvation history and within the narrative presentation of Mary in the New Testament. For example, those employing extra-biblical typology often have seen feminine royal figures of the Old Testament, such as Judith, Esther, or Wisdom, as prefiguring Mary's royalty but have not attempted to demonstrate how those typological connections might be based in the New Testament narrative presentation of Mary. While extra-biblical typology can contribute to our understanding of the queenship, especially when such typologies are demonstrated in the Church Fathers, magisterial teaching or the liturgy, this approach remains a step removed from the narrative portrayal of Mary in the New Testament. Similarly, those employing theological deduction begin with a certain Marian truth revealed in the New Testament (e.g., Mary is the mother of the King) and then make secondary logical conclusions which they argue flow from that biblical truth (e.g., since she is the woman most closely associated with the king, she would be queen; or since she consents to be mother of the king, she shares so intensely in the life of the king that she can be considered queen). Again, these logical conclusions, while they can be helpful for understanding Mary's royal office, remain a step removed from the narrative presentation of Mary in the New Testament.

Going a step further, our approach to the biblical basis for Mary's queenship examines the scriptural portrayal of Mary within the context of salvation history and pays close attention to the narrative framework and intertextual relationships found within the Marian passages of the New Testament which we examined in chapter three. By viewing the mother of the Messiah-King in light of the Davidic kingdom traditions to which those passages allude, we see that she can be understood as a queen mother. This approach of viewing Mary in terms of the queen-mother theme thus can shed even more light from a biblical perspective on the relationship between Mary being the mother of the Messiah-King and her having some share in her Son's royalty—a relationship which theological deduction attempts to arrive at through the theologian's logical argumentation, but which can be more clearly demonstrated through the biblical understanding of queenship in the Davidic kingdom, which these New Testament passages show Christ bringing to fulfillment.

While we have completed the main purpose of this study, which has been to demonstrate a biblical basis for Mary's queenship in light of the queen-mother theme, in closing, we will offer a few brief suggestions on how the approach taken in this study can offer some contributions to understanding the *meaning* of Mary's queenship. Especially in an era when most cultures have moved further away from the monarchical political structures of the past, communicating the significance of Mary being a queen in the life of modern-day Christians has become ever more challenging.[2] While scholars have grappled with the significance of Mary's royal position for a long time, De Fiores notes how common approaches to this doctrine from earlier this century probably would not be very helpful in explaining her queenly role to the modern world.[3] As we looked at in chapter one, the two major schools of thought on this topic begin with an abstract, secular-political notion of royalty and conclude that Mary exercises her queenship either by governing the subjects of the kingdom to their proper end through cooperating in the King's redemptive work and distributing graces (De Gruyter) or through intercession since she, like a queen, would have been able to exert great influence over the King's heart because she was the feminine companion closest to Christ the King and the one who would have been most like the king's spouse (Nicolas). While these approaches can shed some light on Mary's queenship, we saw how they have one shortcoming in that they begin *a priori* with an abstract philosophical and secular-political concept of royalty guiding their interpretation of sources and their understanding of Mary's queenship. Although the biblical presentation of Christ's kingdom may have some points in common with earthly monarchies, it ultimately remains quite different (e.g., Jn. 18:36; Lk. 22:25–26).[4] Thus, as Pius XII taught: "The Queenship of Mary must not be considered—and much less the Kingship of her Son—in analogy with the realities of modern political life."[5]

With secular perspectives at the root guiding many explanations of Mary's royal office, it is not surprising that the very idea of her being a queen has been considered anachronistic and triumphalistic for some,[6] and has been reduced to mere symbolism for others.[7] Especially in a modern age in which most monarchical governments have given way to democratic societies, approaches attempting to view Mary's queenship primarily through the lenses of secular notions of royalty are bound to run into difficulties.[8] For a proper understanding of Mary's queenship, which will avoid these pitfalls, we must begin with the biblical view of Christ's kingdom. Our approach must allow the sacred texts primarily to guide our understanding of queenship—not the other way around. As discussed earlier, we agree with De Fiores's call for a biblical theology that not only will help preserve the traditional content of Mary's royal title, but also enrich it with a broader, timeless, non-politically bound meaning that will have more significance for Christians of our time.[9] We quote again the two-fold approach he proposes: "Return to the Bible in order to understand Mary's queenship in the context of Christ and the people of God and give attention to the culture of our time in order to translate in more simple terms the content and significance of Queen Mary."[10]

In this study, we have taken an important step in that direction. We have returned to the biblical sources and allowed the scriptural view of queenship and the kingdom to guide our understanding of Mary's role in the kingdom of Christ. In doing so, we have seen more clearly from a biblical perspective why, as mother of the King, Mary would be considered a queen. Having already seen how fruitful our salvation-historical approach can be for understanding why Mary might be considered a queen mother, we would suggest that the same biblical theological approach employed in this study also can have important and exciting implications for understanding the meaning and practical significance of Mary's royal office. Thus, in closing, we will offer a few brief suggestions about how further study applying such a biblical methodology to areas related to Mary's queenship might bear much fruit as well.

One area that would benefit from further consideration along these lines is the Christological aspect of Mary's queenship. If Mary has any royal office it should be seen in its relationship with Christ[11]—as dependent upon Him and subordinate to Him (cf. *LG* 62) and as sharing in his reign (cf. *LG* 59). The queen-mother theme certainly underscores this point. Just as the queen mother had no authority on her own but had a royal office based completely on her son's kingship, so too Mary's royal position in the kingdom of God depends entirely on her royal Son, Christ the King.

Following this line of thought, we would suggest that if we continue to view Mary's royal office from more deeply within the biblical perspective on Christ's kingdom, then the authentic meaning of her queenship will continue to shine with greater clarity and help overcome some of the modern difficulties in understanding the practical significance of Mary being a queen. Here, we will see that her queenship is not meant to be understood in terms of secular monarchies. It is not a political authority, nor an aristocratic-like privilege, nor a ceremonial position as is found in monarchies of the West. The kingdom in which Mary reigns—the kingdom of Christ—is presented in the Scriptures as very different from the kingdoms of this earth.[12] Christ's kingship "is not of this world" (Jn. 18:36), and it is not based on political, militaristic, or economic power.[13] Rather, as Serra points out, Jesus is a King of humble origins (Mt. 13:55; Mk. 6:3), who washes the feet of His own disciples (Jn. 13:4–5) and consistently refuses violence (Mt. 5:9–10, 43–47, 26:52; Lk. 9:51–55).[14] He rejected the temptation of Satan for a messiahship that would have been comfortable and politically glorious (Mt. 4:1–11). While rulers of worldly kingdoms "lord it over" their subjects, Christ exercises his reign through humility and becoming a servant, even to the point of giving his life as a ransom for many (Mt. 20:25–28; Phil. 2:5–11).[15] Furthermore, the New Testament describes how because of his humble service, Christ is exalted by the Father and enthroned over all things (Heb. 1:9, 13), victorious over the enemies of sin (Heb. 1:3), the devil (Heb. 2:14), and death (1 Cor. 15:24).[16] This abasement-exaltation of Christ is seen especially in Philippians 2:5–11, which describes how every knee shall bend to Christ and every tongue shall confess Him as Lord, but also emphasizes that His supreme exaltation flows from His abasement—becoming a slave, being obedient unto death, death on a Cross.

All this is important because, as some have suggested, Mary is portrayed in the New Testament as a person who exemplifies this Christ-like abasement-exaltation pattern.[17] She is described as a humble servant of the Lord (Lk. 1:38, 48). She is the first who obediently hears God's word and accepts it (Lk. 1:38, 45; Lk. 11:27–28), and she perseveres even unto suffering (Lk. 2:34–35; Jn. 19:25–27).[18] And it is precisely in her lowliness as the Lord's servant that God has exalted her (Lk. 1:46–55).[19] In this light, De Fiores concludes that the life of Mary is a testimony to the kingdom of God,[20] and it is through her humble, obedient service that she has a share in Christ's reign, reigning with Him over the powers of sin and death.[21]

This is the proper context for understanding the meaning of Mary's queenship. Within such a biblical theology of Christ's kingdom, her queenly role is less likely to be misunderstood as a triumphalistic or aristocratic privilege, as is often found in the kingdoms of the world.[22] Far from any type of political supremacy, Mary's royal position, when viewed through the biblical view of the kingdom, will be seen in light of the way she imitates Christ's reign through humble service, obedience to God, and persevering faith.[23] As Pope John Paul II has taught in *Redemptoris Mater*, this perseverance of Mary as "the handmaid of the Lord" is an important basis for understanding her queenship in the kingdom of Christ.

In this she confirmed that she was a true 'disciple' of Christ, who strongly emphasized that his mission was one of service: the Son of Man 'came not to be served but to serve, and to give his life as a ransom for many' (Mt. 20:28). In this way Mary became the first of those who, 'serving Christ also in others, with humility and patience lead their brothers and sisters to that King whom to serve is to reign,' and she fully obtained that 'state of royal freedom' proper to Christ's disciples: to serve means to reign! (*RM* 41)[24]

A second area worth further consideration in terms of a biblical theology of Mary's queenship is Christ's promise that *all* His faithful disciples would share in His reign. The New Testament describes how those disciples who have been willing to give up everything and follow Christ will "sit on thrones judging the twelve tribes of Israel" (Mt. 19:28–30). Anyone who hears Christ's voice and "opens the door" will sit with Him on His throne (Rev. 3:20–21). His disciples who have continued with him through trials will rule over the new Israel (Lk. 22:28–30), and those who will die with Him will reign with Him (2 Tim. 2:11–12). Serra thus summarizes that those disciples who follow Christ, listen to His voice, and persevere through trials, even unto death, will share in the royal dominion of Christ[25]—a dominion that *Lumen Gentium* describes as a reign over sin, which is meant to be extended throughout all the world.

> He communicated this power to the disciples that they be constituted in royal liberty and, by self-abnegation of a holy life, overcome the reign of sin in themselves (cf. Rom. 6:12)—that indeed by serving Christ in others they may in humility and patience bring their brethren to that king whom to serve is to reign. The Lord also desires that his kingdom be spread by the lay faithful: the kingdom of truth and life, the kingdom of holiness and grace, the kingdom of justice, love and peace. (*LG* 36)

Serra argues that Mary meets the biblical criteria for reigning with Christ.[26] From the Annunciation to Pentecost, Mary is portrayed as a model disciple who heard God's word and accepted it (Lk. 1:38, 45, 8:21, 11:27–28) and persevered throughout her life (Acts 1:14), following her Son even through the torment of His death (Lk. 2:34–35; Jn. 19:25–27).[27] Thus, having been a true disciple of Christ, it is fitting that she would share in the reign Christ promised all of his disciples. O'Donnell concludes: "Mary is portrayed in the New Testament and contemplated in Christian tradition as the one who faithfully followed Jesus, persevered in trials and opened her heart to God—thus fulfilling all the conditions for attaining royal status. . . . She is therefore blessed with heavenly royal dignity. God's free response to her fidelity was to make her Queen."[28]

Third, the biblical understanding of Christ's kingdom places Mary's queenship more clearly in the context of the royalty of the whole people of God, highlighting the ecclesial dimension of her royal office. "The insertion of the queenship of the Virgin in the context of the royal office of the people of God (1 Pet. 2:9; Rev. 1:6, 5:9, 20:4–6), while not detaching the person of Mary from the ecclesial community, helps to understand better the significance of Mary's queenship and its meaning for Christians today."[29] Mary's queenship is not something far removed from the Christian life, an exalted position in heaven that we are to honor only from a distance. "She is not an isolated and extraneous figure, but one who, in communion with all Christians, participates in the same reign of Christ."[30] As such, Mary becomes "an example from within the people of God" of the destiny to which we are all called.[31] We can see in Mary "the concrete possibility" of what all faithful disciples will become.[32]

De Fiores notes that this ecclesial context underscores the fact that Mary's royal dignity is not an individualistic privilege, but rather, that she stands "as a point of reference" for Christians on their pilgrimage of faith.[33] She is a "leader" who inspires God's people to realize the Christian royal vocation in their own lives.[34] "Mary is queen by which she exercises a 'leadership' in regards to the people of God: with her prestige and with the excellence of her existence as first Christian and type of the church, she represents a point of reference necessary for the faithful who intend to discover their own royal identity as children of God and give to the Lord a larger space in their lives."

In this light, we can see that Mary's queenship has great practical significance for Christians of all ages, of all cultures, and in all states of life. As Pope John Paul II taught in an Angelus exhortation in 1981:

> Therefore, fixing our gaze on the mystery of Mary's Assumption, of her 'crowning' in glory, we daily learn to serve—to serve God in our brothers and sisters, to express in our attitude of service the 'royalty' of our Christian vocation in every state or profession, in every time and in every place. To carry over into the reality of our daily life through such an attitude the petition, 'Thy kingdom come,' which we make every day in the Lord's prayer to the Father.[35]

These are some suggestions on how further application of the biblical approach taken in this book can deepen our understanding of the Christological and ecclesial dimensions of this doctrine in a way that will be helpful for expressing the meaning and practical significance of Mary's queenship for modern Christians. In closing, we suggest that this biblical approach to Marian doctrine also may be valuable for ecumenical dialogue. As Mary O'Driscoll points out, Marian devotion needs to include an ecumenical dimension. "This places on all of us the responsibility to present Mary in such a way that, in honoring her, our sisters and brothers in other Christian traditions are not misled as to how we regard Mary theologically."[36] One key principle for presenting Marian doctrine with ecumenical sensitivity is "the law of return to the sources,"[37] which Laurentin highlights in his discussion on Mariology and ecumenism. He notes how Catholic theologians need to "*re-center* all Marian doctrine in the true tradition of the Bible, the liturgy and the Fathers."[38] Such an approach will help minimize formulas and concepts which do not flow from the sources of our faith, so that the authentic content of the doctrine may shine more clearly and may do so in a way that sets up less hindrances for dialogue with other Christians.[39]

In regards to Mary's queenship, we have already seen that abstract philosophical concepts of royalty and secular-political models of queenship guiding the interpretation of sources can lead to misunderstandings and distortions of Mary's royal office. I believe the approach of this study, however, will be more helpful for re-centering the doctrine of Mary's queenship on the source which Laurentin and *Ut Unam Sint* describe as having a primacy for theology: Scripture.[40] Indeed, it has often been pointed out that an ecumenical Mariology must be biblical.[41] Thus, while Mary's queenship admittedly has not been a central topic for ecumenical discussion, at least the biblical *approach* taken here should appeal to a wide segment of ecumenical partners. Furthermore, while the results of this study certainly do not remove all the difficulties surrounding the presentation of Mary's queenship to other Christians, offering a more thoroughly biblical portrait of Mary would at least be more congenial to Christian brothers and sisters from other ecclesial communities. By presenting Mary's royal office in terms of the biblical understanding of queenship and the kingdom, we can offer a basis for expressing her queenship in a way that would be more meaningful to other Christians than approaches to this doctrine beginning with a view of queenship that is primarily guided by abstract metaphysics or Western political monarchies.

Abbreviations

AAS	*Acta Apostolicae Sedis*
AER	*American Ecclesiastical Review*
ASS	*Acta Sanctae Sedis*
BibRev	*Biblical Review*
BS	*Bibliotheca Sacra*
BTB	*Biblical Theology Bulletin*
CBQ	*Catholic Biblical Quarterly*
CTR	*Criswell Theological Review*
EphMar	*Ephemerides Mariologicae*
EstMar	*Estudios Marianos*
EtMar	*Etudes Mariales*
JBL	*Journal of Biblical Literature*
JSOTSup	Journal for the Study of the Old Testament Supplement Series
JSNTSup	Journal for the Study of the New Testament Supplement Series
MI	*Miles Immaculatae*
RB	*Revue Biblique*
RevThom	*Revue Thomiste*
TynBul	*Tyndale Bulletin*
TS	*Theological Studies*
VT	*Vetus Testamentum*
VTSup	Vetus Testamentum Supplements
ZAW	*Zeitschrift für die Alttestamentliche Wissenschaft*

Notes

The Letter & Spirit Project
[1] Second Vatican Council, *Dei Verbum* (November 18, 1965), hereafter cited in text as *DV*.

[2] Thomas Aquinas, *Summa Theologica*, I, 1, 10 *ad* 1, as quoted in the *Catechism*, no. 166.

[3] Augustine, *De doctrina* 1.2; see also *Dei Verbum*, nos. 15–16.

Foreword
[1] Joseph Cardinal Ratzinger, "Crisis in Catechetics," *Canadian Catholic Review* (June 1983): 178.

[2] International Theological Commission, *On Interpretation of Dogmas* (1989), as quoted in *Origins* 20 (May 17, 1990): 10.

Chapter One
[1] Some of the major works I will be drawing from in this section are E. Carroll, "Our Lady's Queenship in the Magisterium of the Church," *Marian Studies* 4 (1953): 29–81; M. Donnelly, "The Queenship of Mary During the Patristic Period," *Marian Studies* 4 (1953): 82–108; W. Hill, "Our Lady's Queenship in the Middle Ages and Modern Times," *Marian Studies* 4 (1953): 134–69; G. Kirwin, *The Nature of the Queenship of Mary* (Ann Arbor, MI: UMI Dissertation Services, 1973), pp. 37–136; N. Peña, "La Encíclica 'Ad Caeli Reginam' y su influjo en el magisterio posterior," *EphMar* 46 (1996): 485–501; F. Schmidt, "The Universal Queenship of Mary," in J. Carol, ed., *Mariology*, vol. 2 (Milwaukee: Bruce Publishing Company, 1957), pp. 501–20, 524–41; L. Gambero, "La Regalità di Maria nel Pensiero dei Padri," *EphMar* 46 (1996): 433–52.

[2] L. Gambero, "La Regalità," p. 435.

[3] Ibid., p. 434.

[4] "Sciendumque quod Maria sermone Syro domina nuncupetur." Jerome, *Liber de Nominbus Hebraicis* (PL 23:842). See also M. Donnelly, "Queenship of Mary During the Patristic Period," p. 90.

[5] Peter Chrysologus, *Sermon 142* (PL 52:579c).

[6] L. Gambero, "La Regalità," pp. 441–42; M. Donnelly, "Queenship of Mary During the Patristic Period," pp. 99–100.

[7] M. Donnelly, "Queenship of Mary During the Patristic Period," p. 87.

[8] Ibid., p. 87.

[9] *Fragmenta Origenis, Ex Macarii Chrysocephali Orationibus in Lucam* (PG 13:1902). "Cur me igitur prior salutas? Nunquid ego sum quae Salvatorem pario? Oportebat me ad te venire: tu enim super omnes mulieres benedicta: tu Mater Domini mei: tu mea Domina."

[10] Ephrem, *Ed. Assemani* III.524, as cited in M. Donnelly, "Queenship of Mary During the Patristic Period," p. 87.

[11] Jerome, *Homilia in die Dom. Paschae*, D. Morin, ed., *Anecdota Maredsolan*, t. III, pars. II, p. 414, as cited in M. Donnelly, "Queenship of Mary During the Patristic Period," p. 88; Augustine, *In Joannis Evangelium VIII* (PL 35:1456). Also see M. Donnelly, "Queenship of Mary During the Patristic Period," p. 88. On the significance of this title, *Domina*, see G. Kirwin, *Nature of the Queenship*, p. 39: "The name 'Domina' indicates a great dignity and the fact that it is applied to Mary who is the Mother of the 'Dominus' leads us easily to the conclusion that she too is a sovereign."

[12] For example, Gregory of Nanzianzus, *Poemata Dogmatica* (PG 37:485a); Hesychius, *De Sancta Maria Deipara Homilia* (PG 93:1465–68); Sedulius, *Opus Paschale* (PL 19:599); cf. John Chrysostom, *In Annuntiationem Deiparae* (PG 62:765).

[13] M. Donnelly, "Queenship of Mary During the Patristic Period," pp. 88–89; L. Gambero, "La Regalità," pp. 438–41.

[14] Chrysippus of Jerusalem, *In S. Mariam Deiparam* (PO 93:339).

[15] G. Kirwin, *Nature of the Queenship*, p. 40.

[16] Cf. L. Gambero, "La Regalità," p. 433.

[17] Idelfonse of Toledo, *Liber de Virginitate Perpetua S. Mariae* (PL 96:106).

[18] M. Donnelly, "Queenship of Mary During the Patristic Period," p. 97 (PG 97:872, 833, 820, 1045).

[19] Andrew of Crete, *In Dormitionem S. Mariae* (PG 97:1107).

[20] Germain of Constantinople, *In Annuntiationem SS. Deiparae* (PG 98:324–25); Germain of Constantinople, *In Praesentationem SS. Deiparae I* (PG 98:304).

[21] John Damascene, *Homilia III in Dormitionem B.V. Mariae* (PG 96:760); John Damascene, *De Fide Orthodoxa Lib. IV* (PG 96:1157, 1162).

[22] John Damascene, *Homilia II in Dormitionem B.V. Mariae* (PG 96:721).

[23] W. Hill, "Our Lady's Queenship in the Middle Ages and Modern Times," pp. 135–43.

[24] Ibid., pp. 139, 143; F. Schmidt, "Universal Queenship of Mary," p. 530.

[25] W. Hill, "Our Lady's Queenship in the Middle Ages and Modern Times," p. 148.

[26] Ibid., p. 152.

[27] G. Kirwin, *Nature of the Queenship*, p. 53. Conrad of Saxony drew a similar conclusion. F. Schmidt, "Universal Queenship of Mary," p. 531.

[28] G. Kirwin, *Nature of the Queenship*, p. 53.

[29] W. Hill notes Bonaventure, the *Mariale,* Richard of St. Lawrence, Bernardine of Siena, and Denis the Carthusian as examples. "Our Lady's Queenship in the Middle Ages and Modern Times," pp. 146, 149–52.

[30] Ibid., p. 153.

[31] G. Kirwin, *Nature of the Queenship*, p. 55; W. Hill, "Our Lady's Queenship in the Middle Ages and Modern Times," pp. 159, 161.

[32] G. Kirwin, *Nature of the Queenship*, p. 55. W. Hill, "Our Lady's Queenship in the Middle Ages and Modern Times," pp. 164–67.

[33] W. Hill, "Our Lady's Queenship in the Middle Ages and Modern Times," p. 168.

[34] G. Kirwin, *Nature of the Queenship*, pp. 62–63.

[35] G. Kirwin, *Nature of the Queenship*, p. 63. See n. 162: "In Greek liturgical language the title 'Despoina' always implies sovereignty."

[36] Pius XII, *Ad Caeli Reginam,* no. 28, in C. Carlen, ed., *The Papal Encyclicals: 1939-1958* (Wilmington, NC: McGrath Publishing, 1981), hereafter cited in text as *AC. AAS* 46 (1954): 631.

[37] G. Kirwin, *Nature of the Queenship*, p. 63.

[38] Ibid., p. 64.

[39] E. Lodi, "Preghiera Mariana," in S. De Fiores and S. Meo, eds., *Nuovo Dizionario di Mariologia* (Milan: Edizioni San Paolo, 1996), p. 1029. C. O'Donnell, *At Worship with Mary: A Pastoral and Theological Study* (Wilmington, DE: Michael Glazier, 1988), p. 153.

[40] *AAS* 46 (1954): 627, 638.

[41] Paul VI, *Marialis Cultus,* no. 6 (Boston: St. Paul Books and Media, 1974), hereafter cited in text as *MC.* "The Solemnity of the Assumption is prolonged in the celebration of the Queenship of the Blessed Virgin Mary, which occurs seven days later. On this day we contemplate her who, seated beside the King of Ages, shines forth as Queen and intercedes as Mother." See also *AAS* 66 (1974): 121.

[42] G. Besutti, "Litanie," in S. De Fiores and S. Meo, eds., *Nuovo Dizonario di Mariologia* (Milan: Edizioni San Paolo, 1996), p. 684.

[43] G. Kirwin, *Nature of the Queenship*, pp. 40–41, 68–79; Pius XII, *Ad Caeli Reginam* (*AAS* 46 [1954]: 632–33).

[44] G. Kirwin, *Nature of the Queenship*, p. 80.

[45] E. Carroll, "Our Lady's Queenship in the Magisterium," pp. 38–39.

[46] "Council of Nicea II," in H. Denzinger, ed., *The Sources of Catholic Dogma* (St. Louis: Herder, 1957), p. 121.

[47] G. Kirwin, *Nature of the Queenship*, p. 81.

[48] E. Carroll, "Our Lady's Queenship in the Magisterium," p. 41.

[49] Benedict XIV, *Gloriosae Dominae*, in Benedictine Monks of Solesmes, ed., *Papal Teachings: Our Lady* (Boston: St. Paul Editions, 1961), pp. 25–29.

[50] Benedict XIV, *Gloriosae Dominae*, in *Papal Teachings*, p. 26.

[51] E. Carroll, "Our Lady's Queenship in the Magisterium," pp. 43–44.

[52] Ibid., pp. 39–42, 44, emphasis added.

[53] Pius IX, *Ineffabilis Deus*, in Benedictine Monks of Solesmes, ed., *Papal Teachings: Our Lady* (Boston: St. Paul Editions, 1961), p. 82.

[54] For example: *Supremi Apostolatus Officio* (*ASS* 16 [1883]: 116); *Octobri Mense* (*ASS* 24 [1891–1892]: 202); *Magnae Dei Matris* (*ASS* 25 [1892–1893]: 140); *Laetitiae Sanctae* (*ASS* 26 [1893–1894]: 193); *Iucunda Semper* (*ASS* 27 [1894–1895]: 177); *Adiutricem Populi* (*ASS* 28 [1895–1896]: 129); *Fidentem Piumque* (*ASS* 29 [1896–1897]: 204). See E. Carroll, "Our Lady's Queenship in the Magisterium," pp. 47–53.

[55] Pius X, *Ad Diem Illum*, in Benedictine Monks of Solesmes, ed., *Papal Teachings: Our Lady* (Boston: St. Paul Editions, 1961), pp. 165–82 (*AAS* 36 [1903–1904]: 454).

[56] See E. Carroll, "Our Lady's Queenship in the Magisterium," pp. 55–56.

[57] Pius XI, *Rerum Ecclesiae*, in Benedictine Monks of Solesmes, ed., *Papal Teachings: Our Lady* (Boston: St. Paul Editions, 1961), p. 207 (*AAS* 18 [1926]: 83); Pius XI, *Lux Veritatis*, in Benedictine Monks of Solesmes, ed., *Papal Teachings: Our Lady* (Boston: St. Paul Editions, 1961), p. 218 (*AAS* 23 [1931]: 515).

[58] "If we should wish to determine from the documents we have what truth Pius XII has above all illuminated in Our Lady, it seems no mistake to say: the Queenship. . . . On this point the teaching of Pius XII far surpasses in richness and development that of his predecessors." D. Bertetto, "La Dottrina Mariana di Pio XII," *Salesianum* 11 (1949): 22–23, as quoted in E. Carroll, "Our Lady's Queenship in the Magisterium," pp. 61–62. Note how this statement was made about Pius XII even before the definition of the Assumption and his encyclical on Mary's queenship, *Ad Caeli Reginam*!

[59] Pius XII, "Mais de uma vez" (*AAS* 34 [1942]: 345–46). See also E. Carroll, "Our Lady's Queenship in the Magisterium," p. 63.

[60] G. Kirwin, *Nature of the Queenship*, p. 92.

[61] Pius XII, *Mystici Corporis*, in Benedictine Monks of Solesmes, ed., *Papal Teachings: Our Lady* (Boston: St. Paul Editions, 1961). *AAS* 35 (1943): 248.

[62] Pius XII, *Munificentissimus Deus,* in Benedictine Monks of Solesmes, ed., *Papal Teachings: Our Lady* (Boston: St. Paul Editions, 1961), pp. 311–12 (*AAS* 42 [1950]: 763).

[63] Pius XII, *Munificentissimus Deus*, in *Papal Teachings*, pp. 314–15 (*AAS* 42 [1950]: 765–66).

[64] Pius XII, *Munificentissimus Deus*, in *Papal Teachings*, p. 318 (*AAS* 42 [1950]: 768–69).

[65] Pius XII, *Ad Caeli Reginam* (*AAS* 46 [1954]: 626–27). For more extensive treatments on this encyclical, see N. Peña, "La Enciclica 'Ad Caeli Reginam,'" *EphMar* 46 (1996): 485–501; R. Peinador, "Propedeutica a la Encíclica 'Ad Caeli Reginam,'" *EphMar* 5 (1955): 291–316; G. Roschini, "Breve commento all'Enciclica 'Ad Caeli Reginam,'" *Marianum* 16 (1954): 409–32.

[66] Pius XII, *Ad Caeli Reginam* (*AAS* 46 [1954]: 627–33).

[67] *AAS* 46 (1954): 633.

[68] *AAS* 46 (1954): 633.

[69] *AAS* 46 (1954): 634.

[70] *AAS* 46 (1954): 635.

[71] *AAS* 46 (1954): 636.

[72] *AAS* 46 (1954): 636.

[73] *AAS* 46 (1954): 637.

[74] *AAS* 46 (1954): 636–37.

[75] G. Kirwin, *Nature of the Queenship*, pp. 131–33; N. Peña, "La Encíclica 'Ad Caeli Reginam,'" p. 492.

[76] "Tu, mater pulchrae dilectionis, agnitionis et sanctae spei, *Ecclesiae regina* et propugnatrix. Tu Nos, consultationes, labores nostros in tuam maternam fidem tutelamque recipias: ac Tuis age apud Deum precibus, ut in uno semper spiritu maneamus et corde." John XXIII, "Portiamo con noi" (*AAS* 53 [1961]: 36–37). See also G. Kirwin, *Nature of the Queenship*, p. 134; N. Peña, "La Encíclica 'Ad Caeli Reginam,'" p. 493.

[77] Peña notes how *Lumen Gentium* no. 59 presents Mary's queenship (along with her Immaculate Conception and Assumption) in the context of her being "more fully conformed" to Christ: "La perfecta conformidad de María con su Hijo es lo que da sentido y fundamento a sus dones y privilegios: para que en todo se asemeje más perfectamente a Cristo, su Hijo, vencedor del pecado (he ahí el

fundamento de la Inmaculada Concepción), y de la muerte (razón de ser de la Asunción gloriosa), Señor de los señores, Rey universal (razón de ser y fundamento del título de María, Reina)." N. Peña, "La Encíclica 'Ad Caeli Reginam,'" p. 494.

[78] Ibid.

[79] Paul VI, *Mense Maio* (*AAS* 57 [1965]: 353).

[80] *AAS* 66 (1974): 119.

[81] *AAS* 66 (1974): 119.

[82] *AAS* 66 (1974): 121.

[83] Among these attitudes, Paul VI considers "the loving service, when she sees in the humble handmaid of the Lord the queen of mercy and the mother of grace." *AAS* 66 (1974): 33.

[84] John Paul II, *Redemptoris Mater* (Boston: Pauline Books, 1987), no. 41, hereafter cited in text as *RM*. *AAS* 79 (1987): 417.

[85] *AAS* 79 (1987): 417. See N. Peña, "La Encíclica 'Ad Caeli Reginam,'" p. 499: "Existe una extrecha relación entre la kénosis de Cristo y su exaltación como Señor de los señores, glorificado a la derecha del Padre. Lo mismo sucede en María: su ser de 'esclava del Señor' y su fidelidad durante toda su vida a lo que ese nombre significa hasta la cruz, fue lo que después la exaltó en su Asunción y por ello ha conseguido aquel 'estado de libertad real, propio de los discípulos fieles de Cristo."

[86] *AAS* 79 (1987): 417–18.

[87] *AAS* 79 (1987): 418. See N. Peña, "La Encíclica 'Ad Caeli Reginam,'" p. 499: "De este modo, María, desde su rango y condición, únicos privilegiados ciertamente, está en comunión con todos los elegidos y todos los santos."

[88] The *Catechism* (no. 1053) does not treat Mary's queenship specifically, but it does show how all the saints will share in Christ's royal rule in heaven. "We believe that the multitude gathered around Jesus and Mary in Paradise forms the Church of heaven . . . where they are also to various degrees, associated with the holy angels in the divine governance exercised by Christ in glory, by interceding for us and helping our weakness by their fraternal concern [Paul VI, *CPG* § 29]." This would seem to place Mary's royal status in an ecclesial context, as we saw Pope John Paul II do explicitly in *Redemptoris Mater*, no. 61. See N. Peña, "La Encíclica 'Ad Caeli Reginam,'" p. 500.

[89] See G. Kirwin, *Nature of the Queenship*, pp. 5–6.

[90] On these two predominant schools of thought, see E. Carroll, "Our Lady's Queenship in the Magisterium," pp. 32–34; K. Moore, "The Queenship of the Blessed Virgin in the Liturgy of the Church," *Marian Studies* 3 (1952): 218–19; S. De Fiores, "Regina: Approfondimento Teologico Attualizzato," in S. De Fiores and S. Meo, eds., *Nuovo Dizionario di Mariologia* (Milan: Edizioni San Paolo, 1996), pp. 1077–78. For an extensive treatment on this, see A. Luis, "La Realeza de María en los Últimos Veinte Años," *EstMar* 11 (1951): 221–51; G. Kirwin, *Nature of the Queenship*, pp. 137–97.

[91] S. De Fiores, "Regina," pp. 1077–78; G. Kirwin, *Nature of the Queenship*, pp. 155–57, 175–84.

[92] L. De Gruyter, *De Beata Maria Regina: Disquisitio Positivo-Speculativa* (Turin: Marietti, 1934), pp. 55–58.

[93] Ibid., p. 57. "Quidquid vero sit, certum est *solis* illis S. Scripturae verbis nullum argumentum afferri pro thesi quod B. Maria sit Regina, quovis etiam modo vox 'regina' sumatur."

[94] Ibid., p. 58. "S. Scriptura *sola* ad summum unicum affert argumentum pro assertione quod S. Virgo sit proprie et formaliter Regina. Accedit vero quod unicum illud argumentum scripturisticum *ut tale* non gaudeat vi probativa apud omnes. Ideoque *eo solo* thesim, quam probandam suscipimus, stabilire forsan non possumus—at certo non volumus. Insistemus super S. Scriptura et Traditione *simul.* Duo enim illi unius revelationis fontes, per modum unius sumpti, invictum tradunt argumentum ad probationem theseos."

[95] Ibid., pp. 124–36. See his summary conclusion on p. 136: "Probavimus quod B. Maria est illa benedicta quae ceteras omnes creaturas antecellit in unione cum Deo et ideo in perfectione ac dignitate tum ratione Maternitatis divinae tum ratione excellentiae gratiarum. B. Maria ergo vere est ac recte dicitur Regina sensu improprio et analogo."

[96] Ibid., pp. 137–44. See p. 141: "Charitati huic in B. Virgine respondet potestas maxima apud Deum et Filium suum incarnatum ita ut Regina nostra recte voceture 'Omnipotentia supplex.'"

[97] Ibid., pp. 144–73.

[98] Ibid., pp. 146–50, 150–54, 145–46.

[99] Ibid., pp. 168–70. De Gruyter argues that Mary's queenship is primarily spiritual and interior. It is universal, and it primarily consists of distributing graces upon humanity, the principle activity by which she reigns as queen.

[100] Ibid., pp. 171–72.

[101] M. Nicolas, "Nature de la Souveraineté de Marie," in *Mater et Ecclesia*, vol. 5 (Congressus Mariologicus Lourdes, 1958), p. 194.

[102] M. Nicolas, "La Vierge-Reine," *Revue Thomiste* 45 (1939): 12. "Peut-on trouver dans le pouvoir universel d'intercession de la Sainte Vierge les caractéristiques essentielles du pouvoir royal? Or nous pensons qu'on ne le peut pas en rigueur de langage. Le pouvoir royal, si on s'en tient à son essence, nous a paru s'exercer formellement par l''imperium.' De même que l'individu se commande à lui-même ses acts en vue d'une fin qui lui est strictement personnelle, de même le roi commande leurs actes aux membres de la Société dont il est le chef, en vue de la fin qui leur est commune à tous et qui les réunit sous lui."

[103] Ibid., pp. 208–12. See p. 208: "Le pouvoir royal est cette vertu qu'a la volonté d'un homme de déterminer efficacement les actions des autres et de les diriger en vue d'une fin commune á tous. L'homme dont la volonté a ce pouvoir en elle-même et sans appel à un autre qu'à la Cause Première et transcendante, est proprement le roi."

Also, p. 210: " Si le roi est vraiment roi et monarque, la volonté de la reine n'a en elle-même ni force de loi, ni autorité intrinsèque. Le roi peut, bien entendu, lui déléguer son pouvoir comme à tout autre et se servir de son ministère pour les tâches où elle lui paraît propre à le seconder. Si sa confiance en elle est manifeste, reconnue et approuvée de tous, cette délégation peut même être tacite. Mais il s'agit toujours d'une délégation et d'un ministère, non pas proprement d'une autorité souveraine."

[104] M. Nicolas, "Nature de la Souveraineté de Marie," p. 198; M. Nicolas, "La Vierge-Reine," pp. 18–29.

[105] M. Nicolas, "La Vierge-Reine," pp. 14–29.

[106] Ibid., pp. 21–26.

[107] Ibid., pp. 26–29. See p. 26: "Lorsqu'on a compris que le grand principe de l'association de Marie et de Jésus dans l'oeuvre de la Rédemption est enraciné dans le lien de Mère à Fils qui les unit, et que Marie devient proprement la Nouvelle Éve quand le Verbe devient lui-même le Nouvel Adam, on comprend qu'elle doive rester sa compagne dans toute son oeuvre d'Homme-Dieu, comme la première Ève devait rester la compagne du premier Adam pour tout son oeuvre d'homme."

[108] Ibid., pp. 212–23. On p. 216: "Cette Reine a dans la communauté humaine un rôle vraiment officiel et indispensable, qui n'est pas un pouvoir de gouvernement, mais un pouvoir d'intercession en faveur du peuple, sans lequel le gouvernement du Christ-Roi ne s'exerce jamais."

[109] M. Nicolas, "Nature de la Souveraineté de Marie," p. 198: "Parmi tous ceux qui prient, Marie—et très précisément comme reine—étant *unie* aux intentions mêmes, à la charge même, à la mission royale du Christ, a une place unique et indispensable."

[110] M. Nicolas, "La Vierge-Reine," pp. 212–23.

[111] Ibid., pp. 221–22.

[112] Ibid., p. 213.

[113] G. Kirwin, *Nature of the Queenship*, p. 156.

[114] Ibid., p. 178.

[115] Ibid., p. 182.

[116] Ibid., introduction, p. 1.

[117] Pius XII, *Ad Caeli Reginam* (*AAS* 46 [1954]: 627–28).

[118] *AAS* 46 (1954): 633.

[119] G. Kirwin, *Nature of the Queenship*, p. 17, original emphasis. At the same time, Kirwin also notes that the pope does not exclude the possibility of a formal revelation of the queenship, nor the possibility of other scriptural texts containing the doctrine of Mary's queenship. Cf. R. Peinador, "Propedeutica a la Enciclica 'Ad Caeli Reginam,'" p. 299: "No encontramos en ella afirmación explícita de que la realeza de María tenga apoyo en la Sagrada Escritura. . . . Sin embargo, notemos que nues-

tra Encíclica, tanto al hablar del antiguo sentido del pueblo cristiano (n. 8), como de los testimonios de los antiguos Padres (n. 9), como del argumento de la divina maternidad (n. 33), afirma que su fundamento se encuentra en las palabras del ángel y de Santa Isabel a María. Por este lado nuestra Encíclica se acerca más a la *Ineffabilis Deus*, que englobó el argumento escriturístico dentro del tradicional."

[120] N. Peña, "La Enciclíca 'Ad Caeli Reginam,'" pp. 489–90. Similarly, see again R. Peinador, "Propedeutica a la Enciclica 'Ad Caeli Reginam,'" p. 299: "No encontramos en [*Ad Caeli Reginam*] afirmación explícita de que la realeza de María tenga apoyo en la Sagrada Escritura."

[121] A. Luis, *La Realeza de María*, (Madrid: El Perpetuo Socorro, 1942), pp. 27–29. It is worth noting that later in this article, Luis argues that Mary's queenship can find some support in Revelation 12 if "the woman" is seen as having a Marian sense along with an ecclesial sense. See p. 31: "En el Apocalipsis brilla deslumbrante de majestad y de grandeza, coronada con diadema real, y como Madre de 'un Hijo varón que ha de gobernar a todas las naciones con mano férrea', Hijo que es 'arrebatado hacia Dios y hacia su trono'. Una vez más la *Madre del Rey* se ofrece a nuestros ojos ostentando los atributos de su excelsa Realeza." However, in a later article, Luis seems to back up from this position, not even considering the woman of Revelation 12 as a possible basis for the queenship. He concludes that the queenship cannot be proven by the Scriptures alone: "Ahora bien: los destellos que sobre el particular despide la Sagrada Escritura son tenues e indecisos en demasía para iluminar por sí solos problema tan complejo." A. Luis, "La Realeza de María en los Ultimos Veinte Años," *EstMar* 11 (1951): 224.

[122] J. Fenton, "Our Lady's Queenship and the New Testament Teachings," in *Alma Socia Christi* Congressus Mariologicus Romae (Rome: Academia Mariana, 1950), pp. 68–86.

[123] Ibid., p. 80.

[124] Ibid., pp. 82–86. In showing how Mary's close association with Christ must have brought her suffering, Fenton mentions Simeon's prophecy, her fleeing to Egypt to avoid the persecution of Herod, her losing Jesus in the Temple, her probable sadness over watching her fellow townsmen in Nazareth reject her Son, and her suffering at the Cross.

[125] Ibid., p. 82.

[126] F. Vandry, "Nature of Mary's Universal Queenship," *Marian Studies* 4 (1953): 13.

[127] While he alludes to the scene of Mary at the Cross in this article, Vandry concentrates most explicitly on the Annunciation, paying particular attention to Mary's words of consent. In a later article, in which he revised the 1953 paper, Vandry does mention that Mary is the woman of Genesis 3:15 who crushed the head of the serpent, who is the king over all the children of pride (Job 41:25). He argues that this royal victory entitles her to the role of queen. See F. Vandry, "Nature of Mary's Universal Queenship," *Laval Thèologique et Philosophique* 10 (1954): 60.

[128] Vandry also considers how Mary is clothed with royalty in her cooperation in redemption by sharing in Christ's sufferings on Calvary and how she exercises her queenship in heaven as the dispenser of the graces she helped to win. F. Vandry, "Nature of Mary's Universal Queenship" (1953), pp. 19–27. In his 1954 article, he also examines how Mary is Queen by grace, by the divine relationship and by right of conquest. F. Vandry, "Nature of Mary's Universal Queenship" (1954), pp. 59–60. In these treatments, Vandry does not mention Scripture with the exception of the brief mention of Genesis 3:15 as discussed in the previous footnote.

[129] F. Vandry, "Nature of Mary's Universal Queenship," (1953), p. 17. Vandry makes the same point in his 1954 article, "Nature of Mary's Universal Queenship," p. 57. Here, Vandry elaborates on how Mary's *fiat* makes her a unique associate of the Savior. See p. 58: "Thus she becomes an associate of her Son in order to perform with Him the whole of His work and establish that reign which shall never end. All of which amounts to saying that she shall be one with Him inasmuch as He is King. This alone means that she is Queen of the Kingdom over which He rules."

[130] E. Smith, "The Scriptural Basis for Mary's Queenship," *Marian Studies* 4 (1953): 111–12.

[131] Ibid., p. 112.

[132] Ibid., pp. 112–13.

[133] Ibid., p. 113.

[134] Ibid., p. 116.

[135] E. Smith also considers Old Testament texts that may serve as types of Mary in a collaborative way. We will discuss the use of Marian typology later in this chapter.

[136] R. Peinador, "Fundamentos Escriturísticos de la Realeza de María," *EstMar* 17 (1956): 27–48.

[137] Ibid., pp. 27–28. See also G. Kirwin, *Nature of the Queenship*, p. 19.

[138] R. Peinador, "Fundamentos Escriturísticos," p. 28: He writes: "Esta verdad parece o da la impresión de hallarse en un plano inferior en la prueba escriturística. Conviene, no obstante, mirar las cosas más despacio y de cerca, porque a lo mejor se trata de eso, *de una impresión*, la cual se ha de superar y dejar a un lado ante razonamientos de una exégesis seria y segura que, sin salirse del sentido literal, no deje de utilizar cuantos recursos le suministre la hermenéutica católica para penetrar en todo el sentido de la palabra divina."

[139] Ibid., p. 34.

[140] Ibid., pp. 35–36.

[141] Ibid., p. 47.

[142] Ibid.

[143] Ibid., pp. 47–48.

[144] Ibid., p. 48.

[145] Ibid., pp. 40–41, 48.

[146] Ibid., p. 28.

[147] A. Luis, "La Realeza de María," pp. 20–1; cf. E. Smith, "Scriptural Basis for Mary's Queenship," p. 114; De Gruyter, *De Beata Maria Regina*, p. 57.

[148] G. Kirwin, *Nature of the Queenship*, pp. 43, 67; A. Luis, "La Realeza de María," pp. 19–20; A. Iglesias, *Reina y Madre* (Madrid: PS Editorial, 1988), pp. 36–7; cf. E. Smith, "Scriptural Basis for Mary's Queenship," p. 114; R. Peinador, "Fundamentos Escriturísticos," pp. 43–44; L. De Gruyter, *De Beata Maria Regina*, p. 57.

[149] E. Smith, "Scriptural Basis for Mary's Queenship," p. 114; G. Kirwin, *Nature of the Queenship*, p. 68.

[150] A. Iglesias, *Reina y Madre*, pp. 38, 40; R. Peinador, "Fundamentos Escriturísticos," p. 44: "Dependiendo el valor probatorio del sentido típico del hecho que Dios haya querido ordenar determinados hechos y personas del A. Testamento a otros del Nuevo, es evidente que esta determinación absolutamente libre no puede conocerse sino por una revelación posterior e independiente del texto mismo. Esta determinación de la divina voluntad nos puede constar por la misma Sagrada Escritura, cuando, v. gr., cita los pasajes del A. Testamento como realizados en otros paralelos del Nuevo; o por la tradición que así lo ha entendido." See also A. Luis, *La Realeza de María*, pp. 22–24: "Pero para que una persona del A.T. pueda decirse con certidumbre *tipo* de otra del Nuevo, es preciso que la significación típica quede establecida por la misma Sagrada Escritura o por la Tradición" (p. 22).

[151] E. Smith, "Scriptural Basis for Mary's Queenship," pp. 113–15.

[152] Ibid., p. 114.

[153] Pontifical Biblical Commission (PBC), *The Interpretation of the Bible in the Church*, II, B, 3, in J. Fitzmyer, *The Biblical Commission's Document "The Interpretation of the Bible in the Church": Text and Commentary* (Rome: Editrice Pontificio Istituto Biblico, 1995).

[154] Ibid.

[155] Ibid.

[156] Ibid., emphasis added. "For example, the context of Matt 1:23 gives a fuller sense to the prophecy of Isa 7:14 in regard to the *almah* who will conceive, by using the translation of the Septuagint (*parthenos*): 'The virgin will conceive.'"

[157] Raymond Brown has made a similar distinction when discussing the criteria by which one can determine an authentic *sensus plenior*. In *An Introduction to the New Testament*, Brown notes how the "fuller sense" is grounded either in "the use of the OT in the NT" or "the use of the Bible in the post-Biblical church practice and preaching." R. Brown, *An Introduction to the New Testament* (New York: Doubleday, 1997), p. 41. See also Brown's earlier treatment of this topic in the *Jerome Biblical Commentary*: "Once we affirm that the [*sensus plenior*] was not clearly intended by the human author but was intended by God, we have to find a way of determining

the presence of such a deeper meaning; for the ordinary principles of exegesis will tell us only what the human author meant. This special way of determining the presence of a [*sensus plenior*] is through *further divine revelation or development in the understanding of revelation.*" He goes on to elaborate on these two criteria. First, "when we speak of further revelation, the chief instance of such revelation would be through a later passage in the Bible itself, for instance, the NT may point out the [*sensus plenior*] of an OT text." Second, in speaking of "development within the understanding of revelation," Brown refers to the Church's deeper understanding of revelation seen particularly in the Church Fathers and Church pronouncements. R. Brown, "Hermeneutics," in R. Brown, et. al., eds., *The Jerome Biblical Commentary*, (London: Geoffrey Chapman, 1968), pp. 616–17. See also R. Brown, "Hermeneutics," in R. Brown, et. al., eds., *The New Jerome Biblical Commentary*, (Englewood Cliffs, NJ: Prentice Hall, 1990), p. 1157.

[158] Brown defines the "typical sense" as "the deeper meaning that the things (persons, places, and events) of Scripture possess because, according to the intention of the divine author, they foreshadow future things. The typical sense differs from the literal sense and from the [*sensus plenior*] in that it is not a sense of the words of Scripture but is attached to things described in Scripture. Like the [*sensus plenior*] it can be discerned only through further revelation or through development in the understanding of revelation." R. Brown, "Hermeneutics" (1968), p. 618. For more on typology in the New Testament, see G. Lampe and K. Woollcombe, *Essays on Typology* (London: SCM Press, 1957); also L. Goppelt, *Typos* (Grand Rapids: Eerdmans, 1982).

[159] PBC, *The Interpretation of the Bible*, II, B, 2, emphasis added.

[160] Similar to the PBC, Raymond Brown draws attention to the "types that have been pointed out by the NT" and "already existing scriptural patterns" as criteria for recognizing an authentic typical sense. R. Brown, "Hermeneutics," (1968), p. 619; R. Brown, *Introduction to the New Testament*, p. 41. As we will see below, Brown is also open to the possibility of extra-biblical typologies (those that are established not by the New Testament) provided they are found in a consensus of the Fathers, the liturgy, or Church doctrine. Although he recognizes these as authentic typologies, Brown still gives a certain primacy to those types that are supported by the Scriptures themselves.

[161] R. Brown, "Hermeneutics" (1990), p. 1157, emphasis added. Along similar lines, it is significant to note the emphasis that the PBC places on typological connections found in the literal sense of the New Testament when discussing methods of actualizing the biblical message. In this section, the PBC gives primacy to inter-biblical typology—the way Scripture interprets Scripture: "*The most sure and promising method* for arriving at a successful actualization, *is the interpretation of Scripture by Scripture*, especially in the case of the texts of the Old Testament which have been re-read in the Old Testament itself (e.g., the manna of *Exodus* 16 in *Wis* 16:20-29) and/or in the New Testament (*John* 6)" (emphasis added). PBC, *The Interpretation of the Bible*, IV, A, 2. See also Laurentin on the primacy of the literal sense: "It is particularly useful to remember . . . the primacy of the literal sense over the secondary or derived senses (the typical or figurative sense, the plenary sense, and, most of all,

the accommodated sense)." R. Laurentin, *The Question of Mary* (Techny, IL: Divine Word Publications, 1964), p. 107.

[162] While Brown seems to give primacy to the typologies established within the Scriptures themselves (as seen above), he still supports the use of typologies that can be determined by a consensus of the Fathers, liturgical usage, and the doctrinal teaching of the Church. R. Brown, "Hermeneutics" (1990), p. 1157; cf. R. Brown, *Introduction to the New Testament*, p. 41. For a discussion on the importance of typological exegesis for Catholic theology, see A. Nichols, *The Shape of Catholic Theology* (Edinburgh: T&T Clark, 1991), pp. 154–62. Pius XII's encyclical *Divino Afflante Spiritu* (*DAS*) might also be helpful here by offering a balanced perspective on this topic. Although the encyclical teaches that interpreters should seek out *both* the literal and the spiritual senses, it still draws special attention to the literal sense. While interpreters should always "search out and expound upon" the spiritual sense of Scripture (*DAS* 26), the encyclical at the same time stresses that the "foremost and greatest endeavor" of the interpreter is to define the literal sense of the biblical words (*DAS* 24). Pius XII, *Divino Afflante Spiritu* (*AAS* 35 [1943]: 310–11).

[163] H. Cazelles, "La Mère du Roi-Messie dans L'Ancien Testament," in *Mater et Ecclesia*, vol. 5 (Congressus Mariologicus Lourdes, 1958), pp. 39–56.

[164] A. Del Moral, "La Realeza de María Segun La S. Escritura," *EphMar* 12 (1962): 161–82.

[165] D. Stanley, "The Mother of My Lord," *Worship* 34 (1960): 330–32.

[166] B. Ahern, "The Mother of the Messiah," *Marian Studies* 12 (1961): 27–48.

[167] C. Stuhlmueller, "The Mother of Emmanuel (Is. 7:14)," *Marian Studies* 12 (1961): 165–204.

[168] R. Laurentin, *A Short Treatise on the Virgin Mary* (Washington, NJ: AMI Press, 1991), pp. 267–81.

[169] H. Cazelles, "La Mère du Roi-Messie," pp. 40–48; D. Stanley, "The Mother of My Lord," pp. 330–31; B. Ahern, "Mother of the Messiah," pp. 35–41.

[170] H. Cazelles, "La Mère du Roi-Messie," pp. 48–51; A. Del Moral, "La Realeza de María Segun La S. Escritura," pp. 164–66; D. Stanley, "Mother of My Lord," p. 331; B. Ahern, "Mother of the Messiah," pp. 41–44; R. Laurentin, *A Short Treatise on the Virgin Mary*, p. 278.

[171] H. Cazelles, "La Mère du Roi-Messie," pp. 51–53; A. Del Moral, "La Realeza de María Segun La S. Escritura," pp. 166–67; B. Ahern, "Mother of the Messiah," pp. 44–46; R. Laurentin, *A Short Treatise on the Virgin Mary*, pp. 272–81.

[172] H. Cazelles, "La Mère du Roi-Messie," pp. 55–56; A. Del Moral, "La Realeza de María Segun La S. Escritura," pp. 168–82; D. Stanley, "Mother of My Lord," pp. 331–2; B. Ahern, "Mother of the Messiah," pp. 46–48; R. Laurentin, *A Short Treatise on the Virgin Mary*, p. 278–81.

[173] H. Cazelles, "La Mère du Roi-Messie," pp. 55–56; A. Del Moral, "La Realeza de María Segun La S. Escritura," p. 175; cf. C. Stuhlmueller, "Mother of Emmanuel," pp. 195–96.

[174] A. Del Moral, "La Realeza de María Segun La S. Escritura," pp. 176, 182; D. Stanley, "Mother of My Lord," p. 330; B. Ahern, "Mother of the Messiah," p. 28.

[175] G. Kirwin, *Nature of the Queenship*, pp. 1–136.

[176] Ibid., pp. 137–97.

[177] Ibid., pp. 178–80, 198–209, 253–56. See p. 179: "This return to the sources involves a rigorous scientific study of the sources of our faith, *particularly scripture*, and it must be accompanied by an openness to the Spirit" (emphasis added).

[178] Ibid., pp. 279–345.

[179] Ibid., pp. 297–305.

[180] Ibid., pp. 305–10.

[181] Ibid., pp. 287–91.

[182] Ibid., p. 311. Kirwin at this moment begins showing how the queen-mother tradition provides a better understanding of Mary's royal office than do the approaches offered by De Gruyter and Nicolas. While certainly true, this discussion seems somewhat premature. One needs to demonstrate that the queen-mother theme can illuminate the New Testament presentation of Mary. At this point in Kirwin's thesis, this has not yet been done. Pertinent New Testament texts portraying Mary as queen mother have only been mentioned in the context of his presentation of what scholarship has said on this topic. See pp. 28–36.

[183] Ibid., pp. 311–12.

[184] Ibid., pp. 28–36, 292–97, 315–16, 333–35. With the exception of his treatment on Revelation 12 (pp. 292–97), Kirwin does not attempt to exegete any of the key New Testament passages that he mentions as supporting Mary's queenship.

[185] Ibid., pp. 292–97.

[186] Luke 1:26–56 (the Annunciation and the Visitation).

[187] Matthew 1–2 (genealogy, reference to Isaiah 7:14, and visit of the magi).

[188] E.g., John 19:25–27 (Mary at the Cross).

[189] G. Kirwin, *Nature of the Queenship*, pp. 5–37.

[190] N. Andreasen, "The Role of the Queen Mother in Israelite Society," *CBQ* 45 (1983): 179–88; T. Gray, "God's Word and Mary's Royal Office," *Miles Immaculatae* 13 (1995): 372–88; R. Harrison, "Queen Mother," in G. Bromiley, ed., *The International Standard Bible Encyclopedia* (Grand Rapids: Eerdmans, 1988), pp. 7–8. Especially on the intercessory role of the queen mother, see F. Rossier, *L'intercession entre les hommes dans la Bible hébraique* Orbis Biblicus et Orientalis 152 (Gottingen: Vandenhoeck & Ruprecht, 1996), pp. 188–91; cf. P. De Boer, "The Counselor," *VTSup* 3 (Leiden: Brill, 1955), pp. 53–55, 60–61.

[191] B. Nollan, *The Royal Son of God* Orbis Biblicus et Orientalis 23 (Gottingen: Vandenhoeck & Ruprecht, 1979), pp. 42–43; R. Brown, *Birth of the Messiah* (New

York: Doubleday, 1993), p. 192 n. 32; A. Serra, "Regina: Ulteriore Elaborazione Biblica sulla Regalità di Maria," in S. De Fiores and S. Meo, eds., *Nuovo Dizionario di Mariologia* (Milan: Edizioni San Paolo, 1996), p. 1073; J. Bastero de Eleizalde, "Fundamentos Cristológicos de la Realeza de María," *EstMar* 51 (1986): 206–8; A. Del Moral, "Santa Maria, la Guebiráh Mesiánica," *Communio* (Spanish edition) 13 (1980): 28.

[192] G. Montague, *Our Father, Our Mother* (Steubenville, OH: Franciscan University Press, 1990), pp. 95–96; S. De Fiores, "Regina," pp. 1080–81; T. Gray, "God's Word and Mary's Royal Office," p. 384; A. Serra, "Regina," p. 1074; cf. J. McHugh, *The Mother of Jesus in the New Testament* (London: Darton, Longman & Todd, 1975), p. 54.

[193] P. Farkas, *La 'Donna' di Apocalisse 12: Storia, Bilancio, Nuove Prospettive* (Roma: Editrice Pontificia Universitá Gregoriana, 1997), pp. 210–12; I. De La Potterie, *Mary in the Mystery of the Covenant* (NY: Alba House, 1992), pp. 239–64; A. Feuillet, *Jesus and His Mother* (Still River, MA: St. Bede's, 1984), pp. 118–29; T. Gray, "God's Word and Mary's Royal Office," pp. 386–87; J. McHugh, *The Mother of Jesus in the New Testament*, pp. 404–32.

[194] Some emphasize that since Mary is queen mother in the kingdom of her Son, her royal authority must be understood in light of the New Testament perspective on the reign of Christ's kingdom—it is a reign grounded in service, just like Christ's kingship is based on his humble service to the point of death on the Cross. See A. Serra, "Regina," pp. 194–97; S. De Fiores, *Maria Presenza Viva nel Popolo di Dio* (Rome: Edizioni Monfortane, 1980), p. 59; E. Touron, "De María Reina a María Liberadora," *EphMar* 46 (1996): 469–70.

[195] For example, A. Serra notes how Mary's royal maternity is linked with her Assumption, showing how, just as Christ's Resurrection was a royal event, so too was Mary's bodily Assumption. A. Serra, "Bibbia," pp. 1076–77. Cf. Montague, *Our Father, Our Mother*, p. 98. Others have used the advocacy role of the queen mother to demonstrate Mary's intercessory role. T. Gray, "God's Word and Mary's Royal Office," pp. 386, 388; G. Montague, *Our Father, Our Mother*, pp. 99–100.

[196] For example, some have emphasized the ecclesial dimension of the queenship: Her preeminent royal office is not detached from the royal office of the whole people of God (1 Pet. 2:9; Rev. 1:6, 5:9, 20:4–6), but rather stands as a model and eschatological sign of hope for the perfection of the entire Church's reign with Christ. S. De Fiores, "Regina," pp. 1078–82; S. De Fiores, *Maria Presenza Viva nel Popolo di Dio*, pp. 58–59. Cf. A. Serra, "Regina," pp. 1074–76.

[197] A few examples among many: B. Ahern, "The Mother of the Messiah," pp. 27–48; B. Buby, *Mary of Galilee*, vol. 2 (New York: Alba House, 1995), pp. 117–18; R. Brown, *Birth of the Messiah*, p. 192; R. Laurentin, *A Short Treatise on the Virgin Mary*, pp. 278–81; C. Stuhlmueller, "The Mother of Emmanuel (Is. 7:14)," pp. 165–204.

[198] A few works stand out: G. Kirwin, *Nature of the Queenship*, pp. 297–344; A. Serra, "Regina," pp. 1071–77; T. Gray, "God's Word and Mary's Royal Office," pp. 372–88; G. Montague, *Our Father, Our Mother*, pp. 89–101.

[199] S. De Fiores, "Regina," p. 1078. See also S. De Fiores, *Maria Presenza Viva nel Popolo di Dio*, p. 58.

[200] Second Vatican Council, *Dei Verbum*, no. 24.

[201] See W. Thompson, *The Struggle for Theology's Soul* (New York: Crossroad Herder, 1996), pp. 1–32.

[202] On the distinction between "referential" and "auxiliary" languages, see the PBC's 1984 document "Bible and Christology," in J. Fitzmyer, *Scripture and Christology: A Statement of the Biblical Commission with a Commentary* (New York: Paulist Press, 1986), p. 20. "The 'auxiliary' languages employed in the Church in the course of centuries do not enjoy the same authority, as far as faith is concerned, as the 'referential' language of the inspired authors, especially of the New Testament with its mode of expression rooted in the Older."

[203] See S. De Fiores, *Maria Madre di Gesù* (Bologna: Edizioni Dehoniane, 1993), pp. 36–37. His comments here on the biblical foundations for Mariology could offer some insights for systematic theology as a whole: "La logica umana e il metodo deduttivo hanno mostrato la lora inadeguatezza ad organizzare sistematicamente i dati riguardanti la Madre di Gesù. . . . É urgente per la mariologia cambiare statuto epistemologico e adottare un'impostazione storico-salvifical. Questo compito sarà facilitato inserendo il discorso su Maria nel contesto della teologia biblica." See also PBC, *The Interpretation of the Bible*, III, D, 2.

[204] See J. Ratzinger, *Principles of Catholic Theology* (San Francisco: Ignatius Press, 1987), p. 321. Following Bonaventure's "*sacrae scripturae, quae theologia dicitur,*" Ratzinger concludes: "Properly speaking, God himself must be the subject of theology. Therefore, Scripture alone is theology in the fullest sense of the word because it truly has God as its subject; it does not just speak of him but *is* his own speech." Of course, employing Scripture as the soul of theology must be done in union with Sacred Tradition and within the context of the teaching Church. The special place of Scripture in Catholic theology does not lead to *sola Scriptura*. Yet as the Biblical Commission has explained, "[w]ithout being the sole *locus theologicus,* Sacred Scripture provides the privileged foundation of theological studies." PBC, *The Interpretation of the Bible*, III, D, 2. See also *Ut Unum Sint*, which, while emphasizing the indispensable role of Tradition for interpreting the Word of God, at the same time describes Scripture as "the highest authority in matters of faith." John Paul II, *Ut Unum Sint*, no. 79 (Boston: St. Paul Books & Media, 1995) (*AAS* 87 [July–December 1995]: 968–69). For an insightful perspective on the special place of Scripture in theology, see S. Hahn, "Prima Scriptura: Magisterial Perspectives on the Primacy of Scripture for Catholic Theology and Catechetics," in *The Church and the Universal Catechism: Proceedings from the 15th Convention of the Fellowship of Catholic Scholars* (Steubenville, OH: Franciscan University Press, 1992), pp. 83–116. Cf. S. Blanco, "Sola Scriptura o Hermeneutica Biblica," *EphMar* 44 (1994): 393–411; R. Laurentin, *The Question of Mary*, pp. 106–7, 134.

Chapter Two

[1] N. Andreasen, "Role of the Queen Mother in Israelite Society," p. 182. In addition to these functions, Kirwin, while examining Mesopotamian, Egyptian, Ugaritic, and Hittite kingdoms, notes how the queen mother often played an intercessory role with the king. G. Kirwin, *Nature of the Queenship*, pp. 299–305.

[2] Cf. R. De Vaux, *Ancient Israel*, p. 118. For an example of the preeminence of the mother-son relationship over all other relationships in tribal cultures, see H. Kuper, "Kinship Among the Swazi," in A. Radcliffe-Brown and D. Forde, *African Systems of Kinship and Marriage* (New York: Oxford University, 1950), p. 95.

[3] R. De Vaux, *Ancient Israel*, pp. 115–16.

[4] D. Stanley, "The Mother of My Lord," p. 331.

[5] B. Ahern, "Mother of the Messiah," p. 35. Also see G. Kirwin, *Nature of the Queenship*, pp. 298–99: "Because the king had many wives he left the upbringing of his children to their mothers. Consequently when the king died and one of his children succeeded to the throne this was largely due to the influence (and at times the machinations) of his mother. Thus the heir to the throne owed his life and his ruling position to his mother."

[6] The pertinent Ugaritic and Hittite literature has been reviewed by a number of scholars, including N. Andreasen, "Role of the Queen Mother in Israelite Society," pp. 179–94; R. De Vaux, *Ancient Israel*, pp. 115–19; L. Schearing, "Queen," in D. Freedman, ed., *The Anchor Bible Dictionary* (New York: Doubleday, 1992), pp. 583–88; H. Cazelles, "La Mère du Roi-Messie dans l'Ancien Testament," pp. 43–46.

[7] R. De Vaux, *Ancient Israel*, p. 118; N. Andreasen, "Role of the Queen Mother in Israelite Society," p. 182.

[8] Epistles 89, 95, 117 in C. Gordon, *Ugaritic Literature* (Rome: Pontificium Istitutum Biblicum, 1949), pp. 116–17. Cf. J. Pritchard, ed., *Ancient Near Eastern Texts Relating to the Old Testament* (Princeton University Press, 1955), p. 146 (hereafter cited as *ANET*); B. Ahern, "Mother of the Messiah," p. 40.

[9] G. Kirwin, *Nature of the Queenship*, p. 302; B. Ahern, "Mother of the Messiah," p. 38.

[10] Harper Letters, nos. 303, 254, 263, 324, 368, 569, in R. Pfeiffer, *State Letters of Assyria* (New York: Krause, 1967). Numerated in Pfeiffer as nos. 181, 188, 274, 187, 230, 229. See also P. De Boer, "The Counselor," p. 64.

[11] J. Pritchard, *ANET*, pp. 75–76, 81. See also B. Ahern, "The Mother of the Messiah," p. 37.

[12] G. Kirwin, *Nature of the Queenship*, p. 301; J. Montgomery, *Daniel* (Edinburgh: T&T Clark, 1964), pp. 257–58; B. Ahern, "Mother of the Messiah," p. 38; R. Harrison, "Queen Mother," p. 8.

[13] B. Ahern, "Mother of the Messiah," p. 38. See also R. Harrison, "Queen Mother," p. 8: "Most scholars agree that in Dnl. 5:10 Aram. *malkâ* ('queen') refers

not to Belshazzar's consort but to his mother (or possibly grandmother), Nebuchadnezzar's widow. The manner of her entry (without being summoned), the authoritative tone of her counsel, and her knowledge of Daniel's accomplishments during the reign of Nebuchadnezzar (vv. 11f.), all suggest that she held the important position of queen mother."

[14] R. De Vaux, *Ancient Israel*, p. 117.

[15] "It is remarkable that the Old Testament only once used the word 'queen', the feminine of *melek*, 'king', in connection with Israel, and that is in a poetical passage and in the plural, to describe the 'queens' of the 'King' in the Song of Songs, as distinct from his concubines (Ct 6:8)." R. De Vaux, *Ancient Israel*, p. 117.

[16] H. Kosmala, "gabhar," in G. Botterweck and H. Ringgren, eds., *Theological Dictionary of the Old Testament* (Grand Rapids: Eerdmans, 1975), p. 373. L. Schearing, "Queen," p. 583. A. Del Moral, "Santa María, La Guebiráh Mesiánica," p. 23.

[17] R. De Vaux, *Ancient Israel*, p. 117.

[18] "*Gebhirah* is a term applied to a woman in contrast to a girl, and indicates that she has some official position." H. Kosmala, "gabhar," p. 373. The word *gebirah* is found fifteen times in the Old Testament with the meaning "great lady" or "queen" (Gen. 16:4, 8–9; 1 Kings 15:13; 2 Kings 5:3, 10:13; Is. 24:2, 47:5, 7; Jer. 13:18; 29:2; Ps. 123:2; Prov. 30:23; 2 Chron. 15:16. Sometimes it is translated "mistress" (Gen. 16:4, 8; 2 Kings 5:3; Ps. 123:2; Prov. 30:23), and once it is used to describe the wife of an Egyptian pharaoh (1 Kings 11:19). Yet in the Judaic kingdom, the term is always used to describe the king's mother as the "queen mother." N. Andreasen, "Role of the Queen Mother in Israelite Society," pp. 179–80; R. De Vaux, *Ancient Israel*, p. 117; R. Harrison, "Queen Mother," pp. 7–8.

[19] See R. Brown, *Birth of the Messiah*, p. 192: "The Queen Mother had an official position in the Davidic monarchy in Judah (but not in the Northern Kingdom), and her name is always mentioned in the introduction to each reign in the Book of Kings." See also R. De Vaux, *Ancient Israel*, pp. 115–19; B. Ahern, "Mother of the Messiah," p. 43: "This was no token honor. The *gebirah* held an actual court office which was probably bestowed upon her at the enthronization of her son."

[20] N. Andreasen, "Role of the Queen Mother in Israelite Society," p. 180.

[21] Like 1 and 2 Kings, the narrative of 1 and 2 Chronicles introduces the queen mother along with each Judean monarch from King Rehoboam to Hezekiah. However, the Chronicler stops mentioning the queen mother with the introduction of King Manasseh in 2 Chronicles 33:1. Del Moral argues that this omission of the queen mother's name fits into the Chronicler's progressive disinterest in the institutional Davidic monarchy in general. See A. Del Moral, "Santa María, La Guebiráh Mesiánica," p. 26.

The accounts of King Jehoram (2 Kings 8:17–18) and King Ahaz (2 Kings 16:2–3) begin with no woman being named, and the account of King Asa (1 Kings 15:10) begins with his grandmother's name mentioned. Some have speculated on why the mother is not mentioned for these three kings. As for the absence of Asa's mother's name, this is probably due to the fact that his grandmother

Maacah continued to reign as queen mother even after the death of her son. Cf. R. De Vaux, *Ancient Israel*, p. 117; N. Andreasen, "Role of the Queen Mother in Israelite Society," p. 180 n. 4. As for the other two kings, Miguens notes how Chronicles also does not mention the mother of Jehoram (2 Chron. 21:6) and Ahaz (28:1) and thus concludes that their names were unknown to the narrator, "probably because they were not found in the documentary sources." M. Miguens, *Mary, "The Servant of the Lord": An Ecumenical Proposal* (Boston: St. Paul Editions, 1978), p. 62 n. 50. It is also worth noting Moral's proposal that the narrator purposely omits the names of these two kings because of their wicked deeds. This is an example of what Del Moral calls "*Damnatio Memoriae*" in which "la Biblia, muy prudente, no quiere acordarse de su madre." These kings were so wicked that Del Moral concludes: "Una perla! Como para recordar el nombre de la madre!" A. Del Moral, "Santa María, La Guebiráh Mesiánica," p. 25. While this theory might be possible, it fails to take into consideration the many other kings who "did what was evil in the sight of the Lord" but whose mothers were mentioned nonetheless (1 Kings 14:21–22; 1 Kings 15:1–3; 1 Kings 22:41–43; 2 Kings 8:25–27; 2 Kings 21:1–2; 2 Kings 21:19–22; 2 Kings 23:31–32; 2 Kings 23:36–37; 2 Kings 24:8–9; 2 Kings 24:18–19).

[22] The practice of naming the king's mother in the royal histories was not followed for the accounts concerning the northern kingdom of Israel. "It is remarkable that the mother's name is given only for the kings of Judah, not those of Israel. . . . This seems to indicate that their prominence was confined to Judah, since Judaism has always paid honor to women. The kingdom of Israel, on the other hand, . . . may have held women in less esteem in conformity with the general ancient attitude." H. Freedman, *Jeremiah* (London: Soncino Press, 1950), p. 96. Miguens notes the sharp contrast between the narrator's introduction of Judean kings and Israelite kings: "The author never uses a formula of this sort for the kings of the north, never does he give the full identity of the mother of a given king, never does he call her 'the mother of the king,' as a title, never is she called *gevirah*—even when the author may occasionally refer to the mother of some of the kings." M. Miguens, *Mary, "The Servant of the Lord"* pp. 63–64. R. De Vaux notes how Jezebel is referred to as a *gebirah*, but the word is found in the mouth of Judean princes (2 Kings 10:13). De Vaux explains that the institution of the queen mother requires a dynastic stability that was generally not found in the northern kingdom. He concludes that "there is no direct evidence of the existence of a Great Lady in the northern kingdom." R. De Vaux, *Ancient Israel*, p. 118. Andreasen agrees with this view. N. Andreasen, "Role of the Queen Mother in Israelite Society," p. 180.

[23] "The wife of the king, the queen, is never mentioned in this connection, whereas the 'mother of the king' is consistently mentioned and, significantly, with her full identity: name followed by her family name." M. Miguens, *Mary, "Servant of the Lord"* p. 62. In footnote 52, Miguens mentions that the family name is missing only in the introduction of Manasseh's mother (2 Kings 21:1). Actually, the family name is not given in the case of Zibiah (2 Kings 12:1), Jehoaddin (2 Kings 14:2) and Jecoliah (2 Kings 15:2) as well. In these cases, the queen mothers' geographic origins are given, e.g. "Zibiah of Beer-sheba," "Jehoaddin of Jerusalem," "Jecoliah of Jerusalem." Also, Rehoboam's mother, Naama, is introduced as "the Ammonitess" (1 Kings 14:21).

[24] G. Montague, *Our Father, Our Mother*, p. 92. Also B. Ahern, "Mother of the Messiah," pp. 43–44.

[25] T. Gray, "God's Word and Mary's Royal Office," p. 377. See also N. Andreasen, "Role of the Queen Mother in Israelite Society," p. 192: "She appeared with the king as coregent (Jer. 13:18) and accompanied him and the entire court into captivity shortly thereafter (2 Kings. 24:12, 15; Jer. 29:2)."

[26] M. Miguens, *Mary, "The Servant of the Lord"* p. 65. In n. 61, Miguens notes how Nahum 3:10 describes those who are bound in chains during the Babylonian exile as the "honoured men" and the "great men." Interestingly, when examining this passage, Miguens also draws attention to the fact that 2 Kings 24:15 speaks of "the mother of the king" when the narrator could have simply said "his mother." He argues that this phrase "the mother of the king" is a real title bestowed upon the queen mother. In this regard, Miguens also looks at 1 Kings 2:13–22 in which the narrator refers to Bathsheba as "the mother of the king" (v. 19). "Instead of this descriptive clause the personal pronoun could be used, as it is, in fact, used three times in the same verse ['her']." *Mary, "The Servant of the Lord"* pp. 63–64.

[27] L. Schearing, "Queen," p. 585; R. Harrison, "Queen Mother," p. 8; R. De Vaux, *Ancient Israel*, p. 118; B. Ahern, "Mother of the Messiah," p. 44.

[28] A. Serra, "Regina," p. 1192; B. Ahern, "Mother of the Messiah," p. 42; G. Kirwin, *Nature of the Queenship*, pp. 307–8; G. Montague, *Our Father, Our Mother*, p. 91; cf. N. Andreasen, "Role of the Queen Mother in Israelite Society," p. 189.

[29] T. Gray, "God's Word and Mary's Royal Office," p. 377.

[30] This is seen in particular in the messianic Psalm 110 ("Sit at my right hand until I make your enemies your footstool"). In fact, the New Testament refers to the "right hand" imagery of Psalm 110 to express Christ's reign with the Father over the whole universe. For example, the author of Hebrews cites this verse from Psalm 110 to show how Christ is above all the angels since He sits at the right hand of the Father, sharing in His Father's dominion over all creation (Heb. 1:13, cf. 1:3).

[31] N. Andreasen, "Role of the Queen Mother in Israelite Society," p. 189 n. 59.

[32] See B. Ahern, "Mother of the Messiah," p. 43; N. Andreasen, "Role of the Queen Mother in Israelite Society," p. 188.

[33] "It is difficult to imagine this happening unless she possessed a strong power base." L. Schearing, "Queen," p. 585. See also B. Ahern, "Mother of the Messiah," p. 44; G. Kirwin, *Nature of the Queenship*, pp. 309–10.

[34] N. Andreasen, "Role of the Queen Mother in Israelite Society," p. 192: "She appeared with the king as coregent (Jer. 13:18)." See also G. Montague, *Our Father, Our Mother*, p. 91.

[35] T. Gray, "God's Word and Mary's Royal Office," pp. 378–79. See also L. Schearing, "Queen," p. 585; M. Miguens, *Mary, "The Servant of the Lord"* pp. 64–65.

[36] "The queen mother could circumscribe royal power to some extent and could represent the interests of people or court before the king, thereby providing a sort

of buffer between king and people." N. Andreasen, "Role of the Queen Mother in Israelite Society," p. 194.

[37] P. De Boer, "The Counselor," pp. 60–61: "The mother of the king is treated with honour. She sits on the right hand of the king and her demands are not refused. . . . She is able to be an intermediary, an intercessor who can appeal to the king because she is versed in royal matters as nobody else." Also see T. Gray, "God's Word and Mary's Royal Office," p. 381: "The ritual that surrounds Bathsheba's intercession suggests that her interceding was a common courtly event. Clearly, the Gebirah had an office [in] which intercession was a significant part. Adonijah's request testifies to the people's recognition of the queen mother's intercessory power."

[38] See F. Rossier, *L'intercession Entre les Hommes dans la Bible Hébraique*, p. 189. "On a même vu en elle, dans cette perspective, quelqu'un susceptible de représenter les intérêts du peuple à la cour. Dans de telles circonstances, Adoniah n'aurait pu choisir meilleure avocate ou meilleur intercesseur. Le fait que la reine-mère jouit de l'autorité sur toutes les femmes de la maison royale a son importance pour Adoniah vu que sa requête a justement une de ces femmes pour object." Also see Gray's important footnote: "The fact that Solomon denies the request in no way discredits the influence of the Gebirah. Adonijah wanted Abishag the Shunammite for the treacherous purpose of taking over the kingdom from Solomon. [Taking the king's concubine was a sign of usurping the throne in the ancient Near East. For example see how Absalom (Adonijah's older brother), in his attempt to take the throne from David, took his concubines (2 Sam. 16:20-23).] Thus *the wickedness of Adonijah's intention is the reason for denial, which in no way reflects negatively upon the Gebirah's power to intercede. The narrative bears out the fact that the king normally accepted the Gebirah's request,* thus Solomon says, 'Ask, I will not refuse you.' To say then that this illustrates the weakness of the Gebirah's ability to intercede would be to miss the whole point of the narrative, which tells how Adonijah uses the queen mother's position in an attempt to become king" (emphasis added). T. Gray, "God's Word and Mary's Royal Office," p. 381 n. 16. For more on the political symbolism of usurping a member of a king's harem, see R. De Vaux, *Ancient Israel,* p. 116.

[39] P. De Boer, "The Counselor," p. 54. See also N. Andreasen, "Role of the Queen Mother in Israelite Society," pp. 190–91.

[40] N. Andreasen, "Role of the Queen Mother in Israelite Society," pp. 192–93. See also G. Montague, *Our Father, Our Mother,* p. 92; T. Gray, "God's Word and Mary's Royal Office," p. 381.

[41] N. Andreasen, "Role of the Queen Mother in Israelite Society," p. 190; P. De Boer, "The Counselor," pp. 54, 60. T. Gray, "God's Word and Mary's Royal Office," p. 382.

[42] For discussions on the development of messianism in Israel, see J. McKenzie, "Royal Messianism," *CBQ* 19 (1957): 41–43; R. Brown, "God's Future Plans for His People," in *The New Jerome Biblical Commentary* (London: Geoffrey Chapman, 1989), pp. 1310–12.

[43] R. Laurentin, *A Short Treatise on the Virgin Mary,* pp. 278–81. Kirwin similarly notes how these texts "are centered around a woman who has a special role to play

in the dynastic succession which appears as the vehicle for God's salvific activity among His people. There is no mention in these prophecies of a father according to the Davidic line, but a very clear reference to a mother who is being viewed according to the queen-mother tradition in Israel. The solemnity of these prophecies is derived from the importance of the message: salvation is to come from Yahweh in the person of the Messiah from the kingly line of David. Salvation will come through the cooperation of one who, as queen mother, responds in faith to Yahweh's promises." G. Kirwin, *Nature of the Queenship*, p. 311. In reference to Genesis 3:15 in particular, Kirwin argues that since this text received its literary form in the period of the Davidic dynasty, it "may well be that the woman of Gen. 3:15 is understood by the author in terms of the queen-mother tradition in Judah." See also C. Stuhlmueller, "The Mother of Emmanuel," pp. 192–95; B. Ahern, "Mother of the Messiah," p. 45. Laurentin, Kirwin, Stuhlmueller, and Ahern also view the woman figure in Micah 5:3 as a queen mother. (See n. 68 in this chapter for a brief evaluation of this view). The following discuss the queen-mother background to Isaiah 7:14, but do not treat Genesis 3:15: G. Montague, *Our Father, Our Mother*, pp. 93–95; T. Gray, "God's Word and Mary's Royal Office," pp. 382–83.

[44] J. Scullion notes Davidic overtones to this passage in which the warning that if Ahaz does not believe he shall not be established resembles how Nathan told David that "your house and your kingdom shall be made sure forever before me; your throne shall be established for ever" (2 Sam. 7:16). "Nathan tells David that his house shall be made sure or established. David believed; Ahaz did not. . . . One should not press too far this verbal resemblance. . . . Yet a resemblance there is, and both passages are in the context of the permanence of the dynasty." J. Scullion, "An Approach to the Understanding of Isaiah 7:10–17," *JBL* 87 (1968): 289.

[45] For a brief survey of the various perspectives, see H. Wildberger, *Isaiah 1–12* (Minneapolis: Fortress, 1991), pp. 308–11; J. Watts, *Isaiah 1–33* (Waco: Word Books, 1961), pp. 98–99.

[46] E. Young, *The Book of Isaiah*, vol. 1 (Grand Rapids: Eerdmans, 1965), pp. 283–91; C. Feinberg, "The Virgin Birth in the Old Testament," *BS* 119 (1962): 251–58.

[47] It is sometimes argued that if Isaiah 7:14 wished to emphasize the virginity of Immanuel's mother, the Hebrew word *betulah* could have been used, since it is found some fifty times in the Old Testament in reference to a virgin. R. Brown, *Birth of the Messiah*, p. 147 n. 43. Indeed, the word *almah* is more ambiguous as it describes a young woman of marriageable age up to the birth of her first child without necessarily highlighting her virginity. Of the nine times *almah* is found in the Old Testament, it is never used of a woman who is clearly already married or sexually experienced. Nevertheless, the word itself says nothing about virginity directly. As Brown explains, "It puts no stress on her virginity, although *de facto*, in the light of Israelite ethics and social standards, most girls covered by the range of this term would be virgins" (p. 147). Also see C. Stuhlmueller, "The Mother of Emmanuel," p. 187; J. Oswalt, *The Book of Isaiah* (Grand Rapids: Eerdmans, 1986), p. 210.

[48] R. Brown, *Birth of the Messiah*, p. 146.

[49] "Since the birth of this child was to be a sign to Ahaz, it is only logical to conclude that the birth took place during the lifetime and reign of Ahaz." W. Mueller, "A Virgin Shall Conceive," *EQ* 32 (1960): 206. Also J. Oswalt, *The Book of Isaiah*, p. 208; J. Jensen, *Isaiah* (Wilmington, DE: Michael Glazier, 1986), p. 96; M. Buber, *The Prophetic Faith* (New York: Harper, 1949), p. 135.

[50] This critique of the traditional view does not necessarily exclude *any* foreshadowing of Mary and Jesus. For a perspective that sees the prophecy as having a partial fulfillment in the immediate future and an ultimate fulfillment in Mary and Christ, see below.

[51] W. McKane, "The Interpretation of Isaiah VII 14–25," *VT* 17 (1967): 214: "What is being said then is that within a period of nine months the danger occasioned by the Syro-Ephraimitic coalition will have passed and mothers will mark this experience of deliverance and liberation by giving their children the name Immanuel. The name will be in vogue since it answers to a new sense of security and assurance." See also Duhn, Marti, Kohler, "Zum Verstandis von Jes. 7,14," *ZAW* 67 (1955): 48, as cited in O. Kaiser, *Isaiah 1–12* (Philadelphia: Westminister Press, 1983), p. 157 n. 30.

[52] Mowinkel notes that the most natural interpretation of the definite article preceding *almah* is that it refers to a particular woman known to the king. He concludes that this makes an interpretation that does not see the *almah* as a specific woman highly unlikely. S. Mowinkel, *He That Cometh* (New York: Abingdon, 1954), p. 113. Brown agrees with this view. "The presence of the definite article, 'the young girl,' makes it likely that Isaiah was referring to someone definite whose identity was known to him and to King Ahaz, perhaps someone whom the king had recently married and brought into the harem." R. Brown, *Birth of the Messiah*, pp. 147–48.

[53] Cf. S. Mowinckel, *He That Cometh*, p. 113.

[54] Different variations on this interpretation include: W. Mueller, "A Virgin Shall Conceive," p. 206. Mueller argues that the events surrounding Isaiah's son Maher-shalal-hash-baz in 8:4 parallel those of the Immanuel child in 7:15–16. He concludes that Isaiah 7:14 refers to the prophetess in 8:3 and her son. Gottwald reaches a similar conclusion by highlighting how Isaiah 6–8 is concerned with signs, "namely 'the children whom Yahweh has given to me' [Is. 8:18]. Naturally that includes Shear-jashub and Maher-shalal-hash-baz and, unless the immediate context forbids, Immanuel is to be understood in the same way, especially since the very term 'sign' addressed to Ahaz in vii 10 and 14 is echoed in the summary of viii 18." N. Gottwald, "Immanuel as the Prophet's Son," *VT* 8 (1958): 37. Wolf proposes that the mother of Isaiah's older son Shear-jashub died and Isaiah re-married the prophetess in 8:1–3 who bore him another son, Maher-shalal-hash-baz, who is to be understood as the Immanuel child of 7:14. The mother named the child Immanuel to portray how God would "be with" the kingdom in defeating Syria and Israel, while Isaiah named the son Maher-shalal-hash-baz (meaning "the spoil hastens, the plunder comes quickly") to describe how Assyria would take the riches of Syria and Israel before devastating the land of Judah. H. Wolf, "A Solution to the Immanuel Prophecy in Isaiah 7:14–8:22," *JBL* 91 (1972): 449–56.

[55] "As a woman is not called *almah* after her first pregnancy, the [Immanuel] son must necessarily be [the Isaiah 7:14 *almah's*] first child." O. Kaiser, *Isaiah 1–12*, p. 160. Wildberger and Brown conclude that the *almah* could not be Isaiah's wife since she already had a child. H. Wildberger, *Isaiah 1–12*, p. 309; R. Brown, *Birth of the Messiah*, p. 148. Furthermore, if Jensen's appraisal of these two signs is correct, the birth of Maher-shalal-hash-baz will accompany the end of the Aram-Israel crisis (Is. 8:3–4), while the Immanuel child will reach a point of maturity through enduring the trials of the Assyrian threat (Is. 7:14–17). This would make Maher-shala-hash-baz and Immanuel two different children and two different signs. For this interesting discussion, see J. Jensen, "The Age of Immanuel," *CBQ* 41 (1979): 220–39; J. Jensen, *Isaiah*, pp. 97–98.

[56] "The context and constant references or allusions to the House of David, its permanence or its state of jeopardy (cf. vss. 2a, 3, 6b, 13a, 17) give (vs. 9b) dynastic overtones. King and people must take their stand on Yahweh; he will assure permanence to the dynasty." J. Scullion, "An Approach to the Understanding of Isaiah 7:10–17," p. 289.

[57] "Isaiah addresses Ahaz as 'house of David' because that is precisely what is at stake, the dynastic succession promised to David through the prophecy of Nathan," G. Montague, *Our Father, Our Mother*, p. 94.

[58] Wildberger notes 2 Samuel 7:9, 1 Kings 1:37, Psalm 89:22, 25, and especially 1 Kings 11:38, which says, "I will be with you, and will build you a sure house, as I built for David." H. Wildberger, *Isaiah 1–12*, pp. 311–12. "The child about to be born, therefore, may be the young Hezekiah in whose birth Judah would see the continuing presence of God among his people and another renewal of the promise made to David." F. Moriarty, "Isaiah 1–39" in R. Brown, et. al., eds., *The Jerome Biblical Commentary* (Englewood Cliffs, NJ: Prentice Hall, 1968), p. 271. See also J. Watts, *Isaiah 1–33*, p. 101; J. Scullion, "An Approach to the Understanding of Isaiah 7:10–17," p. 295.

[59] "Most probably the prophet is here foretelling the birth of a royal heir, through whom the promises to the Davidic dynasty would find fulfillment." R. Clements, *Prophecy and Covenant* (Naperville, IL: Alec R. Alleson, 1965), p. 51 n. 51. The further description of the child knowing how to reject evil and choose good (Is. 7:16) also might point to the child's royalty. Knowing how to reject evil and choose good (e.g., 1 Kings 3:9; 2 Sam. 24:17) was more than a moral or religious quality, but also referred to a king's role as a ruler, particularly in his exercise of judgment. As Scullion explains, "The king discerns between good and evil in fulfilling his functions as God's chosen one. He is to dispense justice, defend the rights of the widow, care for the orphan, etc." J. Scullion, "An Approach to the Understanding of Isaiah 7:10–17," p. 298. Jensen similarly notes how "just judgment is a kingly prerogative" and the Immanuel child will possess this. J. Jensen, "The Age of Immanuel," p. 232. If the Immanuel child is indeed a royal heir, it is fitting to find him described as having the qualities of a good ruler, knowing how to reject evil and choose good.

[60] H. Wildberger, *Isaiah 1–12*, p. 312. Also S. Mowinckel, *He That Cometh*, p. 117: "In the situation to which the promise in Isa. vii refers, the continued existence of

the Davidic dynasty is at stake. The enemy's plan was to depose Ahaz, and make another, the son of Tabeel (possibly an Aramean), king in Jerusalem. But if this is so . . . it can hardly be doubted that the reference is to the wife of King Ahaz, to the queen and not simply to any of the ladies of the harem." Further, Mowinckel views Hezekiah as the partial fulfillment of this prophecy with complete fulfillment coming in Christ.

[61] R. Brown, *Birth of the Messiah*, p. 148. Similarly, Watts concludes, "The view that the child to be born is a royal heir and that his mother belongs to the king's household does justice to the evidence, fits the context, and provides the potential of messianic intention that is needed." J. Watts, *Isaiah*, p. 99. Many conclude that the child is most likely Ahaz's son and successor, Hezekiah (2 Kings 16:20, 18:1–2). For this view, see J. McKenzie, "Royal Messianism," pp. 41, 43; R. Brown, "God's Future Plans for His People," p. 1311; R. Laurentin, *A Short Treatise on the Virgin Mary*, pp. 275–76; J. Scullion, "An Approach to the Understanding of Isaiah 7:10–17," pp. 295, 300; J. Watts, *Isaiah*, pp. 99–101; W. Wildberger, *Isaiah 1–12*, p. 310. This Hezekian view is not without its difficulties, though they are not insurmountable. Wildberger addresses two objections to viewing Immanuel as an heir to the Davidic throne and the *almah* as his queenly mother. First, he addresses the objection that the mother generally does not name the child: "It is certainly not outside the realm of possibility that the *mother* named the child particularly since the king had many wives, and that the form of speech in the annunciation oracle shows that this was an ancient custom, which may well have continued to be popular right within the palace." He cites as examples Genesis 4:25, 35:18; Judges 13:24; and 1 Samuel 1:20 (p. 310). Another objection is that the Immanuel child cannot be Hezekiah because, according to the chronologies of 2 Kings 16:2 and 2 Kings 18:2, he already would have been born at the time of the Syro-Ephraimitic War when this prophecy took place. North, Watts, and Stuhlmueller, however, note that the chronologies are far from certain. C. North, "Immanuel," in *The Interpreter's Dictionary of the Bible*, vol. 2 (New York: Abingdon, 1962), p. 687; J. Watts, *Isaiah*, p. 99; C. Stuhlmueller, "The Mother of Immanuel," pp. 196–97. Along these lines Wildberger responds, "But the chronology for this era is by no means clearly established. If the Syro-Ephraimitic War took place in 734/3 and Hezekiah was five years old when he ascended the throne in 728/27, as the chronology of Pavovsky/Vogt . . . maintains, then it is at least not impossible that this might refer to Hezekiah" (p. 310). For more discussion on this point, see J. Watts, *Isaiah*, p. 99; C. Stuhlmueller, "The Mother of Immanuel," pp. 196–97; O. Kaiser, *Isaiah 1–12*, p. 158.

[62] M. Buber, *The Prophetic Faith*, p. 139: "If Ahaz, as he hears the word *almah*, knows to whom it refers (and only then does the sign truly concern him), it can only be a woman near him, and moreover hardly another than the young queen."

[63] A. Serra identifies the *almah* as the Queen Mother Abia (Hezekiah's mother and wife of Ahaz) when he considers Matthew's use of Isaiah 7:14 to describe Mary: "Come ella diede alla luce un figlio che garantì la continuità della casa di Davide, così Maria dà alla luce un figlio che regnerà per sempre sul trono di Davide, nella casa di Giacobbe, nell'Israele di Dio' (cf Mt 28,20; 16,18; Gal 6,16; 2 Sam 7,16); si noti la 'regalità' delle due madri." A. Serra, "Bibbia," in S. De Fiores and S. Meo,

eds., *Nuovo Dizionario di Mariologia* (Milan: Edizioni San Paolo, 1996), p. 219. See also the following scholars who have drawn attention to the *almah*'s queenship: J. Scullion, "An Approach to the Understanding of Isaiah 7:10–17," p. 300; G. Montague, *Our Father, Our Mother*, pp. 93–94; H. Wildberger, *Isaiah 1–12*, pp. 310–11; B. Vawter, *The Conscience of Israel* (New York: Sheed and Ward, 1961), pp. 184–85; H. Cazelles, "La Mère du Roi-Messie," pp. 51–52; J. Watts, *Isaiah*, p. 99; C. Stuhlmueller, "The Mother of Emmanuel," pp. 185–92.

[64] C. Stuhlmueller, "The Mother of Emmanuel," p. 190. Stuhlmueller describes how the queen mother played an important part in dynastic succession—a key theme here in Isaiah 7. In the kingdom of Judah, "the throne always remained within the Davidic family. . . . The prophet Nathan had promised that through the *Davidic* king, God would fulfill the promises made to the patriarchs and to Moses. . . . Each new king received these royal prerogatives through his father and queen mother" (pp. 190–91).

[65] G. Montague, *Our Father, Our Mother*, p. 93. Also significant is the fact that the mother is given the role of naming the child. "El profeta, al atribuir a la madre la imposición del nombre, piensa más en las funciones de guebiráh en el ceremonial de la futura entronización." A. Del Moral, "Santa María, La Guebiráh Mesiánica," p. 31.

[66] G. Montague, *Our Father, Our Mother*, p. 92: "On the throne the queen mother represented the king's continuity with the past, the visible affirmation of God's ongoing plan for his people, the channel through which the Lord's dynastic promise to David was fulfilled."

[67] G. Montague, *Our Father, Our Mother*, p. 94.

[68] This oracle is sometimes linked with Micah 5:1–4, which, like Isaiah 7:14, involves a woman figure who will give birth to a royal Davidic son signaling for God's people a period of freedom from their enemies. L. Allen, *The Books of Joel, Obadiah, Jonah, and Micah* (Grand Rapids: Eerdmans, 1976), p. 345; S. Mowinckel, *He That Cometh*, p. 185; R. Smith, *Micah-Malachi* (Waco, TX: Word, 1984), p. 44; H. Wolff, *Micah: A Commentary* (Minneapolis: Ausburg, 1990), p. 145. These scholars conclude that Micah was influenced by the Immanuel oracle and that he alludes to it in Micah 5:3. Others have gone even further by viewing the woman in travail in Micah 5:3 as a queen mother giving birth to a Davidic king. "Because the child will be a Davidic king, Michea spoke explicitly of his mother, the *gebirah*." C. Stuhlmueller, "The Mother of Emmanuel," p. 192. Also G. Kirwin, *Nature of the Queenship*, p. 33; R. Laurentin, *A Short Treatise on the Blessed Virgin Mary*, pp. 277–81; B. Ahern, "Mother of the Messiah," p. 45; T. Gray, "God's Word and Mary's Royal Office," p. 383. This latter view of the woman in Micah 5:3 as a queen mother, however, may be overstated, especially in light of the immediate context wherein we find Jerusalem—not an individual queen mother—described as a woman in travail in Micah 4:9–10. As Shaw notes, "Within the context of the discourse the 'one who is in labor' probably refers to Jerusalem, which in 4.9–10 is described as a woman in labor. Thus in 5.2 the prophet is probably proclaiming that the defeat of some within Israel will continue until the time that Jerusalem's labor has ended; that is, until she has defeated

her enemies." C. Shaw, *The Speeches of Micah: A Rhetorical-Historical Analysis* (JSOTSup 145), p. 153. Along similar lines, see J. Mays, *Micah* (Philadelphia: Eerdmans, 1976), p. 205.

[69] J. McKenzie, "Royal Messianism," p. 41: "The child mentioned is historical, but again he is viewed as the representative of the dynasty, the bearer of covenant promises and of the messianic hope of the future." Scullion notes: "The sign is dynastic. It concerns that which touches the dynasty most intimately, its continuance." J. Scullion, "An Approach to the Understanding of Isaiah 7:10–17," p. 300. Considering how wicked kings like Ahaz tarnished the glory of the Davidic line in the eighth century, R. Brown views this prophecy as pointing to the near future, summing up hopes for "an inbreak of the power of Yahweh that would revive the dynasty and ensure its permanence. Yahweh would soon raise up a successor of David who would be worthy of the name of Davidic king; he would be an example of charismatic power, just as David had been when the royal line was instituted." R. Brown, "God's Future Plans for His People," p. 1311.

[70] Jensen for example links Isaiah 7:14 with the child in Isaiah 9 and 11. "He did not think of Immanuel as simply another Davidide, but as the messianic king who was to rule in the new order. We have perhaps been too concerned about putting Isaiah in the proper stage of that well-known development from dynastic messianism to personal messianism. But if 11:1–9 is attributed to him, it is difficult to keep Isaiah in the stage of dynastic messianism; the idyllic picture painted there, the universal peace, is the new order with a vengeance. And 'a shoot from the stump of Jesse' accompanies it and helps actualize it. This oracle no doubt comes late in Isaiah's career, its fulfillment projected to the distant future." J. Jensen, "The Age of Immanuel," p. 233. See also pp. 232–39.

[71] C. North, "Immanuel," p. 688: "The possibility must be considered that a prophecy may have a proximate fulfillment which nevertheless does not exhaust its meaning. If we say that the original Immanuel was Hezekiah, we are not saying that the further application of the sign to Jesus in the NT was unwarranted fancy." North goes on to explain that royal texts such as Psalms 2, 45, and 100 are generally accepted as referring to individual kings reigning in Israel or Judah, but New Testament writers, such as the author of Hebrews, give them a messianic-christological interpretation. Laurentin views the proximate aim of Isaiah 7:14 as pointing to Hezekiah as a pledge that the threatened dynasty will continue. "But this immediate realization was far from exhausting the content of the oracle. The sequel of events clearly showed this. In many a regard Hezekiah's career was a disappointment. He failed in his reform. Exile followed. Hence the readers of Isaiah 7:14 found themselves ready to look for the realization of the promise in a more distant future." R. Laurentin, *A Short Treatise on the Virgin Mary*, p. 276. Mowinckel and Stuhlmueller hold similar positions. S. Mowinckel, *He That Cometh*, pp. 118–19; C. Stuhlmueller, "The Mother of Emmanuel," pp. 181–82. Cf. PBC, *The Interpretation of the Bible in the Church*, II, B, 3.

[72] PBC, *The Interpretation of the Bible in the Church*, II, B, 3: "The context of Matt 1:23 gives a fuller sense to the prophecy of Isa 7:14 in regard to the *almah* who will conceive, by using the translation of the Septuagint (*parthenos*)." Also see R. Brown, *Birth of the Messiah*, pp. 149–53.

[73] W. Brueggemann, "From Dust to Kinship," *ZAW* 84 (1972): 1–18; W. Brueggeman, "David and His Theologian," *CBQ* 30 (1968): 156–181; W. Witfall, "The Breath of His Nostrils," *CBQ* 36 (1974): 237–40; W. Witfall, "Gen. 3:15—A Protevangelium?" *CBQ* 36 (1974): 361–65; P. Kearney, "Gen. 3:15 and Johannine Theology," *Marian Studies* 27 (1976): 99–109; G. Wenham, *Genesis 1–15* (Waco: Word Publishing, 1987), pp. 27–40; E. Merrill, "Covenant and the Kingdom: Genesis 1–3 as Foundation for Biblical Theology," *Criswell Theological Review* 1 (1987): 295–308. M. Guinan, "Davidic Covenant," in D. Freedman, ed., *The Anchor Bible Dictionary*, vol. 2 (New York: Doubleday, 1992), p. 70. Cf. G. Von Rad, *Genesis* (London: SCM Press, 1972), pp. 59–60, 83.

[74] "Only human beings have been given dominion in God's creation. This dominion is expressly stated to be over all other living creatures: sky, sea, and land creatures." J. Sailhamer, *The Pentateuch as Narrative* (Grand Rapids: Zondervan, 1992), p. 95.

[75] Von Rad explains how humanity is God's representative in the world, "summoned to maintain and enforce God's claim to dominion over the earth. The decisive thing about man's similarity to God, therefore, is his function in the nonhuman world." G. Von Rad, *Genesis*, p. 58. Wenham makes a similar point: "God's purpose in creating man was that he should rule over the animal world (v. 26). Here [in v. 28] this injunction is repeated and defined more precisely. 'Rule the fish of the sea, the birds of the sky and every living creature . . . on earth.' Because man is created in God's image, he is king over nature. He rules the world on God's behalf." G. Wenham, *Genesis 1–11*, p. 33. Also E. Merrill, "Covenant and Kingdom," p. 298.

[76] Name-giving was an exercise of royal authority in the ancient Near East. As Von Rad has observed while commenting on Genesis 2:19, "Let us remind ourselves once more that name-giving in the ancient Orient was primarily an exercise of sovereignty, of command. This passage [Gen. 2:19], therefore, stands close to [Gen. 1:28b]." G. Von Rad, *Genesis*, p. 83. See affirmation of this view in W. Brueggemann, "From Dust to Kingship," p. 5.

[77] For an extensive summary of the various views, see G. Wenham, *Genesis 1–11*, pp. 29–32.

[78] G. Von Rad, *Genesis*, pp. 59–60. Merrill similarly concludes: "Man was created, then, to serve as the agent of God in implementing God's sovereign will and sway over the universe. . . . That man is to serve as vice-regent of God is seen clearly in the fact that he is the 'image' and 'likeness' of God." E. Merrill, "Covenant and the Kingdom," p. 298.

[79] G. Wenham, *Genesis 1–15*, p. 30: "That man is made in the divine image and is thus God's representative on earth was a common oriental view of the king. Both Egyptian and Assyrian texts describe the king as the image of God. . . . Furthermore, man is here bidden to rule and subdue the rest of creation, an obviously royal task (cf. 1 Kgs 5:4 [4:24], etc.), and Ps 8 speaks of man as having been created a little lower than the angels, *crowned* with glory and made to *rule* the works of God's hands."

[80] Ibid., pp. 30–31, emphasis added.

[81] H. Wolff, "The Kerygma of the Yahwist," *Interpretation* 20 (1966): 129–58. While showing the comparisons between Genesis 12–50 and the politics of the Davidic kingdom, Wolff characterizes the Genesis stories of the patriarchs as the Yahwist's "sermon on the Solomonic kingdom" (p. 149). R. Clements also argues: "When the Yahwist historian came to write of Israel's origins he saw in the Abrahamic covenant an expression of the divine providence which pointed forward to the rise of the great Davidic empire. The promises to the patriarch were interpreted as foretelling the rise of the kingdom of Israel, and its possession of the land of Canaan." *Abraham and David* (London: SCM Press, 1967), p. 80. Cf. M. Weinfield, "*berith*," in *Theological Dictionary of the Old Testament*, vol. 2, pp. 270–72. Weinfield shows how the Abrahamic covenant is promissory, based on God's choice and fidelity, and how it involves a promise of land and offspring, just like the Davidic covenant.

[82] W. Brueggemann, "From Dust to Kingship," pp. 1–18; W. Brueggemann, "David and His Theologian," pp. 156–181; W. Brueggemann, "Kingship and Chaos: A Study in Tenth Century Theology," *CBQ* 33 (1971): 317–32; W. Brueggemann, "Weariness, Exile and Chaos: A Motif in Royal Authority," *CBQ* 34 (1972): 19–38. W. Witfall, "The Breath of His Nostrils," pp. 237–40; W. Witfall, "Gen. 3:15—A Protevangelium?" pp. 361–65. Other treatments include M. Guinan, "Davidic Covenant," p. 70; P. Ellis, *The Yahwist: The Bible's First Theologian* (Notre Dame: Fides Publishers, 1968), pp. 189–211; D. Spires, "Yahwist Patterns: Genesis 2:4b-25:11," (Ann Arbor: UMI Dissertation Services, 1978), pp. 197–220.

[83] W. Brueggemann, "David and His Theologian," p. 158. On pp. 159–164, Brueggemann interestingly argues that the story of David's fall into sin with Bathsheba finds parallels with Adam's fall. Just as David (1) was attracted to one who was forbidden him, (2) was aware that he has done wrong, (3) was judged by Yahweh mercifully, even though his actions merited death, and (4) had his shattered hopes allayed by the birth of a son, Solomon, so also do we find in Genesis Adam (1) being attracted to what was forbidden him, (2) being aware of his wrong actions, (3) being judged by Yahweh mercifully and spared death, and (4) having his sadness from his expulsion from the garden allayed by the granting of a son, Seth. If this is true, this may add further grounds for seeing the Davidic kingdom as an important background for understanding Genesis 2–3.

[84] W. Brueggemann, "From Dust to Kingship," pp. 1–18; W. Witfall, "The Breath of His Nostrils," p. 1; P. Kearney, "Gen. 3:15 and Johannine Theology," p. 99.

[85] W. Brueggemann, "From Dust to Kingship," pp. 1–4. Brueggemann shows how Genesis 2:7, 1 Kings 16:2–3, Psalm 113:7, and 1 Samuel 2:6–8 "all speak of being raised from dust to power, a formula which best makes sense if understood as an enthronement formula" (p. 4).

[86] Ibid., p. 2. Similarly, see V. Hamilton, *Genesis*, p. 158: "Especially interesting for possible connections with Gen. 2:7 are those passages which speak of an exaltation from dust, with the dust representing pre-royal status (1 K. 16:2), poverty (1 Sam. 2:8; Ps. 113:7), and death (Isa. 26:19; Dan. 12:2). To 'be raised from the dust' means to be elevated to royal office, to rise above poverty, to find life. Hence man is formed from dust to be in control of the garden. . . . He is raised from the dust to reign."

[87] W. Brueggemann, "From Dust to Kingship," p. 12.

[88] W. Witfall, "The Breath of His Nostrils," pp. 237–40. "Although the term for 'breath' is *nesama* in Gen. 2:7b and *ruah* in Lam 4:20, both terms are used in conjunction in Gen 7:22 and 2 Sam 22:16 and in synonymous parallelism in Job 27:3" (p. 238). Also M. Kline, *Images of the Spirit* (Grand Rapids: Baker, 1980), pp. 21–22.

[89] Even though the Hebrew word for "breath" in Gen. 2:7 (*nesama*) is different for the word used in Is. 11:1–2 (*ruah*), Walter Witfall has shown how the two words are used in synonymous parallelism in the Old Testament (see previous footnote). "The Breath of His Nostrils," pp. 238–39. See also P. Kearney, "Gen. 3:15 and Johannine Theology," p. 99: "The breath of life given him by God (Gen 2:7) likewise denotes a divine gift to the king (cf. Isa 11:2) known also from Egyptian royal theology."

[90] W. Witfall, "The Breath of His Nostrils," p. 240.

[91] Brueggemann shows how licking the dust or being beaten down to the dust was a sign of defeat or fall from power. He examined the following texts to make this point: Gen. 2:7; Ps. 72: 9–11, 22:15, 29, 44:25, 7:6, 119:25, 104:29; Lam. 3:28–30; Mic. 7:16–17; Is. 47:1, 49:22, 41:2, 25:10–12, 26:4–5. W. Brueggemann, "From Dust to Kingship," pp. 5–13. Others note how the idea of eating the dust is used in Isaiah 49:23 and Micah 7:17 to describe "total defeat" (Sailhamer), "the plight of conquered foes" (Cassuto) and "abject humilation, especially of enemies" (Wenham). J. Sailhamer, *The Pentateuch as Narrative*, pp. 106–7; U. Cassuto, *A Commentary on the Book of Genesis* (Jerusalem: Magnes Press, 1961), p. 160; G. Wenham, *Genesis 1–15*, p. 79.

[92] W. Brueggemann, "From Dust to Kingship," p. 9.

[93] The same Hebrew verb is used to describe what the woman's seed will do to the serpent and what the serpent will do to the woman's seed. The RSV translates this word (*shuph*) as "bruise" in both instances. For other options in translation (such as "crush" or "strike at"), see V. Hamilton, *Genesis*, pp. 197–98. Hamilton concludes: "In order to maintain the duplication of the Hebrew verb, whatever English equivalent one decides on must be used twice" (p. 198).

[94] "Further light on the Davidic background of Gen 3:15 can be found in such 'royal' Psalms as Ps 89 and 2 Sam 22. David is addressed as God's 'anointed' or 'messiah' (Ps 89:21,39; 2 Sam 22:51) whose 'seed' will endure forever under God's favor (Ps 89:5,30,37). As Yahweh has crushed the ancient serpent 'Rahab' (Ps 89:11), so now David and his sons will crush their enemies in the dust beneath their feet (Ps 89:24; 2 Sam 22:37-43)." W. Witfall, "Gen. 3:15—A Protevangelium?" p. 363. Witfall adds further support for the royal Davidic background to Genesis 3:14–15 as he considers how Psalm 72:9 uses the similar imagery of the king's enemies bowing before him and "licking the dust."

[95] W. Witfall, "Gen. 3:15—A Protevangelium," p. 363.

[96] Referring to the seed of Genesis 3:15, Hamilton notes: "Would this individual, or these individuals, be among the kings of Israel and Judah who are the 'offspring' of their father (2 Sam. 7:12; Ps. 89:5 [Eng. 4]), who 'crush' their enemies (Ps. 89:24

[Eng. 23]) 'under their feet' (2 Sam. 22:39), so that the enemies lick the dust' (Ps. 72:9)?" V. Hamilton, *Genesis*, p. 200. Indeed, the notion of the seed itself was important to the Davidic dynasty (2 Sam. 7:12; Ps. 89:4, 29, 36). Important Davidic texts "take the key word *zera'* from 2 S. 7:12 (cf. 1 Ch. 17:11), according to which Yahweh will raise up a son after David and will establish him and his kingdom." H. Preuss, "*zera'* " in G. Botterweck and H. Ringgren, eds., *Theological Dictionary of the Old Testament*, vol. 4 (Grand Rapids: Eerdmanns, 1980), p. 157. Witfall sees a direct link between the seed of Genesis 3:15 and the Davidic seed. W. Witfall, "Gen. 3:15—A Protevangelium?" p. 363. Ellis develops this point even further by arguing that the Yahwist gradually relates the seed of the woman with the royal seed of David (2 Sam 7:13). The Yahwistic texts of the Pentateuchal narrative subtly narrow down the seed's identity "by eliminating from the seed of the first woman all except that elect line of blessed descendants which begins with Seth, runs through Noah, Shem and Abraham and terminates with the royal, conquering seed of Judah in Gn 49:8-12 and Nm 24:17. The audience, if it is following the foreshadowing and the story that flows from it, must conclude that it is the seed of Judah, the dynasty of David, which will, according to God's will and plan, conquer the seed of the serpent and recover for mankind that blessed communion with God which was man's glory before the fall." P. Ellis, *The Yahwist*, p. 200. Cf. R. Laurentin, *A Short Treatise on the Virgin Mary*, pp. 273–74.

[97] P. Kearney, "Gen. 3:15 and Johannine Theology," p. 99. Ellis has elaborately discussed the relationships between Genesis 3:15 and the Davidic kingdom. He argues that the basic Yahwistic themes such as the curse on God's enemies and the seed defeating those enemies are found in Genesis 3:15 and then are elaborated upon in other Yahwistic texts such as Genesis 49:8–12 and Numbers 24:17–18 and are to be understood in relation with the Davidic dynasty's conquest over the false religions such as that of the Canaanites. P. Ellis, *The Yahwist*, pp. 196–202. Similarly, see W. Witfall, "Gen. 3:15—A Protevangelium?" pp. 363–65. "The royal and 'Davidic' significance of this passage for both the OT and NT cannot be overlooked. Apparently, Gen. 3:15 owes its present form to the Yahwist's adaptation of both the David story (2 Sam -1 Kgs 2) and ancient Near Eastern royal mythology to Israel's covenant faith and history. The Yahwist has thus presented Israel's history and pre-history within a 'Davidic' or 'messianic' framework" (p. 365).

[98] G. Aalders, *Genesis*, vol. 1 (Grand Rapids: Zondervan, 1981), pp. 107–8; H. Stigers, *A Commentary on Genesis* (Grand Rapids: Zondervan, 1976); F. Schaeffer, *Genesis in Space and Time* (Downers Grove: InterVarsity Press, 1972), pp. 103–4. Some have argued not only that Genesis 3:15 is a clear messianic prophecy, but also that the woman of Genesis 3:15 is a direct prediction of Mary in the literal sense. See J. Cantinant, *Mary in the Bible* (Westminster: Newman, 1965), pp. 34–37; E. May, "Mary in the Old Testament," in J. Carol, ed., *Mariology*, vol. 1 (Milwaukee: Bruce, 1955), pp. 56–62; F. Peirce, "The Protevangelium," *CBQ* 13 (1951): 239–52.

[99] "It will certainly be advisable not to use any longer the conception of protevangelium in connection with Gen. 3:15." O. Loretz, "Schopfung und Mythos," *SBS* 32 (1968): 137, as cited in H. Ruger, "On Some Versions of Genesis 3:15, Ancient and Modern," *The Biblical Translator* 27 (1976): 109. Similar perspectives are found in: C. Westermann, *Genesis: A Practical Commentary* (Grand Rapids: Eerdmans, 1987), p. 25; D. Gowan, *From Eden to Babel* (Grand Rapids: Eerdmans,

1988), p. 57; B. Vawter, *On Genesis* (Garden City, NY: Doubleday, 1977), p. 84; S. Mowinckel, *He That Cometh*, p. 11.

[100] "Real snakes are obviously the subject of v. 14, and an etiology is provided for two of their peculiarities, that they can move very well indeed without legs and that they eat dust (as people of antiquity thought)." D. Gowan, *From Eden to Babel*, p. 57. "When taken literally the verse seems to say no more than that the serpent species . . . will struggle violently and unremittingly with every generation of humans." M. Maher, *Genesis*, p. 46. For similar views, see B. Vawter, *On Genesis*, p. 82; M. Maher, *Genesis* (Wilmington, DE: Michael Glazier, 1982), pp. 45–46.

[101] "The traditional interpretation of the clause '. . . it will crush your head and you will snap at its heel' as a protoevangelium is therefore impossible, if only because the 'seed' of the woman and the serpent can mean only the generations to come, not an individual (Mary or Jesus)." C. Westermann, *Genesis*, p. 25. Similarly, Ruger concludes: "This means that the interpretation of Gen. 3:15 as being the first witness to Christ and/or Mary has no base in either the Hebrew text or in any of the ancient versions, and therefore it is only natural that both Protestant and Roman Catholic Old Testament scholars emphatically deny that this verse has to be regarded as the protevangelium." H. Ruger, "On Some Versions of Genesis 3:15," p. 109.

[102] G. Von Rad, *Genesis*, p. 93.

[103] A. Feuillet, *Jesus and His Mother*, p. 22; S. De Fiores, *Maria, Madre di Gesù*, p. 40; W. Witfall, "Gen. 3:15—A Protevangelium," pp. 361–65; W. Lasor, "Prophecy, Inspiration, and *Sensus Plenior*," *TynBul* 29 (1978): 56–57; G. Wenham, *Genesis*, pp. 78–81; V. Hamilton, *Genesis*, pp. 197–200; W. Kaiser, *The Messiah in the Old Testament* (Grand Rapids: Zondervan, 1995), pp. 37–42. Cf. A. Serra, "Bibbia," p. 264.

[104] J. McKenzie, "The Literary Characteristics of Genesis 1–3," *TS* 15 (1954): 541–72; G. Von Rad, *Genesis*, pp. 92–93; G. Wenham, *Genesis*, pp. 1–91; J. Sailhamer, *The Pentateuch as Narrative*, pp. 81–111.

[105] "One has to take this passage symbolically, not literally. Therefore, it is fruitless to see in this particular verse an etiology of why snakes no longer walk on legs and why they lost their legs. If one is prepared to see in the decree *On your belly shall you crawl* a change in the snake's mode of locomotion, then to be consistent one must also see in the decree *dust shall you eat* a change in the snake's diet. The writer clearly intends these two facts to be expressions of humiliation and subjugation (as in Ps. 72:9; Isa. 49:23; Mic 7:17)." V. Hamilton, *Genesis*, pp. 196–97. Even Von Rad, who does not support any messianic reading of Genesis 3:15, still recognizes that the serpent figure represents more than a reptile creature in the narrative. He argues that one must not stop with a literal understanding of the serpent, "for the things with which this passage deals are basic, and in illustrating them, the narrator uses not only the commonplace language of every day, but a language that also figuratively depicts the most intellectual matters. Thus by serpent he understands not only the zoological species (which in a Palestinian's life plays a quite different role from in ours), but at the same time, in a kind of spiritual clearheadednesss, he sees in it an evil being that has assumed form, that is inexplicably present within our created world. . . . The same thing applies to the forbidden fruit; one must

guard against understanding it simply as symbolical, and yet no reader thinks of stopping with the realistic understanding. So too the serpent; a real serpent is meant; but at the same time, in it and its enigmatic relation to man, man's relation to the evil with which he has become involved becomes vivid." G. Von Rad, *Genesis*, pp. 92–93. McKenzie offers another symbolic view. He notes how the serpent was a phallic symbol associated with male and female fertility rites outside of Israel, but within Israel it represented an evil opponent to Yahweh: ". . . the serpent appears in other forms in the Bible, and I do not believe that these should be left out of consideration. In Isa 27:1, Job 25:13, the serpent is a monstrous adversary of Yahweh. The serpent on the floor of the sea in Amos 9:3 must be the same mythological monster. . . . I do not think this significance of the serpent was altogether absent from the author's mind. It would not be difficult for the Hebrew to identify the chaotic monster of evil with the serpent of those rites which he found so offensive to his moral sense." J. McKenzie, "The Literary Characteristics of Genesis 2–3," pp. 563–64. Also, Peter Ellis sees the serpent as "a symbol representing the false religion of the Canaanites" and Genesis 3:15 as referring to the conquest of Canaan, "the conquest of the forces of anti-God—represented by the false religion of Canaan in the time of the Yahwist." P. Ellis, *The Yahwist*, pp. 196–97.

[106] G. Wenham, *Genesis 1–15*, p. 80. Thus, a symbolic view of the serpent seems more probable and may find confirmation in the Pentateuchal narrative itself. Wenham notes how the serpent, as a swarming animal that swarms on the earth and crawls on its belly (Cf. Gen. 3:14; Lv. 11:41–42), is depicted as the unclean animal *par excellence* in the Pentateuch (Lv. 11 and Dt. 14), placed at the farthest distance away from the pure animals which can be offered in sacrifice. "So for any Israelite familiar with the symbolic values of different animals, a creature more likely than a serpent to lead man away from his creator could not be imagined" (p. 73). Moreover, Sailhamer notes how a literalistic understanding of the serpent in Genesis 3:15 does not fit well into a narrative reading of Genesis. "It is unlikely that at such a pivotal role in the narrative the author would intend no more than a mere reference to snakes and their offspring and the fear of them among humankind." J. Sailhamer, *The Pentateuch as Narrative*, p. 107. Further, a canonical reading of the passage also would confirm the symbolic view. Leviathan in Isaiah 27:1 is a serpent-figure who is an enemy of God. And the New Testament writers also seem to build upon the view of the serpent in Genesis 3 as an anti-God symbol (Rom. 16:20; Heb. 2:14; Rev. 12), with Revelation 12 specifically identifying the serpent with the anti-God figure, Satan, the devil himself.

[107] "It must be remembered that this is a curse on the serpent, not on mankind, and something less than a draw would be expected." G. Wenham, *Genesis 1–15*, p. 80. "Since this verse is part of the curse of the temptor, we can justly argue to a victory for the woman's seed." S. Rowe, "An Exegetical Approach to Gen. 3:15," *Marian Studies* 12 (1961): 66. Also R. Laurentin, *A Short Treatise on the Virgin Mary*, p. 273.

[108] Brueggemann shows how Psalms 18, 22, and 72 each "regards the destiny of the enemy as an essential part of the process by which the king receives dominion over the realm. . . . The wish for the enemy to be in the dust is the counterpart of the enhancement of the king." W. Brueggemann, "From Dust to Kingship," p. 9. In

light of this biblical symbolism, it seems that the serpent being cursed to eat the dust all the days of his life would again support the view of an eventual defeat of the serpent. It is true that man is told that he will return to the dust (3:19), but here man is not cursed, only the ground. Further, as Sailhamer points out, "So strongly was the imagery of the snake's defeat felt by later biblical writers that in their description of the ultimate victory and reign of the righteous 'seed,' when peace and harmony are restored in creation, the serpent remains under the curse: 'dust will [still] be the serpent's food' (Isa 65:25)." J. Sailhamer, *The Pentateuch as Narrative*, p. 107.

[109] Maher does not think the imagery points to an advantageous position of the woman's seed over the serpent: "To say that victory for humankind is implied in the fact that a human being will crush the head of the serpent while the latter will only wound the heel of the other, seems to be going beyond the meaning of the text. In accord with the imagery called for by the situation, the biblical words simply oppose humankind's crushing of the serpent's head to the latter's deadly sting." M. Maher, *Genesis*, p. 46. However, since (as we have seen above) crushing the head under one's feet is often used in the Old Testament as a symbol for subjecting one's enemies, the picture in Genesis 3:15 presents the woman's seed in a stronger position over the serpent. This allows us to see in this verse something more than a never-ending dual between the two seeds. Some have thus concluded that this image points to an eventual victory of the woman's seed. "Sta comunque il fatto che la sconfitta del serpente è mortale, dal momento che gli viene schiacciata la testa." A. Serra, "Bibbia," p. 264. "The contrast between crushing the head and crushing or bruising the heel is the difference between a mortal blow to the skull and a slight injury to the victor." W. Kaiser, *The Messiah in the Old Testament*, p. 41. Similarly, see W. La Sor, "Prophecy, Inspiration and *Sensus Plenior*," p. 56; G. Wenham, *Genesis 1–15*, p. 80; J. Sailhamer, *The Pentateuch as Narrative*, p. 108. Interestingly, Rigaux suggests that the serpent is portrayed in a defensive position and that the reason the serpent only strikes at the heel is because the woman's seed is raised above the serpent, ready to strike its head. B. Rigaux, "The Woman and her Seed in Genesis 3:14–15," *Theology Digest* 6 (1958): 28.

[110] "One may note in passing the similarity of the basic notion in Gn 3:15 with the common symbolic description of conquest by the foot upon the head as in Ps 110:1; Jos 10:24-25. If this interpretation is correct then Gn 3:15 would be only an obscure expression of what is clearly said in Ps 110:1 '. . . I will make your enemies a footstool for you.'" P. Ellis, *The Yahwist*, p. 200 n. 71.

[111] Interestingly, Rigaux and Feuillet have also argued that since Yahwistic passages often attribute to the heads of families (e.g., Esau, Moab, sons of Jacob) the characteristics of their descendants and since they associate women with the work of salvation (e.g., Sarah, Rebecca, Rachel), it is at least plausible to see that the woman in Genesis 3:15 is meant to be understood as a starting point through which some future work of redemption will be accomplished. B. Rigaux, "The Woman and Her Seed," pp. 30–31; A. Feuillet, *Jesus and His Mother*, p. 119. Cf. R. Laurentin, *A Short Treatise on the Virgin Mary*, pp. 273–74.

[112] A. Feuillet, *Jesus and His Mother*, p. 22. Also S. De Fiores, *Maria, Madre di Gesù*, p. 40; E. Smith, "The Scriptural Basis for Mary's Queenship," p. 111; R.

Laurentin, *A Short Treatise on the Virgin Mary*, pp. 273–74; G. Wenham, *Genesis 1–15*, pp. 80–81; J. Sailhamer, *The Pentateuch as Narrative*, p. 108; cf. A. Serra, "Bibbia," p. 264.

[113] Wenham concludes: "While a messianic interpretation may be justified in the light of subsequent revelation, a *sensus plenior*, it would perhaps be wrong to suggest that this was the narrator's own understanding. Probably he just looked for mankind eventually to defeat the serpent's seed, the powers of the devil." G. Wenham, *Genesis 1–15*, p. 81. La Sor similarly concludes, "I do find the fullness of meaning in some as-yet-unspecified member of the human race who would destroy the satanic serpent, thus playing a key role in God's redemptive plan. In that sense, the passage is indeed the first enunciation of the good news." W. La Sor, "Prophecy, Inspiration and *Sensus Plenior*," p. 57. For more on the possibilities of finding messianic significance in Genesis 3:15 in terms of a *sensus plenior*, see R. Brown, *Mary in the New Testament*, pp. 29–30; R. Laurentin, *A Short Treatise on the Virgin Mary*, pp. 272–74. Later pre-Christian Jewish belief seems to reflect a messianic understanding of Genesis 3:15 as seen in the Septuagint. R. Martin, "The Earliest Messianic Interpretation of Genesis 3:15," *JBL* 84 (1965): 425–27. And a canonical reading of this passage would confirm such an interpretation since this passage was understood by the New Testament writers as having messianic significance (cf. Rom. 16:20; Heb. 2:14; Rev. 12). While it is true that Vatican II was cautious on its use of Genesis 3:15 as having Marian significance, *Lumen Gentium* 55 nevertheless taught that Mary "is already prophetically foreshadowed in the promise of victory over the serpent which was given to our first parents after their fall into sin (cf. Gn. 3:15)," and our study of this passage seems to confirm the council's teaching in this regard. See also *Catechism*, nos. 410–11, which refers to Genesis 3:15 as a "protoevangelium."

[114] R. Laurentin, *A Short Treatise on the Virgin Mary*, p. 279.

[115] A. Robert and A. Feuillet, *An Introduction to the Old Testament* (New York: Desclee Company, 1968), p. 139; H. Cazelles, "La Torah ou Pentateuque" in *Introduction à la Bible*, vol. 1 (Tournai, 1957), p. 354, as cited in C. Stuhlmueller, "The Mother of Emmanuel," p. 193; B. Ahern, "The Mother of the Messiah," p. 45; P. Kearney, "Genesis 3:15 and Johannine Theology," p. 100; R. Laurentin, *A Short Treatise on the Virgin Mary*, pp. 279–81.

[116] Whatever hypothesis one may hold about the dating of texts considered Yahwistic, a canonical approach to these passages would render similar conclusions. By studying Genesis 3:15 in its final form within the Old Testament canon, one can observe the notion of a mother being linked with the hope surrounding a royal offspring as an Old Testament theme found prototypically in Genesis and seen in the queen-mother tradition of the Davidic kingdom and in the messianic prophecy of Isaiah 7:14.

[117] B. Ahern, "Mother of the Messiah," p. 45.

[118] "It is very possible that [the Yahwist] has seen in the salvific maternity of Eve the prototype of the royal maternity." H. Cazelles, "La Torah ou Pentateuque," p. 354. Similarly, Robert and Feuillet suggest that the Yahwist saw in the woman's moth-

erhood "a prototype of the royal maternity (cf. Is 7,14; Mi 5,2, and the persistent mention of queen mothers in the Books of Kings) and hence of Messianic motherhood." A. Robert and A. Feuillet, *An Introduction to the Old Testament*, p. 139. See also C. Stuhlmueller, "Mother of Emmanuel," pp. 192–93; R. Laurentin, *A Short Treatise on the Virgin Mary*, pp. 278–81.

[119] P. Kearney, "Genesis 3:15 and Johannine Theology," p. 100.

Chapter Three

[1] Recognizing the importance of the Davidic kingdom themes in Matthew 1–2 is not meant to diminish other backgrounds to Matthew's infancy narrative, such as the Old Testament figures of Abraham, the patriarch Joseph, Moses, or Israel. See R. Brown, *Birth of the Messiah*, pp. 68–69, 213–19, 228.

[2] L. Hurtado, "Christ," in J. Green, et. al., eds. *Dictionary of Jesus and the Gospels*, (Downers Grove, IL: InterVarsity Press, 1992), p. 107. R. Menninger, *Israel and the Church in the Gospel of Matthew* (New York: Peter Lang, 1994), p. 82.

[3] "Though the term 'Anointed One' is usually associated with the king, it was apparently not until around 50 BC that 'Messiah" was used in the technical sense of an ideal King-Redeemer [Pss Sol 17:32]." R. Menninger, *Israel and the Church*, p. 82. L. Hurtado, "Christ," p. 107. See Brown, who discusses how Israel's hopes in a future Davidic Messiah who would restore the kingdom grew out of Israel facing the Babylonian exile: "When the Babylonian Exile of 586-39 B.C. brought an end to the reigning Davidic monarchy, and when in the early post-exilic period the dreams centered around Zerubbabel and the Davidic descendancy came to nought, the expectations surrounding the anointed kings of the House of David shifted to an anointed king of the indefinite future. And thus hope was born in the Messiah, the supreme anointed one who would deliver Israel. This hope is given voice in the first century B.C. in the Psalms of Solomon 17:23 (21): 'O Lord, raise up for them their king, the son of David at that time in which you, O God, see that he may reign over Israel your servant.'" R. Brown, *The Birth of the Messiah* (New York: Doubleday, 1993), p. 67 n. 9. For a more extensive treatment on the view of messiahship in the Jewish world of Jesus' day, see N. Wright, *Jesus and the Victory of God* (Minneapolis: Fortress, 1996), pp. 481–86.

[4] R. Brown, *Birth of the Messiah*, pp. 59, 67; C. Wright, *Knowing Jesus Through the Old Testament* (Downers Grove, IL: InterVarsity Press, 1992), p. 143; D. Hagner, *Matthew 1–13* (Dallas: Word Books, 1993), pp. 9, 11.

[5] "Matthew shows a particular interest in the title 'son of David' for Jesus. John never uses it and Mark and Luke use it only four times, but Matthew uses it a total of 10 times." R. Brown, *Birth of the Messiah*, p. 134.

[6] Also, the prophets spoke of a Davidic descendant as a "righteous branch" from David's line who would reestablish Israel, free them from their oppressors, and gather people from all nations into Jerusalem to behold Yahweh's glory (Jer. 23:5–8, 30:21–22; Ezek. 37:21–23; Zech. 3:8–10, 6:12–15; Hag. 2:21–22). The Psalms of Solomon 17–18 also speak of a "son of David" who will cast out foreign oppres-

sors, judge the nations, and cause all peoples to serve him. R. Menninger, *Israel and the Church*, p. 88: "The OT anticipated a king of Davidic descent who would free Israel. . . . The hope that a scion of David would sit on Israel's throne was appropriated by Israel through the covenant (2 Sam 7:16; cf. Ps 89:3–4). This was a view contemporary with Jesus (Ps Sol 17:21)."

[7] "But Jesus is not simply a son of David; he is *the* Son of David. As Son of David, Jesus is the Messiah-King in the line of David who has been sent by God specifically to the people of Israel." D. Bauer, "Son of David," in J. Green, et. al., eds. *Dictionary of Jesus and the Gospels*, (Downers Grove, IL: InterVarsity Press, 1992), p. 769. Also C. Wright, *Knowing Jesus Through the Old Testament*, p. 5.

[8] "David is the only one designated king in the genealogy (1:6). This does not mean that Matthew was ignorant of the fact that others in the genealogy were also kings; rather it is his way of highlighting the royal Messiahship of Jesus." R. Menninger, *Israel and the Church*, p. 75. B. Viviano, "The Gospel According to Matthew," in *The New Jerome Biblical Commentary* (London: Geoffrey Chapman, 1989), p. 634. Cf. J. Meier, *Matthew* (Wilmington, DE: Michael Glazier, 1980), p. 4.

[9] Cf. D. Hagner, *Matthew 1–13*, p. 11: The addition of "the king" in verse 6 "strengthens the link between David and Jesus as messianic king."

[10] In commenting on this section, Brown notes the dynastic importance of Zerubbabel (v. 13), who not only was the focus of royal messianic expectations in the return from exile, but also serves as the last link in Matthew's genealogy about whom there is any Old Testament record. R. Brown, *Birth of the Messiah*, pp. 61, 69.

[11] "Nella terza filza di nomi, conseguente alla deportazione in Babilonia (vv. 12-16), compaiono persone destituite di insegne regali. Cristo, allora, darà vita ad un nuovo tipo di regalità, che è di tutt'altro genere. Come Figlio di Dio (Mt. 2,15), egli stabilisce un'altra 'casa' di Davide, un regno che trascende le leggi della carne e del sangue." A. Serra, "Bibbia," p. 215.

[12] M. Johnson, *The Purpose of the Biblical Genealogies, with Special Reference to the Setting of the Genealogies of Jesus* (Cambridge University, 1969), p. 192. Also R. Menninger, *Israel and the Church*, pp. 74–75: "The practice of assigning values to the letters of the Hebrew alphabet and then taking the sum is a rabbinical literary device . . . called 'gematria' (i.e. play on numbers). Recognition of this rabbinical practice helps explain the somewhat artificial and selective nature of Matthew's genealogy." J. Meier, *Matthew*, p. 4: "Mt may be playing with the numerical values given Hebrew letters (a technique called 'gemetria'). The consonants in the Hebrew name David add up to fourteen (D + W + D = 4 + 6 + 4). When you 'add up' the meaning of Israel's history, the bottom line is Jesus Christ, the Son of David." See also J. Jones, "Subverting the Textuality of Davidic Messianism: Matthew's Presentation of the Genealogy of the Davidic Title," *CBQ* 56 (1994): 266; S. Ackerman, "The Queen-Mother and the Cult in the Ancient Near East," in K. King, ed., *Women and Goddess Traditions*, (Minneapolis: Fortess, 1997), p. 196; K. Stendahl "Quis et Und?" in *The Interpretation of Matthew*, ed. G. Stanton (Edinburgh: T&T Clark, 1995), p. 74; R. Brown, *Birth of the Messiah*, p. 80; G. Montague, *Companion God: A Cross-Cultural Commentary on the Gospel of Matthew*

(New York: Paulist Press, 1989), p. 17. Interestingly, David himself appears as the *fourteenth* generation in the family tree of Matthew 1.

[13] P. Perkins, "Mary in the Gospels: A Question of Focus," *Theology Today* 56 (1999): 300. J. Kingsbury, *Matthew: Structure, Christology, Kingdom* (Philadelphia: Fortress, 1975), p. 43. Cf. B. Nolan, *The Royal Son of God* Orbis biblicus et orientalis 23 (Gottingen: Vandenhoeck & Rupprecht, 1979), p. 31.

[14] "By naming the child, Joseph acknowledges him as his own. The Jewish position on this is lucidly clear and is dictated by the fact that sometimes it is difficult to determine who begot a child biologically. Since normally a man will not acknowledge and support a child unless it is his own, the law prefers to base paternity on the man's acknowledgment. The Mishna *Baba Bathra* 8:6 states the principle: 'If a man says, "This is my son," he is to be believed.'" R. Brown, *Birth of the Messiah*, p. 139. Kingsbury makes a similar point: "Jesus can be designated the Son of David because Joseph son of David obeys the instruction he receives from the angel of the Lord and gives Jesus his name (1:20, 25). In other words, Jesus, born of Mary but not fathered by Joseph, is legitimately Son of David because Joseph son of David adopts him into his line." J. Kingsbury, *Matthew as Story* (Minneapolis: Fortress, 1988), p. 47. See also D. Bauer, "Son of David," pp. 768–69.

[15] R. Brown, *Birth of the Messiah*, p. 138.

[16] S. Klassen-Wiebe, "Matthew 1:18–25," *Interpretation* 46 (1992): 392. Also R. Brown, *Birth of the Messiah*, p. 150: "Matthew has been trying to explain that Jesus is truly of the House of David, a Davidic descent that is not at all negated by the fact that Joseph begot him legally rather than naturally. And here he has a text addressed to the House of David which speaks of a virgin being with child and giving birth to a son. . . . Through this virgin foretold in His word spoken by the prophet, God had prepared for the birth of Jesus the Messiah 'in this way' (Mt. 1:18)."

[17] B. Nolan, *The Royal Son of God*, p. 39; D. Hagner, *Matthew 1–13*, p. 26.

[18] R. Menninger, *Israel and the Church*, pp. 85–86. Menninger notes how the title "King of the Jews" is related directly to "Messiah" and would signify the fulfillment of Israel's hopes for God to send the great messianic king.

[19] See R. Brown, *Birth of the Messiah*, pp. 170–71.

[20] "The rising of the star heralds the appearance of the King of Israel, as Numbers 24:17 had foretold (along with Numbers 24:9 and the allusion to Genesis 49:9–10 concerning the prince of Judah, to whom 'shall be the obedience of the peoples')." B. Nolan, *The Royal Son of God*, p. 44. "In this phenomenon, whatever it was, the magi-astrologers perceived the sign of the fulfillment of the Jewish eschatological expectation concerning the coming king and so would have set off on their journey toward Jerusalem." See also Nolan's comments on p. 74. Cf. D. Hagner, *Matthew 1–13*, p. 27; D. Senior, "Matthew 2:1–12," *Interpretation* 46 (1992): 395–96.

[21] Brown notes the interchangeability between "king of the Jews" and "messiah" in Matthew 2:2–4: "The magi asked for 'the King of the Jews'; Herod speaks of 'the Messiah.'" R. Brown, *Birth of the Messiah*, p. 175.

[22] Matthew's wording agrees verbatim with the LXX of 2 Samuel 5:2: "It was rabbinic practice to combine quotations referring to the same thing, particularly when linked by a key word or common concept, in the present instance 'ruling' and 'shepherding.' The messianic king, the Son of David, would shepherd his people. The special appropriateness of a Davidic context for Matthew is obvious." D. Hagner, *Matthew 1–13*, p. 29.

[23] Psalm 72:10–11 speaks of all kings falling down before the king, serving him and offering him gifts, including gifts of gold (v. 15). Isaiah 60:1–6 describes all nations coming to the light and kings coming "to the brightness of your rising" with "the wealth of the nations" being offered, including gold and frankincense. In considering these two Old Testament passages, Hagner makes the following conclusion: "Theologically these passages are saying in part the same thing that Matthew says: the newborn king is king of all the world, and the appropriate homage shall be paid to him by all nations." D. Hagner, *Matthew 1–13*, p. 31. On this, see also R. Brown, *Birth of the Messiah*, pp. 187–88; D. Senior, "Matthew 2:1–12," p. 396. Nolan suggests that the magi's gifts would also recall the gifts offered to King Solomon by the Queen of Sheba (1 Kings 10:2,10). He also notes how these types of gifts were featured in Jewish royal wedding songs (Song of Songs 3:6, 5:13; Ps. 45:8–9) and were displayed by King Hezekiah as part of the Davidic heritage. B. Nolan, *The Royal Son of God*, pp. 45–46. See also G. Montague, *Companion God*, p. 27: "Gold, frankincense and myrrh were common stock of magicians, but Jewish tradition also saw them as gifts suitable for a king (Ps. 45:8; 72:10, 11, 15; Is. 60:6; Sg. 3:6) and that is probably Matthew's understanding of them here."

[24] R. Brown, *Birth of the Messiah*, pp. 187–88. "The implicit citation of Isa 60:6 and Ps 72:10-11 in [this scene] emphasizes his role as son of Abraham in whom all the nations of the earth are blessed, for at his birth are fulfilled the expectations that people, nay kings, from Sheba and Saba would bring gifts and pay the King homage. The star that rose in the east is the star of the King of the Jews, but this King rules over the nations as well."

[25] Hagner points out that of the ten fulfillment formulas employed by Matthew, only here in 2:23 is the plural "prophets" used. In other places, a specific prophet is named or is referred to as "the prophet." Thus, 2:23 may suggest not a direct reference to a prophet, but to a common theme shared by a number of prophets. In this light, messianic hopes were associated with the "branch" image not only by Isaiah, but also by prophetic texts such as Jeremiah 23:5, 33:15 and Zechariah 3:8, 6:12. D. Hagner, *Matthew 1–13*, p. 41.

[26] R. Brown, *Birth of the Messiah*, p. 219: "The gentilic designation 'Nazarene' also reminds us that Jesus is the messianic 'branch' (neser)—the blossom from the Davidic root predicted in Isa 11:1, as part of Isaiah's continued description of Emmanuel. Thus, with ingenious symmetry Matthew brings together Isaian themes in his first and last citations in the infancy narrative: 'They will call his name Emmanuel' (Isa 7:14) and 'He will be called a Nazarene' (the *neser* of Isa 11:1)." Nolan argues that this interpretation is to be preferred for three reasons: (a) *neser* was part of the messianic hope found in "the prophets," (b) these messianic hopes were continued at Qumran, and (c) the *neser* theme fits well into Matthew's theology. B. Nolan, *The Royal Son of God*, pp. 212–15. See also D. Hagner,

Matthew 1–13, pp. 40–41; G. Segalla, "Il Bambino con Maria sua Madre in Matteo 2," *Theotokos* 4 (1996): 636. For a summary of the various views of this text, see R. Brown, *Birth of the Messiah*, pp. 211–13; D. Hagner, *Matthew 1–13*, pp. 39–41; J. Meier, *Matthew*, p. 16.

[27] B. Nolan, *The Royal Son of God*, p. 42.

[28] In Matthew's narrative telling of Jesus' origins (Mt. 1–2), we do not learn about Gabriel's annunciation to Mary or her response. We do not read about Mary's family, her visit to Elizabeth, the shepherds at Jesus' birth, nor a visit to the Temple. All this is found only in Luke. In contrast, throughout the Matthean narrative, Mary is silent.

[29] "Matthew's version of Jesus' origins focuses on Joseph, whose adoption of the child provides the point of entry into the Davidic line (1:2–17)." P. Perkins, "Mary in the Gospels," p. 300.

[30] In Matthew 12:46–50, Jesus' mother and brothers come to Him and ask to speak to Him. Jesus responds: "Who is my mother and who are my brethren?" Then pointing to His disciples He says, "Here are my mother and my brethren! For whoever does the will of my father in heaven is my brother, and sister, and mother." Softer than Mark's account—which seems to contrast Jesus' physical family, who do not understand Him, from His spiritual family of disciples (Mk. 3:31–35)—Matthew's account simply shows Jesus using the occasion to teach about how His disciples are to Him as family. "Matthew's emphasis falls on the eschatological family of disciples, with the physical family serving more as a catalyst rather than a contrast to the remarks." R. Brown, *Mary in the New Testament*, p. 99. In Matthew 13:53–58, Jesus is rejected by His own countrymen, who say, "Where did this man get this wisdom and these mighty works? Is not this the carpenter's son? Is not his mother called Mary? And are not his brethren James and Joseph and Simon and Judas? And are not all his sisters with us? Where then did this man get all this?" Like the scene in 12:46–50, this scene adds little to our understanding of Mary. "Nothing particularly noteworthy about that family causes the neighbors to expect—or even accept—the possibility that they have produced a 'prophet' (v. 57) or something more than a prophet. As was the case in 12:46–50, the incident focuses on varying responses to Jesus rather than on Mary or other members of Jesus' family." B. Gaventa, *Mary: Glimpses of the Mother of Jesus* (Columbia: University of South Carolina Press, 1995), p. 45.

[31] See discussion below. R. Brown, *Mary in the New Testament*, pp. 77–83.

[32] "Over and over again, Matthew interprets an event in Jesus' life with the formula 'this took place to fulfill what had been spoken by the Lord through the prophet.' Mary's contribution to this governing principle is made quite explicit in the first formula quotation: 'Look, the virgin shall conceive and bear a son, and they shall name him Emmanuel' (1:23). For Matthew, the most important function of Mary is to fulfill this prophecy." B. Gaventa, *Mary*, p. 47.

[33] "The Gospel of Matthew . . . concentrates on the figure of Joseph who came from the tribe of David. Given this, it appears strange for the text to repeat five times in an identical manner the phrase 'the child with his mother' (Mt

2:10,13,14,20,21). This seems to show a special interest in the mother of Jesus."
J. Paredes, *Mary and the Kingdom of God* (Middlegreen: St. Paul Publications,
1991), p. 50. "The persistent use of the phrase 'the child and his mother,' however, should give us pause. While it is true that Matthew 2 refers to Mary only in
connection with Jesus, it is also true that reference to Jesus almost always involves
reference to Mary. With the consistent use of the phrase 'the child and his mother' Matthew reflects a powerful connection between the two." B. Gaventa, *Mary*,
p. 43. For more on this, see discussion below.

[34] S. Ackerman, "The Queen-Mother and the Cult in the Ancient Near East," p.
196; V. Branick, "Mary in the Christologies of the New Testament," *Marian Studies*
32 (1981): 38; B. Buby, *Mary of Galilee*, vol. 2 (New York: Alba House, 1995), pp.
116–18; R. Menninger, *Israel and the Church*, p. 76.

[35] See R. Brown, *Mary in the New Testament*, p. 78; M. Johnson, *The Purpose of the
Biblical Genealogies*, pp. 153–54.

[36] For summaries of various theories on the meaning of the four women in
Matthew's genealogy and their relation to Mary, see *Mary in the New Testament*,
eds. R. Brown, et al. (New York: Paulist Press, 1978), pp. 77–83; R. Brown, *Birth
of the Messiah*, pp. 71–74; G. Montague, *Our Father, Our Mother*, p. 97.

[37] Judah's son came through Tamar who posed as a harlot (Gen. 38:24). Rahab
actually was a Gentile prostitute in Jericho (Josh. 2:1). Ruth was a Moabite, and
Bathsheba was originally married to a Hittite and had an adulterous union with
David. Mary had her own irregular situation as a virgin betrothed to Joseph who
conceived by the Holy Spirit—not only extraordinary, but also potentially scandalous in the eyes of men since she had not yet lived with her husband. R.
Brown, *Mary in the New Testament*, pp. 81–83. The authors of *Mary in the New
Testament* conclude that "what the four women had in common with each other
was not a sinful union (which was true only in Bathsheba's case) but an irregular
or an extraordinary union which might have been despised by outsiders. Yet
through these unions, in which the woman was often the heroic figure, God carried out His promises and plan. Tamar was the instrument of God's grace by get-
ting Judah to propagate the messianic line; it was through Rahab's courage that
Israel entered the Promised Land; it was through Ruth's initiative that she and
Boaz became great-grandparents of King David; and it was through Bathsheba's
intervention that the Davidic throne passed to Solomon. The advantage of this
theory is that it does not go beyond the biblical evidence and that it gives the
women something in common with Mary as she will be described in Matt
1:18–25" (p. 82).

[38] J. Meier, *Matthew*, pp. 4–5.

[39] "This irregularity and hint of scandal gives Mary's marital situation something in
common with that of Tamar, Rahab, Ruth and Bathsheba." R. Brown, *Mary in the
New Testament*, p. 85. Meier notes how the four women "represent 'holy irregularities' in God's orderly plan. . . . All four women point ahead to the supreme holy
irregularity, the supreme discontinuity: the virginal conception of Jesus by Mary."
J. Meier, *Matthew*, p. 5. Also R. Brown, *Birth of the Messiah*, pp. 73–74; D. Hagner,
Matthew 1–13, p. 10.

[40] V. Branick, "Mary in the Christologies of the New Testament," p. 38. Cf. A. Del Moral, "Santa María, La Guebiráh Mesiánica," p. 48.

[41] S. Ackerman, "The Queen-Mother and the Cult in the Ancient Near East," p. 197. See also her footnote 95: "The Bible itself makes explicit this connection between the royal line as descended from Judah to Perez and as descended from Boaz to Obed and then to Jesse, David's father: see Ruth 4:12." See also Ruth 4:18–22, which traces the lineage from Judah through Salmon and Boaz to David.

[42] R. Menninger, *Israel and the Church*, p. 76. After considering Tamar, Ruth, and Bathsheba, Menninger goes on to say "Even Rahab is considered by Matthew to have given birth to an ancestor of David (i.e. Salmon, the father of Boaz) although there is no [Old Testament] evidence to confirm this. What is true of this group is true of Mary: these women bore children which were of the house of David. This common denominator links the four women of the [Old Testament] with Mary. . . . If this conclusion about the four women is correct, then they were included in the genealogy in order to show that Jesus is the Davidic Messiah."

[43] "The statement that Boaz was the child of Rahab . . . has no other biblical support and is curious since the famous Rahab . . . lived at the time of the conquest, nearly two centuries before Boaz' time." R. Brown, *Birth of the Messiah*, p. 60. "Tamar, Ruth, and Bathsheba have their place as wives of Judah-ites and ancestors of David. But Rahab is not associated with the royal house in the Bible. She is absent from the apocrypha or pseudepigrapha and Philo; and she is never explicitly connected with the Davidids in the rabbinic writings." B. Nolan, *The Royal Son of God*, p. 62.

[44] J. Paredes, *Mary and the Kingdom of God*, p. 58. See also V. Branick, "Mary in the Christologies of the New Testament," p. 38; A. Serra, "Bibbia," pp. 218–19; B. Nolan, *The Royal Son of God*, p. 43; S. Ackerman, "The Queen-Mother and the Cult in the Ancient Near East," pp. 197–98; J. Bastero de Eleizalde, "Fundamentos Cristológicos de la Realeza de María," *EstMar* 51 (1986): 207.

[45] As discussed in chapter two.

[46] "Qui richiamo semplicemente il carattere 'regale' del passo matteano. Da una parte abbiamo la *almâh*, ossia la giovane sposa di Achaz, madre dell'Emmanuele, il re Ezechia, la cui nascita e il cui regno assicurano la sopravvivenza della dinastia davidica, allora gravemente minacciata. Dall'altra abbiamo Maria, 'la vergine' che, senza conoscere uomo, diviene madre del Cristo, re-messia; egli è il perfetto Emmanuele, il 'Dio con noi' (Mt 1,23; cf 28,20), che garantisce la continuità perenne della nuova casa di Davide, cioè la chiesa, contro ogni potenza avversa (cf Mt 16,18)." A. Serra, "Regina," p. 1073.

[47] A. Serra, "Bibbia," p. 219. "Come ella diede alla luce un figlio che garantì la continuità della casa di Davide, così Maria dà alla luce un figlio che regnerà per sempre sul trono di Davide, nella casa di Giacobbe, nell''Israele di Dio' (cf Mt 28,20; 16,18; Gal 6,16; 2 Sam 7,16); si noti la 'regalità' delle due madri. Inoltre, come la nascita di Ezechia ebbe carattere di prodigio, in quanto fu preannuciata dal profeta quale 'segno', così la nascita di Cristo fu sommamente prodigiosa in quanto fu concepito da una vergine, per sola virtù dello Spirito (Mt 1,18.20)."

[48] See Mt. 2:11, 13, 14, 20, 21. "Throughout chapter 2, Matthew refers to 'the child with Mary his mother' (Matthew 2:11) or 'the child and his mother' (Matthew 2:13,14,20,21), binding the two figures together in one inextricable image." B. Gaventa, "Glimpses of Mary," *Bible Review* (April 1996): 17.

[49] V. Branick, "Mary in the Christologies of the New Testament," p. 38; B. Nolan, *The Royal Son of God*, p. 43; R. Brown, *Birth of the Messiah*, p. 192 n. 32; G. Segalla, "Il Bambino con Maria Sua Madre in Matteo 2," *Theotokos* 4 (1996): 17.

[50] B. Nolan, *The Royal Son of God*, p. 43. "Matthew's catchphrase 'the child and his mother' has a Davidic resonance which is echoed in prophecies recognized as messianic by the early Church."

[51] V. Branick, "Mary in the Christologies of the New Testament," p. 38. G. Segalla, "Il Bambino con Maria Sua Madre in Matteo 2," *Theotokos* 4 (1996): 17–18: "Maria si presenta *sempre insieme al bambino* come colui che abita nella casa ove i magi trovano il bambino, e poi sempre insieme a lui nella vicenda dolorosa della fuga e del ritorno, sotto la regia dell'angelo del Signore e la guida silenziosa di Giuseppe." He later concludes that Mary is "madre di questo 're' ed è perciò regina-madre." Nolan argues that repetition of "the child and his mother" in Matthew 2 also may recall the Isaiah 7:14 prophecy in which a queen mother gave birth to a royal son, Immanuel, who was referred to as "the child" (7:14) (as discussed above). B. Nolan, *The Royal Son of God*, p. 42. L. Deiss, although he does not explicitly mention the queen-mother theme, does see Mary's motherhood taken up into her son's royalty: "The royalty of the Davidic line thus confers on Mary's motherhood a new dignity, a royal dignity. Mary is not simply the Mother of the 'Child Jesus'; she is also the mother of the King. *Her motherhood is a royal motherhood.*" L. Deiss, *Mary: Daughter of Zion* (Collegeville: Liturgical Press, 1972), p. 40, emphasis added.

[52] Brown shows how this scene moves from Jerusalem toward Bethlehem, where it reaches its climax. R. Brown, *Birth of the Messiah*, p. 178. Aragon notes how the places mentioned in the narrative move from the east (2:1, 2, 9) to Judea (2:1, 5), to Jerusalem (2:1, 3), to Bethlehem (2:1, 5, 6, 8), and finally to the house where the mother and child are (2:11). "Este movimiento geográfico centrípeto pone de relieve que el lugar que Mateo quiere destacar como centro de su relato es precisamente aquella casa." R. Aragon, "La Madre con el Niño en la Casa: Un Estudio Narratologico," *EphMar* 43 (1993): 50.

[53] See discussion on the Davidic themes in this passage above.

[54] "Matthew reflects a poweful connection between [Jesus and Mary]. When the magi finally arrive at the place of the star, they see both the child and Mary. The flight to Egypt involves not two parents and the child they protect but Joseph who is instructed to protect 'the child and his mother.' . . . In Matthew's story, the two belong together." B. Gaventa, *Mary*, p. 43.

[55] R. Aragon, "La Madre con el Niño en la Casa," pp. 54–55. "Su mención en este momento, junto con la omisión de José, subraya que María es una persona especialmente importante para el narrador y por ello la coloca en esta posición tan destacada." Also G. Segalla, "Il Bambino con Maria Sua Madre," p. 19: "Nella sequenza dei magi Maria, madre del bambino, compare sulla scena *da sola*; Giuseppe, protag-

onista nelle altre tre sequenze . . . qui scompare dietreo alle quinte. . . . All'inizio Maria compare come primo personaggio dopo Gesù Cristo. Giuseppe è implicato nella vicenda misteriosa come suo sposo, custode del mistero e mediatore della regia divina nel salvare Gesù. E perciò scompare ove la sua presenza non è necessaria."

[56] "Matthew makes it very clear that the infant is king, Israel's Messiah, son of David (1:1, 20; 2:2, 6, 11). Clearly, Mary is the Gebirah, the queen-mother." G. Montague, *Our Father, Our Mother*, p. 97. "I magi . . . rappresentano perciò le genti che riconoscono in Gesù il Messia-re e in Maria la sua nobile regina-madre." G. Segalla, "Il Bambino Con Maria Sua Madre in Matteo 2," p. 18. Others who see Mary being portrayed in this scene in light of the queen mother of the Old Testament, include V. Branick, "Mary in the Christologies of the New Testament," p. 38; A. Serra, "Regina," p. 1073; O. Lukefahr, *Christ's Mother and Ours* (Liguori, MO: Liguori, 1998), p. 39; G. Del Moral, "Santa María, La Guebiráh Mesiánica," p. 42; G. Segalla, "Il Bambino con Maria Sua Madre," p. 18; J. Bastero de Eleizalde, "Fundamentos Cristológicos de la Realeza de Maria," p. 208. See also E. Smith, "The Scriptural Basis for Mary's Queenship," p. 115: "It is a forceful episode that makes the presence of Our Lady something more than mere association or coincidence. The exegete is compelled to evaluate oriental customs with their stern traditions that permeate this context of Matthew. They predicate a royalty in the mother both temporal and spiritual." Although Smith wrote this before many scholars began emphasizing the Old Testament significance of the queen mother, he still was able to note how this scene points not only to Christ's royalty, but Mary's as well.

[57] R. Brown, *Birth of the Messiah*, p. 192 n. 32.

[58] V. Branick, "Mary in the Christologies of the New Testament," p. 38. Similarly, Serra concludes: "Giuseppe, che pure occupa un ruolo di primo piano in Mt 1-2, quasi scompare. Riemerge forse qui la tradizione veterotestamentaria sulla *gebiráh*: ora *è Maria la regina-madre del neonato re-messia*; le sue ginocchia sono il trono naturale ove siede la maestà regale del bambino." A. Serra, "Regina," p. 1073.

[59] "En el acto de la adoración de los Magos, S. Mateo, buen conocedor de las tradiciones davídicas, pensando en los destinatarios de su evangelio, no omite el detalle significativo de mostrar 'al niño con María, su madre' y de esta forma asocia y confirma a María como la *gebiráh* del reino mesianico. Además es Ella quien entroniza y presenta al Rey-Mesías a la adoración de los Magos, ejercitando una de las misiones específicas de la *gebiráh*." J. Bastero de Eleizalde, "Fundamentos Cristológicos de la Realeza de Maria," p. 208. Bastero de Eleizalde rightly disagrees with Del Moral's assertion that the Magi offer their gifts and homage to both the child Jesus *and* to Mary. "No podemos estar de acuerdo con esta afirmación, pues el texto sagrado dice taxativamente que la adoración y el ofrecimiento de los dones fue exclusivamente al Niño." *Contra*: G. Del Moral, "Santa María, La Guebiráh Mesiánica," p. 42.

[60] While it is possible that the queen-mother theme also may shed light on Mary being linked with the four women in the genealogy, as discussed above, this is less certain since this theory does not necessarily account for Rahab's inclusion in the genealogy.

[61] R. Brown, *Birth of the Messiah*, p. 318. Brown has developed this theme in a number of his works, including "The Annunciation to Mary, the Visitation, and the Magnificat (Luke 1:26–56)," *Worship* 62 (1988): 254–59; "The Meaning of Modern New Testament Studies for an Ecumenical Understanding of Mary," in *Biblical Reflections on Crises Facing the Church* (New York: Paulist, 1975), pp. 87–95; *Birth of the Messiah*, pp. 318–19. See also J. Fitzmyer, *The Gospel According to Luke: I–IX* (Garden City, NY: Doubleday, 1981), p. 341; P. Bearsely, "Mary The Perfect Disciple: A Paradigm for Mariology," *TS* 41 (1980): 474–78; B. Buby, *Mary of Galilee*, pp. 76, 98–99; J. Paredes, *Mary and the Kingdom of God*, pp. 76, 90–91, 101–2; cf. J. McKenzie, "The Mother of Jesus in the New Testament," in H. Kung and J. Moltmann, eds. *Mary in the Churches*, (Edinburgh: T&T Clark, 1983), p. 8. The authors of *Mary in the New Testament* argue that in Luke–Acts, Mary is shown to be the first Christian disciple and first believer in the true family of God. See R. Brown, *Mary in the New Testament*, pp. 125–26, 135–37, 142, 151, 157, 162, 168, 171, 174. They note how the blessed in Christ's eschatological family are those who hear the Word of God and keep it (Lk. 8:21). At the Annunciation, Mary accepts God's word from the Angel Gabriel (1:38). At the Visitation, Elizabeth says Mary is blessed not only for being the physical mother of the Messiah (1:42), but also because she has believed that there would be a fulfillment of what was spoken to her from the Lord (1:45). Responding to the shepherd's report about the message of the angels and to the cryptic words of Jesus after being found in the Temple, Mary *kept* all these things in her heart (2:19, 52). In Simeon's words at the presentation about a sword piercing her soul, Luke shows us that Mary will not be spared the painful test of discipleship (2:34–35). "If thus far [Luke] has shown Mary as passing the test of obedience (1:38, 45), he has also hinted that the learning process is an ongoing one (2:19); here he insists that it is a process that is not without its peril and its sufferings [2:34–5]" (p. 157). Furthermore, Luke shows that Jesus' mother and brothers have met the criteria for being part of His eschatological family since they too "hear the word of God and keep it" (8:21, cf. 11:27–28). Finally, after the Ascension, Mary is mentioned as being devoted to prayer with the disciples in Jerusalem. In all these things, Luke shows us that Mary meets the criteria of discipleship and was the first to meet the standards of what it means to be part of the eschatological family. "In the overall Lucan picture of Mary, 11:28 stresses that Jesus' mother is worthy of a beatitude, yet not simply because she has given birth to a child. Her beatitude must be based on the fact that she has heard, believed, obeyed, kept and pondered the word, and continued to do it (Acts 1:14)" (p. 172).

[62] J. Fitzmyer, *Luke*, p. 341; J. Paredes, *Mary and the Kingdom of God*, pp. 72, 89; J. McHugh, *The Mother of Jesus*, p. 54; L. Deiss, *Mary: Daughter of Zion*, p. 54.

[63] M. Strauss, *The Davidic Messiah in Luke–Acts: The Promise and Its Fulfillment in Lukan Christology* (JSNTSup 110) (Sheffield Academic Press, 1995), p. 87. The virginal conception in no way would diminish Joseph's fatherhood, since his legal paternity would have been viewed as a realistic fatherhood which would have brought Jesus into Joseph's family heritage. See also I. Marshall, *The Gospel of Luke* (Grand Rapids: Eerdmans, 1978), p. 157. In commenting on the genealogy in Lk. 3 which speaks of Jesus as being "the son (as was supposed) of Joseph . . . the son of David," Marshall explains: "There is no inconsistency in Luke's mind between

the account of the virgin birth and the naming of Joseph as one of the parents of Jesus. From the legal point of view, Joseph was the earthly father of Jesus, and there was no other way of reckoning his descent. There is no evidence that the compilers of the genealogies thought otherwise."

[64] "Joseph—who has scarcely any role in Luke 1-2 and is only mentioned otherwise in 3:23—receives more of an introduction than Mary, the primary character in the birth narrative. Why? Luke is interested in his royal ancestry. He is 'of the house of David' (v. 27), and this prepares for the identification of his (albeit adopted) son as a Davidide." J. Green, *The Gospel of Luke* (Grand Rapids: Eerdmans, 1997), pp. 84–85. See also J. McHugh, *The Mother of Jesus in the New Testament*, p. 53. McHugh notes how there is "a hint" of Jesus' messianic identity already in 1:27, "where Mary is said to have been betrothed to a man named Joseph, 'of the house of David': any child of Mary would trace his legal ancestry through Joseph, and would therefore be a member of the house of David." Also C. Evans, *Luke* (London: SCM Press, 1990), p. 160; M. Strauss, *The Davidic Messiah in Luke-Acts*, p. 87. Brown also notes how this Davidic emphasis in the Annunciation is fitting and prepares the reader for understanding Christ's messianic mission in the rest of Luke: "In this annunciation the place is Nazareth in Galilee and the heritage is Davidic-circumstances befitting gospel characters like Mary and Joseph intimately involved with Jesus, whose public ministry will be in Galilee and who is the Messiah of the house of David." R. Brown, "The Annunciation to Mary, the Visitation and the Magnificat," p. 251.

[65] J. Fitzmyer, *Luke*, p. 337.

[66] Gen. 14:14–20, 22; Num. 24:16; Ps. 7:17; 2 Sam. 22:14. D. Bock, *Proclamation from Prophecy and Pattern: Lukan Old Testament Christology* (JSNTSup 12) (Sheffield: Sheffield Academic Press, 1987), p. 64. Fitzmyer notes how Luke uses this title for God more than any other New Testament author: Luke 1:35, 76, 6:35, 8:28; Acts 7:48, 16:17. J. Fitzmyer, *Luke*, p. 348. See also L. Johnson, *Luke* (Collegeville: Liturgical Press, 1991), p. 37; R. Brown, *Birth of the Messiah*, p. 289.

[67] "According to the angel's words, Jesus will be 'Son of the Most High,' a designation synonymous with 'Son of God.' This will be made clearer in v. 35." J. Green, *The Gospel of Luke*, p. 89. Bock notes this title's messianic significance: Jesus as Son of the Most High "is another reference to the sonship which places Jesus in the context of being the Davidic ruler." D. Bock, *Proclamation from Prophecy and Pattern*, p. 64.

[68] Cf. 2 Sam. 7:14; 1 Chron. 17:13, 22:10, 28:6; Ps. 2:7, 89:26–27. In fact, Luke associates Jesus' kingship and sonship elsewhere (cf. Lk. 4:41, 22:29, 67–70; Acts 9:20–22). "This was one form of the hope of Israel; cf. Ps. So. 17:23, 'Lord raise up for them their king, the Son of David'—which was based on the promise in 2 Sam. 7:12-14 of a son of God from David's line on the throne of his kingdom. For literal fulfillment Jesus as the Son of David (18:38; 20:41) must have David as well as God for *his father*." C. Evans, *Saint Luke*, p. 162.

[69] D. Bock, *Proclamation from Prophecy and Pattern*, p. 64. Also p. 65: "*Luke presents this son of God theme consistently in terms of the Davidic deliverer as found in the regal Christ.*" See also M. Strauss, *The Davidic Messiah in Luke-Acts*, p. 88; R.

Brown, *Birth of the Messiah*, pp. 310, 312; C. Evans, *Saint Luke*, p. 161; J. Green, *The Gospel of Luke*, pp. 89–90.

[70] According to Evans, the child being given by God "the throne of his father David" could be "an extension of Jesus' title 'Son of the Most High' expressed in terms of the Davidic king who was called God's Son (Ps. 2:7)." C. Evans, *Saint Luke*, p. 162. Also J. Fitzmyer, *Luke*, p. 348. See Ellis who notes how 4QFlor intertwines the messianic 'Son of God' with a never-ending kingship by using the same passage 2 Samuel 7:10–14. E. Ellis, *The Gospel of Luke* (London: Nelson, 1966), p. 71.

[71] "Jacob" was an ancient designation for Israel (Gen 46:27; Ex. 19:3; Is. 8:17). Thus, these words refer to the child being king over all of Israel. See L. Johnson, *Luke*, p. 37. With this background, the child reigning "over the house of Jacob" probably recalls how David was the king who ruled over all of Israel. As Deiss explains, "Like David Jesus possesses the throne of Jerusalem and at the same time is king over the house of Jacob. The unification of the North and the South achieved under David was thus a prophetic foreshadowing of the spiritual unification that Jesus would accomplish, a thousand years later, in the messianic kingdom." L. Deiss, *Mary: Daughter of Zion*, p. 39.

[72] "Possibly Luke alludes here to Isa 9:6 (LXX) or to Daniel 7:14, where promise of an everlasting kingdom is made. The endless character of this kingship is thus one of the qualities of the messianic kingdom. At this point in the Lukan Gospel the kingship should be understood in terms of the OT theme of kingdom (e.g. as in Ps. 45:7). Jesus in some sense is to be anointed descendant of David and restorer of ancient kingship (Amos 9:11)." J. Fitzmyer, *Luke*, p. 348.

[73] Numerous scholars have discussed these parallels. For example: E. Schillebeeckx, *Mary, Mother of the Redemption* (New York: Sheed and Ward, 1964), p. 9; J. Fitzmyer, *Luke*, pp. 338–39; J. Green, *The Gospel of Luke*, p. 88; L. Deiss, *Mary: Daughter of Zion*, pp. 38–39. R. Brown, *Birth of the Messiah*, pp. 310–11. R. Nelson, "David: A Model for Mary in Luke?" *Biblical Theology Bulletin* 18 (October 1988): 139; A. Valentini, "Editoriale: L'Annuncio a Maria," *Theotokos* 4 (1996): 286.

[74] R. Brown, *Birth of the Messiah*, pp. 310–11. Brown shows how Gabriel quotes that promise from 2 Samuel 7 "in a slightly rephrased manner" (which he notes was customary at the time, as is seen in the Dead Sea Scrolls). R. Brown, "The Annunciation to Mary, the Visitation, and the Magnificat," p. 253.

[75] R. Brown, *Birth of the Messiah*, p. 310.

[76] Similar to Luke, the Qumran interpretation of 2 Samuel 7:10–14 viewed Nathan's oracle as promising a single Davidic king, the messianic 'shoot' who will rule with wisdom and justice in the last days. J. Fitzmyer, *Luke*, pp. 338–39; L. Johnson, *The Gospel of Luke*, p. 37; R. Brown, *Birth of the Messiah*, p. 311.

[77] J. Green, *The Gospel of Luke*, p. 88. Similarly, Bock argues that in addition to 2 Samuel 7, Luke has in mind the entire prophetic tradition about the Davidic kingdom. "Thus, for Luke, Jesus fulfills the promise made to David by Nathan of a future son, who in the Prophets and Psalms was raised to a status of climactic pro-

portions (2 Sam. 7:8-17, esp. 13, 16; 1 Kings 2:24-25 refers to Solomon as the ful-fillment to the establishment of a Davidic house; Ps. 89, esp. 1-3, 19-29, 35-37; Isa. 9:6-7; 11:1-5, 10; and Jer. 23:5-6). Luke has this whole developed prophetic motif in view and not one specific passage. The added descriptive elements of Jesus' ruling 'over the house of Jacob forever' and that 'his kingdom shall not end' makes the Davidic emphasis clear." D. Bock, *Proclamation from Prophecy and Pattern*, pp. 62–63.

[78] M. Strauss, *The Davidic Messiah in Luke-Acts*, p. 89: "This indicates, at the least, that this Davidic-messianic motif has a prominent place in Luke's Christological presentation." See N. Wright, who shows how the story of David may be a possi-ble framework for the story of Luke-Acts. N. Wright, *The New Testament and the People of God* (Minneapolis: Fortress, 1992), pp. 378–84.

[79] J. Fitzmyer, *Luke*, p. 337.

[80] R. Brown, *Birth of the Messiah*, pp. 311–12.

[81] Strauss suggests that Luke 1:35 may be joining the theme of the Spirit coming on the king and the divine begetting of the king in Psalm 2:7. He notes how the idea of the Spirit descending on men and the theme of divine sonship are found in the Old Testament, but there is no precedent in Judaism for the divine generation of a son of God by the Spirit like that found here in Luke 1:35. Strauss argues that Luke's combination of these two themes can be understood in light of the Davidic king upon whom the Spirit would fall (1 Sam. 16:13; Is. 11:1–4) and the 'beget-ting' of the royal Messiah in Psalm 2:7. "The verse [Lk. 1:35] thus appears to be an *original application* of the creative role of the Spirit, perhaps linking it to the idea of the begetting of the king as in Ps. 2:7." M. Strauss, *The Davidic Messiah in Luke-Acts*, p. 91. See also R. Brown, *Birth of the Messiah*, pp. 311–12.

[82] "Luke seems to be consciously opposing the view that Jesus' divine sonship is merely 'functional'—a special relationship with God by virtue of his role as king. He is rather the Son of God from the point of conception, before he has taken on any of the functions of kingship." M. Strauss, *The Davidic Messiah in Luke-Acts*, p. 93. Strauss continues: "In verse 35, then, Luke clarifies the meaning of the Davidic Messiah's father-son relationship with God by linking Jesus' divine sonship to his conception by the Spirit, thus connecting this sonship to his divine origin rather than merely to his *role* as king" (p. 94).

[83] J. Fitzmyer, *Luke*, p. 339–40. Similarly, see J. Green, *The Gospel of Luke*, p. 91. "Jesus is 'Son of God' not as a consequence of his assuming the throne of David (as in Ps. 2:7), but as a result of his conception, itself the work of the Spirit. . . . [T]hough Luke is not working with Johannine or later Trinitarian categories, he is nonetheless moving toward a more ontological (and not only functional) under-standing of Jesus' sonship."

[84] J. Fitzmyer, *Luke*, p. 340.

[85] Strauss explains that a development in the Jewish understanding of the Messiah-king's sonship explains the different emphasis in Luke 1:32 (sonship by role as king) and 1:35 (sonship by origin as seen in the divine intervention). Certainly, Luke did not see these two verses as contradictory since he has placed them side-

by-side. M. Strauss, *The Davidic Messiah in Luke-Acts*, p. 93 n. 1. See also R. Brown, *Mary in the New Testament*, pp. 116–17. After noting how Romans 1:3–4 moves from "son of David" to "Son of God," the authors conclude that in Luke 1:32–35, "there is no conflict in progressing from a Davidic portrait to the description of Jesus as Son of God."

[86] Cf. R. Tannehill, *The Narrative Unity of Luke-Acts* (Philadelphia: Fortress, 1986), p. 25: "To be sure, 1:35 indicates that the title Son of God belongs to Jesus in light of his wondrous conception, a motif which goes beyond the Old Testament idea of the king as God's son. However, this does not mean that the traditional royal Messiah is being replaced with a different sort of Son of God. Jesus as Davidic Messiah and fulfiller of Israel's hope for a messianic king has greater continuing importance in Luke-Acts than the virgin birth does. For the author, the virgin birth is an indication of God's purpose and power at the very beginning of Jesus' life, and *this wondrous beginning does not compete with the view that he is Son of God as Davidic king but attributes his kingship to prevenient divine action*" (emphasis added).

[87] M. Strauss, *The Davidic Messiah in Luke-Acts*, p. 93. Although Bock is open to the ontological meaning of Jesus' sonship in Luke 1:35, he stresses that Jesus' divine sonship should be understood primarily in terms of his being the Davidic Messiah. D. Bock, *Proclamation from Prophecy and Pattern*, pp. 65–66: "Luke presents this Son of God theme consistently in terms of the Davidic deliverer as found in the regal Christ. . . . Thus, if Luke is stressing a divine element in Jesus' birth in calling him Son of God, it is *not* in an explicit statement of metaphysical divinity but only an assertion that his origins are divinely grounded in the Spirit's creative power. He is from God in a unique way. An ontological statement may be implied here but it is *not* what Luke *emphasizes* in using and in describing this title."

[88] J. McHugh, *The Mother of Jesus in the New Testament*, p. 54. Similarly, Strauss concludes: "The description of the birth in v. 31 is verbally similar to Gen. 16:11 and Isa. 7:14 (cf. Judg. 13.3, 5), and may be a conscious allusion to the latter with the name 'Immanuel' changed to Jesus." M. Strauss, *The Davidic Messiah in Luke-Acts*, p. 88. See also E. Ellis, *The Gospel of Luke*, p. 70. A. Valentini, "L'Annuncio a Maria," p. 285; R. Tannehill, *Luke* (Nashville: Abingdon Press, 1996), p. 49.

[89] For the similarities between these texts and Genesis 16:11 LXX, see M. Bock, *Proclamation from Prophecy and Pattern*, p. 62. Bock compares Isaiah 7:14 LXX and Luke 1:31 as follows:

Isaiah 7:14 (LXX)	ιδοὺ ἡ παρθένος ἐν γαστρὶ ἕξει καὶ τέξεται υἱὸν καὶ καλέσεις τὸ ὄνομα αὐτοῦ Ἐμμανουηλ
Luke 1:31	καὶ ἰδοὺ συλλήμψη ἐν γαστρὶ καὶ τέξη υἱὸν καὶ καλέσεις τὸ ὄνομα αὐτοῦ Ἰησουν

Although Bock argues that "verbally Lk. 1.31 is not closer to Isa. 7.14 than to Gen 16.11," the Davidic context of Luke 1:31 and the emphasis on Mary as παρθένος shows us that Luke must have had Isaiah 7:14, and not Genesis 16:11, *primarily* in mind. Also see M. Strauss, *The Davidic Messiah in Luke-Acts*, p. 88: "While the language of the verse is as close to Gen. 16.11 LXX as to Isa. 7.14 LXX . . . the description of Mary as (Lk. 1.27, 34; cf. Isa. 7.14 LXX), the reference to the οἶκος Δαυιδ

(Lk. 1.27; Isa. 7.13 LXX), and the greeting 'the Lord is *with you* ' [sic] (Lk. 1.28; cf. Isa. 7.14, 'Immanuel')—all in the context of Davidic expectations—suggest that Luke indeed had Isa. 7.14 in mind."

[90] J. Fitzmyer, *Luke*, p. 336.

[91] J. Green, *The Gospel of Luke*, p. 85 n. 15. Also M. Strauss, *The Davidic Messiah in Luke-Acts*, p. 88 n. 1.

[92] J. Fitzmyer, *Luke*, pp. 336, 348–9. For example, Fitzmyer argues that the description of Mary as "*a virgin betrothed to a man*" in Luke 1:27 is much closer to Deuteronomy 22:23 than to Isaiah 7:14 (pp. 336, 343). Further, "the House of David" is a stereotyped phrase from the Old Testament (e.g. 1 Kings 12:19; 2 Chron. 23:3), not just from Isaiah 7:14 (p. 344). Also, "The Lord is with you" is found throughout the Old Testament, but was used specifically as a greeting in Ruth 2:4 and Judges 6:12. When considering Luke 1:31, Fitzmyer argues: "The message to Mary is couched in rather stereotyped [Old Testament] phraseology for announcing the conception and birth of an extraordinary child" (p. 346). Here, the language seems to echo not just Isaiah 7:14, but Genesis 16:11 as well: "Behold, you are with child and shall bear a son; you shall call his name Ischmael" (cf. Judg. 13:3, 5).

[93] Brown holds a similar position. He lays out two principle arguments for opposing an Isaiah 7:14 background to Luke 1:31. First, just because both Luke 1:26–32 and Isaiah 7:13–14 refer to the "House of David" does not mean that Luke was necessarily dependent on Isaiah since the House of David theme is found in Nathan's oracle (2 Sam. 7:8ff.) which, as we have seen, is clearly in the background of Luke 1:32–33. Second, Luke's mention of a virgin who is told "you will conceive in your womb and bear a son, and you shall call his name . . ." (Lk. 1:31) is not necessarily dependent on Isaiah 7:14, since these phrases and themes are common to numerous birth annunciations in the Old Testament (see Gen. 16:11). He concludes, agreeing with Fitzmyer, that "there is no way of knowing that Luke was drawing upon Isa 7:14." R. Brown, *Birth of the Messiah*, p. 300. See also, Bock who admits that Isaiah 7:14 may have been in Luke's mind, but it is not central. "If it is present, it is but a small piece of a portrait with many other larger elements." D. Bock, *Proclamation from Prophecy and Pattern*, pp. 61–62.

[94] Marshall, for example, recognizes a resemblance with other Old Testament annunciation scenes, but also recognizes that it reflects Isaiah 7:14. I. Marshall, *The Gospel of Luke*, p. 66.

[95] "Le parole 'Ecco concepirai un figlio e lo darai alla luce' evocano non solo in generale i diversi annunci dell'Antico Testamento, ma in particolare Is 7,14, con la sola differenza che il nome *Gesù* prende il posto di *Emmanuele*." A. Valentini, "Lc 1,39-45: Primi Indizi di Venerazione della Madre del Signore," *Marianum* 58 (1996): 342; Also H. Cazelles, "La Mère du Roi-Messie," p. 55: The words of Luke 1:31 evoke "non seulement les annonces faites dans l'Ancien Testament (Gen. XVI, 11; Jud. XIII, 7) mais surtout Is VII, 14. Il en est de même du nom, sauf que Jésus, Sauveur, remplace Emmanuel."

[96] J. Green, *The Gospel of Luke*, p. 85. Although Green does not think Luke is attempting to narrate the explicit *fulfillment* of Isaiah 7:14, he nevertheless sees

Isaiah 7:14 as playing an important part in the shaping of Luke 1:31. See p. 88 as well. For a view which does see Luke 1:31 as an actual fulfillment of Isaiah 7:14, see B. Buby, *Mary of Galilee: Mary in the New Testament*, p. 73: "In verses 31 and 32 we have Luke's more subtle way of showing fulfillment of a promise made in the Scriptures. Luke does not use a direct citation of Isaiah 7:14 as Matthew had done, but rather implies it. The birth of Jesus is foretold in this Lukan Annunciation in the light of the Emmanuel passage (compare Lk 1:31 with Mt 1:23 [Is 7:14]). Luke in a subtle way uses the thought of the text so that it fits into the actual calling of Mary to respond in trust and faith to the angel."

[97] M. Strauss, *The Davidic Messiah in Luke-Acts*, p. 88 n. 1. Another link between the two texts is seen in the fact that both the woman of Isaiah 7:14 and Mary are singled out as the ones who are to name the royal child. The husbands are not mentioned in this regard. A. Valentini, "L'Annuncio a Maria," p. 285. Unlike Matthew's Gospel, in which Joseph is highlighted as the one giving the name to the child (Mt. 1:21), Luke portrays Mary as the one who "shall call his name Jesus" (Lk. 1:31). Valentini concludes: "Diversamente da Lc 1,13 (cf Mt 1,21), è lei che attribuisce il nome (come in Is 7,14 TM): l'averlo sottolineato è un discreto accenno alla maternità verginale." Similarly, Montague sees an allusion to Isaiah 7:14 in the words "and *you* shall call him" (Lk. 1:31), thus establishing another link between the Virgin Mary in Luke and the young woman in Isaiah 7:14 who will bear the royal child and "*who shall call his name* Immanuel." G. Montague, *Our Father, Our Mother*, pp. 95–96.

[98] J. McHugh, *The Mother of Jesus*, p. 54, emphasis added. See also L. Deiss, *Mary: Daughter of Zion*, p. 39: "Christ, the Son of David, is King. Mary is the Mother of the King, the Mother of the true Son of David." J. Fitzmyer, *Luke*, p. 341; J. Paredes, *Mary and the Kingdom of God*, pp. 72, 89.

[99] S. De Fiores, "Regina," pp. 1080–81; A. Serra, "Regina," pp. 1073–74; D. Bertetto, *Maria la Serva del Signore* (Napoli: Edizioni Dehoniane, 1988), pp. 439–40; J. Ibánez and F. Mendoza, *La Madre del Redentor* (Madrid: Ediciones Palabra, 1988), p. 290; G. Del Moral, "Santa María, La Guebiráh Messiánica," p. 44; T. Gray, "God's Word and Mary's Royal Office," p. 384; G. Kirwin, *Nature of the Queenship*, pp. 21–22; H. Cazelles, "La Mere du Roi-Messie," pp. 55–56; O. Lukefahr, *Christ's Mother and Ours*, p. 39.

[100] See T. Gray, "God's Word and Mary's Royal Office," p. 384: "Because the kingship of Jesus is described by Gabriel in Davidic terms, it is easy to conclude that Mary's role can likewise be understood in the context of the Davidic tradition. And since it was customary, in Israel, that the mother of the king was queen, . . . it would make sense to conclude that Mary as the mother of Christ was de facto Gebirah."

[101] S. Ackerman, "The Queen-Mother and the Cult of the Ancient Near East," p. 196. Similarly, De Fiores argues that Mary has the role of queen mother in this passage because she is being invited to become mother of the messianic king. De Fiores concludes "Maria è pertanto la *ghebiráh* del NT." S. De Fiores, "Regina," p. 1081. R. Laurentin, *The Truth of Christmas* (Petersham, MA: St. Bede's, 1986), p. 46: "Whenever in Luke Jesus is identified with the Messiah, Mary is identified with the

Gebirah, mother of the king, a very important character according to the background of Jewish culture."

[102] A Valentini, "Lc 1,39-45," p. 348: "Genitrice del Messia davidico, Maria è la *gebirah*, la gloriosa regina-madre alla quale va l'omaggio e la venerazione di tutto il popolo messianico."

[103] "Grazie all'intreccio di questi annunci [Isaiah 7:14 and 2 Sam 7], il testo lucano si sofferma anche sulla madre vergine del Messia. Ella è la madre del Re, la *Gebirah*, la Regina-madre, con tutta la dignità che questa figura riveste nella cultura del Medio Oriente e nella tradizione d'Israele." A. Valentini, "Editoriale," p. 290. In another article, Valentini explains, "In questa luce, su questo sfondo di ideologia regale, nella quale la *gebirah* gode di un prestigio unico accanto al re, è da intendere l'espressione piena di stupore di Elisabetta portavoce della comunità lucana: 'A che debbo che la Madre del mio Signore venga a me?'" A. Valentini, "Lc 1,39-45," p. 342.

[104] G. Kirwin, *Nature of the Queenship*, pp. 21–22. Kirwin shows how the angel's words in Luke 1:31–32 allude to the prophecies of the Old Testament which spoke of the Messiah and his royal mother and show their fulfillment in Jesus and Mary. "The Isaian prophecies (7:7, 9:6) and Miceas, 6:2 clearly allude to the regal dignity of the Messiah. They do not *directly* indicate the same dignity in the woman who will give birth to him. But, does not the messianic concept in the Old Testament, the Davidic kingship of the Messiah, and the special importance given to the women of these prophecies seem to indicate that *her regal dignity is supposed?*")emphasis added). Cf., S. Ackerman, "The Queen-Mother and the Cult of the Ancient Near East," p. 197. Ackerman makes a similar case for finding Matthew's use of Isaiah 7:14 as possibly pointing to Mary as queen mother. See also G. Montague, *Our Father, Our Mother*, pp. 95–96.

[105] "On ne pouvait plus explicitement annoncer la naissance du Messie attendu et annoncé par les prophètes. Mais, implicitement parlant directement à la mère du Messie, l'ange évoquait ce qu'etait la mère du Roi, associée à son fils. C'est ainsi que ces paroles recèlent une théologie mariale de la royauté de Marie." H. Cazelles, "La Mère du Roi-Messie," p. 56.

[106] G. Montague, *Our Father, Our Mother*, pp. 95–96.

[107] B. Witherington, "Lord," in J. Green, et. al., eds., *Dictionary of Jesus and the Gospels* (Downers Grove, IL: InterVarsity Press, 1992), p. 489.

[108] C. Evans, *Saint Luke*, p. 170; J. Green, *The Gospel of Luke*, p. 96; M. Miguens, *Mary, "The Servant of the Lord,"* p. 61; cf. J. Fitzmyer, *Luke*, pp. 364–65.

[109] D. Bock, *Proclamation from Prophecy and Pattern*, pp. 69–70; cf. J. Fitzmyer, *Luke*, p. 203.

[110] "Luke's readers may well have understood this fuller sense of κύριος, but the choice of Luke to postpone the defining of this term is still a significant literary point to note." D. Bock, *Proclamation from Prophecy and Pattern*, p. 300 n. 61.

[111] Bock continues: ". . . but in view of Luke's later development of this term, clearly something more is in mind here, though this deeper intention is *not clear by this*

text alone. It only emerges from later Lucan usage." D. Bock, *Proclamation from Prophecy and Pattern,* p. 70. See also A. Feuillet, *Jesus and His Mother,* p. 13; M. Strauss, *The Davidic Messiah in Luke-Acts,* p. 96. While Strauss agrees that "the significance of *kurios* in Lukan theology as a whole must be considered in interpreting this reference," he also stresses that "it is of even greater importance to follow Luke's narrative development and not read ideas into a passage which Luke has not yet presented or clarified." Thus, Strauss also argues that "Lord" here in 1:43 is primarily to be understood in a royal messianic sense. Cf. J. Fitzmyer, *Luke,* p. 96.

[112] "The Semitic form of the question here in v. 43 parallels the query with which Araunah disclaims his worthiness to receive King David (2 Sam. 23:21)." F. Danker, *Jesus and the New Age* (Philadelphia: Fortress, 1988), p. 41. "David's response that he wishes to build an altar to the Lord (τῷ κυρίῳ) shows that it is not unusual to find κύρις used of Yahweh and of the king in the same context." M. Strauss, *The Davidic Messiah in Luke-Acts,* p. 95 n. 4. See also R. Brown, *Birth of the Messiah,* p. 345; J. Fitzmyer, *Luke,* p. 364; I. Marshall, *The Gospel of Luke,* p. 81.

[113] "If Elizabeth's inspired words in 1,43 echo Ps 110,1 or 2 Sam 24,21, then the title has a royal connotation here." F. Fearghail, *The Introduction to Luke-Acts: A Study of the Role of Lk 1,1-4,44 in the Composition of Luke's Two-Volume Work* (Rome: Editrice Pontificio Istituto Biblico, 1991), p. 134. M. Strauss, *The Davidic Messiah in Luke-Acts,* pp. 95–96. D. Bock, *Proclamation from Prophecy and Pattern,* pp. 70, 300 n. 60; R. Brown, *Birth of the Messiah,* p. 345; cf. J. Fitzmyer, *Luke,* p. 364.

[114] J. Nolland notes how "my Lord" was a royal court expression that also reflected messianic use in Psalm 110:1. J. Nolland, *Luke 1–9:20* (Dallas: Word Books, 1989), pp. 67, 75. Miguens explains that Luke 20:41 and Mark 12:36ff. provide evidence that in New Testament times, "Yahweh said to *my* Lord" (Ps. 110:1) was interpreted messianically. After noting how the phrase "my Lord" was used in Old Testament times to address the king himself and the Messiah, he concludes that 'my Lord' is "a respectful and courtly description of the Messiah; it is, in practical terms, a messianic title related to the royal dignity of 'the son of David' to whom the 'throne' of David is given, who will 'be king over the house of Jacob,' and whose 'kingdom' will have no end." M. Miguens, *Mary, "The Servant of the Lord,"* p. 61. See also Bock: "Note that its presence here is *not* an absolute usage, that is the mere title Lord by itself. It can be paralleled in the [Old Testament] as a reference to a regal figure (2 Sam. 24.21). The figure there is David." D. Bock, *Proclamation from Prophecy and Pattern,* p. 300 n. 60.

[115] R. Brown, *Birth of the Messiah,* p. 344.

[116] "Elisabetta riconosce al tempo stesso l'identità di Maria (la Madre) e di Gesù (il mio Signore)." B. Maggioni, "Esegesi di Lc 1,39-45," *Theotokos* 5 (1997): 19.

[117] M. Miguens, *Mary, "The Servant of the Lord,"* p. 61.

[118] Strauss notes how the context surrounding the narrative of the visitation supports a messianic interpretation for Elizabeth's words "mother of my Lord." Following the description of Jesus as the Davidic Messiah in 1:32–33, mother of my Lord in 1:43 "suggests that *kurios* has a 'messianic' sense somewhat equivalent to 'the mother of

my king.' Furthermore, the next time the title appears in Luke is in 2:11 where it stands alongside the messianic title '*Christos*,'" showing its close association with the Messiah. M. Strauss, *The Davidic Messiah in Luke-Acts*, p. 96. See also R. Brown, *Birth of the Messiah*, p. 344.

[119] X. Pikaza, "La Madre de mi Señor (Lc 1,43)," *EphMar* 46 (1996): 421–26; G. Perez, "La Visitacion: El Arca Nuevamente en Camino," *EphMar* 43 (1993): 201; D. Stanley, "The Mother of My Lord," *Worship* 34 (1960): 330–32; B. Ahern, "The Mother of the Messiah," pp. 27–28, 46–48; A. Feuillet, *Jesus and His Mother*, p. 13; A. Valentini, "Lc 1,39-45," pp. 341–42; M. Miguens, *Mary, "The Servant of the Lord,"* pp. 60–61; G. Kirwin, *Nature of the Queenship*, pp. 27–32; D. Bertetto, *Maria La Serva del Signore* (Napoli: Edizioni Dehoniane, 1988), pp. 349–50; M. Cuellar, *María, Madre del Redentor y Madre de la Iglesia* (Barcelona: Editorial Herder, 1990), p. 108; G. Del Moral, "La Realeza de María segun la Sagrada Escritura," p. 176; J. Bastero, "Fundamentos Cristológicos de la Realeza de María," p. 209; T. Gray, "God's Word and Mary's Royal Office," pp. 384–85; A. Serra, "Regina," p. 1074. As we noted above, J. Nolland shows how "my Lord" was a royal court expression which also reflected messianic use in Ps. 110:1, although he does not mention this in relationship with the queen mother. J. Nolland, *Luke 1–9:20*, pp. 67, 75.

[120] "The title 'Mother of my Lord' bears a wealth of meaning for those familiar with the Old Testament. In the court language of the ancient Near East it designated the mother of the reigning monarch who was addressed as 'My Lord' (2 Sam. 24:21)." B. Ahern, "Mother of the Messiah," p. 28. "The phrase 'mother of my Lord' seems to be a technical phrase referring to the fact that Mary was the mother of the Messiah-King and therefore queen-mother." G. Kirwin, *Nature of the Queenship*, p. 29 n. 72. Also G. Del Moral, "La Realeza de María segun la Sagrada Escritura," p. 176; D. Stanley, "Mother of My Lord," p. 330; M. Miguens, *Mary, "The Servant of the Lord,"* pp. 60–62.

[121] Serra argues that since "my Lord" has a royal character derived from the messianic Psalm 110:1 ("The Lord said to *my lord* . . ."), Mary's designation as "the mother of my Lord" points to her role as mother of the Messiah-king. "É a tutti noto che il salmo 110 ebbe delle riletture escatologico-messianiche, in riferimento privilegiato all'atteso re-messia (cf Mc 12,35-37; Mt 22,41-46; Lc 20,41-44). Elisabetta, dunque, saluta in Maria la madre del re-messia: quel re nascituro di cui ha parlato l'angelo a Maria (Lc 1,32-33)." A. Serra, "Regina," p. 1074. Also M. Miguens, *Mary, "The Servant of the Lord,"* pp. 60–62: After demonstrating that the words "my lord" were used to address the king (1 Kings 1:13–47) and the Messiah (Ps. 110:1) in the Old Testament, Miguens shows that Mary as "mother of my lord" in 1:43 is being addressed as the mother of the Messiah-King, i.e. the queen mother. He concludes on p. 65: "The definition of Mary as 'the mother of my lord,' by Elisabeth is, if nothing else, loaded with all that biblical tradition of the kingdom of Judah and with all the significance that the biblical mind attached to the national and official figure of 'the mother of the king.'" A. Feuillet, *Jesus and His Mother*, p. 13: "The dignity recognized in Mary by Elizabeth in greeting her as she did could thus be related to the authority which in ancient Israel was attributed to the Queen-mother or *gebirah*."

[122] "Ciertamente María es ahí reconocida y proclamada por Isabel—y por el evangelist—en su dignidad de Madre del Mesías connotando su participación en la realeza de su Hijo, al modo como lo hacía la madre del rey en el antiguo testamento." G. Perez, "La Visitacion," pp. 200–1. Also, A. Valentini, "Lc 1,39-45," p. 342: "Qui non c'è soltanto l'onore dovuto ad una semplice regina-madre, ma alla madre-vergine del Re messianico Figlio di Dio, di Colui che il Padre ha innalzato nella gloria (cf Rm 1,4) e di fronte al quale si piega ogni ginocchio (cf Fil 2,10). Ella è la madre del Re-Signore, e come tale è oggetto di venerazione da parte di tutta la comunità dei credenti."

[123] G. Kirwin, *Nature of the Queenship*, p. 28. See also D. Stanley, "The Mother of My Lord," p. 330: Interestingly, Stanley concludes that Luke's mention of this title for Mary expresses the most ancient form of Marian devotion in the earliest Christian community. "The title, 'the Mother of my Lord,' provides the clearest and probably the most ancient evidence we possess of the form which devotion to the Mother of God assumed in apostolic Christianity. These words, attributed by Luke to Elizabeth, which he clearly regards as spoken under divine inspiration (Luke 1:41), indicate that it was the queenship of Mary which was honored in the primitive Christian Church." For a contrary view, see J. Fitzmyer, *Luke*, pp. 365–66. Although admitting the possibility of regal overtones in Elizabeth's greeting, Fitzmyer argues that such a view is doubtful because it is too subtle and because "when Luke wants to get across the role of Jesus as king, he calls him precisely that" (p. 365). However, Luke's Gospel does not seem to be locked into alluding to Jesus' kingship only by using the title king. In fact, Luke elsewhere draws attention to Jesus' kingship without explicitly using the title king (Lk 19:14, 27; Acts 2:30–36; 13:34–37). Further, as Brown has shown, Luke uses "my Lord" both in the Gospel (20:41–44) and in Acts (2:34) to show that Jesus is the Messiah as in the Davidic messianic Psalm 110:1. R. Brown, *Birth of the Messiah*, p. 344. Finally, Fitzmyer does not seem to consider the Old Testament use of the royal address "*my* Lord" (as seen in 2 Sam. 24:21 and Ps. 110:1) which likely stands in the background of Elizabeth's greeting.

[124] "The dragon is more than a mere metaphor for an evil kingdom. It also stands for the devil himself as the representative head of evil kingdoms, as 12:9 and 20:2, 10 make explicit. The devil is the force behind the wicked kingdoms who persecute God's people." G. Beale, *The Book of Revelation* (Grand Rapids: Eerdmans, 1999), pp. 633–34. Also p. 655: The dragon is also explicitly identified with the serpent of Genesis 3. "He is called the 'ancient serpent,' which identifies him as the diabolical character of Gen. 3:1, 14."

[125] "The male child of Rev. 12:5 who 'is to rule over all the nations with a rod of iron' echoes the description of the Davidic king of Ps 2:9; and we know that Psalm 2 (especially v. 7) was frequently used in the NT with reference to the Messiah (Luke 3:22; Acts 13:33, etc.). The reuse of this same description and its application to 'The Word of God,' in Rev. 19:15, assure us of the author's intention to refer to Christ here." R. Brown, *Mary in the New Testament*, p. 230. Also D. Aune, *Revelation 6–16* (Nashville: Thomas Nelson, 1998), pp. 687–88; R. Mounce, *The Book of Revelation* (Grand Rapids: Eerdmans, 1998), p. 234.

[126] For a brief summary of various views on the woman's identity in the Church Fathers, see J. McHugh, *The Mother of Jesus in the New Testament*, pp. 470–71. For a more extensive treatment on the patristic interpretation, see B. Le Frois, *The Woman Clothed with the Sun: Individual or Collective* (Roma: Orbis Catholicus, 1954), pp. 1–61. See also the bibliography by Feuillet on modern interpretations of the woman in Revelation 12 from 1922–1960. A. Feuillet, *The Apocalypse* (Staten Island, NY: Alba House, 1965), pp. 112–15. For a study summarizing the scholarship on this topic from 1935–1990, see P. Farkas, *La 'Donna' di Apocalisse 12*, pp. 16–162.

[127] For summaries of these various views, see A. Valentini, "Il 'Grande Segno' di Apocalisse 12," *Marianum* 59 (1997): 31–34; J. McHugh, *The Mother of Jesus in the New Testament*, pp. 406–8; B. Le Frois, "The Woman Clothed with the Sun," *AER* 76 (1952): 170–72; R. Brown, *Mary in the New Testament*, pp. 231–39.

[128] "Certainly some of the imagery of Gen 3:15-16 and the struggle between the serpent and the woman and her offspring are part of the background for chap. 12." R. Brown, *Introduction to the New Testament*, p. 790. A. Feuillet, *Jesus and His Mother*, p. 21: "There is no question that chapter 12 of the Apocalypse does make reference to chapter 3 of Genesis." Similarly A. Collins, *The Apocalypse* (Wilmington, DE: Michael Glazier, 1979), pp. 86–87; J. Ford, *Revelation* (Garden City, NY: Doubleday, 1975), p. 206; G. Beale, *The Book of Revelation*, pp. 679–80; A. Serra, "Bibbia," pp. 264–65; L. Deiss, *Mary, Daughter of Sion*, pp. 139–41; R. Laurentin, *A Short Treatise on the Virgin Mary*, p. 44.

[129] R. Brown, *Mary in the New Testament*, p. 230.

[130] Even the prophetic image of Zion bearing the messianic community in much pain—which many recognize as a backdrop to understanding the woman of Revelation 12 (see below)—itself may draw from the birth pangs of Genesis 3:16. G. Beale, *The Book of Revelation*, pp. 630–31. Also W. Harrington, *Understanding the Apocalypse* (Washington: Corpus Books, 1969), p. 165.

[131] G. Caird, *Commentary on the Revelation of St. John the Divine* (London: A&C Black, 1984), p. 160: "This is a conscious echo of the words of God to the serpent in Eden." A. Feuillet, *Jesus and His Mother*, p. 22: "We have here almost certainly a literary contact with the Greek translation of Gn. 3:15." G. Beale, *The Book of Revelation*, p. 679: "Rev. 12:17 is also a partial fulfillment of the promise in Gen. 3:15 where God prophesies that the individual (messianic) and corporate seed of the woman will bruise fatally the head of the serpent." Beale argues that Genesis 3:15–16 is explicitly alluded to in Revelation 12:17 (p. 630). Also J. Ford, *Revelation*, p. 205.

[132] R. Brown, *The Gospel According to John* (Garden City, NY: Doubleday, 1970), pp. 107–8: "The figure of Eve in Gen iii 15 is the background for the description of the woman in Rev xii."

[133] Referring to the woman giving birth in pain in Revelation 12, De La Potterie explains: "This is a classic image of the apocalyptic tradition. The pains of a woman in childbirth has always been a symbol of the eschatological sufferings of the Daughter Zion in her condition as mother." I. De La Potterie, *Mary in the Mystery*

of the Covenant, p. 250. For his extended treatment on this theme and its significance for Revelation 12, see pp. 246–54. See also G. Beale, *The Book of Revelation*, pp. 630–32; G. Ladd, *A Commentary on the Revelation of John* (Grand Rapids: Eerdmans, 1972), p. 167; J. Court, *Myth and History in the Book of Revelation* (London: SPCK, 1979), pp. 110–18. J. McHugh, The Mother of Jesus in the New Testament, pp. 412–17; R. Brown, *Mary in the New Testament*, pp. 230–31; A. Feuillet, "The Messiah and His Mother," pp. 272–77.

[134] "The imagery of the nation as a woman giving birth to the Messiah already appears in Isaiah 26:18 LXX and more strikingly in the Qumran *thanksgiving Hymn E*." G. Beasley-Murray, *The Book of Revelation* (Grand Rapids: Eerdmans, 1974), p. 198.

[135] "If John has borrowed from Isaiah 26—and we must conclude that this is extremely likely—it provided him with the language and context to explain the condition of the woman (pregnant), the intensity of her labour (full of pain and anguish), and the nearness of the birth (imminent)." J. Fekkes, *Isaiah and Prophetic Traditions in the Book of Revelation* (JSNTSup 93) (Sheffield Academic Press, 1994), p. 182. "Whereas one or more of these expressions is found in a number of biblical passages, the particular combination of ideas chosen by John comes strikingly close to the birth metaphor related in Isa. 26.17" (p. 181). Beale, too, notes the similarities the pregnant woman in Isaiah 26 has with the woman in Revelation 12: "Note the similar pattern in Rev. 12:1-12: Israel as a woman in birth pangs, the resurrection and the resulting defeat of the dragon, God's people fleeing to a protective place where they are hid from the dragon's wrath, which God allows. Strikingly, in Isa 26:20 Israel is commanded to 'enter your closets . . . hide yourself *for a little season* . . . until . . . the Lord . . . brings wrath on the [unbelieving] earth-dwellers' and on the 'dragon' (27:1). This corresponds uniquely with the place of protection given the new Israel in Rev. 12:6, 14. . . . Furthermore, the time of protective hiding is during the 'little time' of the devil's wrath [12:7]." G. Beale, *The Book of Revelation*, p. 632. See also J. Ford, *Revelation*, p. 198; R. Mounce, *The Book of Revelation*, p. 232.

[136] In Isaiah 66, "the son born of the Woman Zion represents all the children of the people of Israel, the new messianic people." I. De La Potterie, *Mary in the Mystery of the Covenant*, p. 251. Also A. Feuillet, *Jesus and His Mother*, pp. 19–20; R. Mounce, *The Book of Revelation*, p. 232; D. Aune, *Revelation 6–16*, p. 687–88.

[137] J. Fekkes notes how in Isaiah 66 "not only does the collective image of Zion giving birth suit the corporate nature of the pregnant woman in Revelation 12, but the ambiguity of the metaphor in Isa 66.7-8 allows for *both* an individual birth (the Messiah), and a collective birth (the salvation community)." J. Fekkes, *Isaiah and Prophetic Traditions in the Book of Revelation*, p. 185. Beale similarly notes how the individuality and plurality of sons in Isaiah 66:7–8 fits well with the woman in Revelation 12:5, 17. G. Beale, *The Book of Revelation*, p. 641.

[138] J. Ford, *Revelation*, p. 196; G. Beale, *The Book of Revelation*, p. 625; I. De La Potterie, *Mary in the Mystery of the Covenant*, p. 248. A. Feuillet, "The Messiah and His Mother," pp. 273–74. Feuillet also notes how the liturgy has linked this passage from the Canticles with Revelation 12.

[139] I. De La Potterie, *Mary in the Mystery of the Covenant*, pp. 247–48. Beale suggests that the Isaian image itself may be based on Cant. 6:20: "This Isaiah text may even be based on the Canticle's imagery, since Isa. 61:10 and 62:3, 5 refer to Zion as Yahweh's bride 'with a crown of beauty and a royal diadem,' which is also comparable to the Revelation 12 depiction of the woman." G. Beale, *The Book of Revelation*, p. 626.

[140] "If the eschatological Zion shines so in all her splendor and magnificence, this is not its own light, but by the glory of God which radiates on her. She is clothed with the glory of Yahweh. In Revelation 21, it is even written that in the eschatological Zion there is no longer sun or moon. The stars are no longer necessary, "because the glory of God illumines her and his light is the Lamb" (Rv 21:23)." I. De La Potterie, *Mary in the Mystery of the Covenant*, pp. 247–48.

[141] Cf. R. Brown, *Mary in the New Testament*, p. 230: "The woman who appears 'clothed with the sun, with the moon under her feet, and on her head a crown of twelve stars' (Rev 12:1) evokes the description in Gen 37:9, in the dream of Joseph where the sun stands for Jacob/Israel, the moon for Rachel, and the twelve stars for the twelve sons of Jacob who would be the founders of the tribes of Israel." Similarly, R. Brown, *Introduction to the New Testament*, p. 791: The woman of Revelation 12 "represents Israel, echoing the dream of Joseph in Gen. 37:9 where these symbols represent his father (Jacob/Israel), his mother, and his brothers (the sons of Jacob who were looked on as ancestors of the twelve tribes)." Also G. Ladd, *A Commentary on the Revelation of John*, p. 168. J. Roloff, *The Revelation of John* (Minneapolis: Fortress, 1993), p. 145; J. Court, *Myth and History in the Book of Revelation*, p. 108.

[142] "Strictly speaking, Joseph is not explicitly identified as a star in Genesis 37, though Philo, *Dreams* 2.113 refers to Joseph as the twelfth star in that dream." G. Beale, *The Book of Revelation*, p. 625.

[143] "The woman-in-the-wilderness motif of Rev 12:6, 14 is probably meant to recall Israel in the Exodus. Certainly the story of the Exodus shows how God protected Israel in the wilderness and even 'nourished' her there (cf. Rev 12:14 and Exod 16:4-17)." R. Brown, *Mary in the New Testament*, p. 231. "Exodus typology is woven throughout this entire episode." R. Mounce, *The Book of Revelation*, p. 240. See also Beale's extensive treatment on the Exodus themes in this passage. G. Beale, *The Book of Revelation*, pp. 643–46.

[144] R. Mounce, *The Book of Revelation*, p. 240. Also G. Caird, *The Revelation of St. John*, p. 152: "To the Israelites escaping from Pharaoh, the Egyptian dragon in the midst of his streams, the desert was the place of safety and liberation; and it was to such a sanctuary that the woman was taken to be protected and sustained by God." G. Beale, *The Book of Revelation*, p. 668: "The exodus themes throughout this chapter may be reflected in the dragon's pursuit of God's people, since Pharaoh is often likened to a dragon in the [Old Testament]." See also A. Johnson, *Revelation* (Grand Rapids: Zondervan, 1983), p. 121. A. Collins, *The Apocalypse*, p. 87.

[145] "The transportation of the woman by 'the two wings of the great eagle' (Rev 12:14) echoes God's words to the house of Jacob/Israel in Exod 19:4: 'I bore you on eagle's wings' (also Deut 32:11-12)." R. Brown, *Mary in the New Testament*, p.

231. Beale argues that in addition to Exodus 19:4, Deuteronomy 1:31–33 and 32:10–12 also are in the background, with all three serving as a foundation for the Psalms alluding to this Exodus imagery "by praying that God's wings will shelter them from persecutors and slanderers, the same protection needed by the 'woman' in Rev. 12:13-17." Beale also argues that Revelation 12:14 recalls Isaiah 40:31, which describes how, in the future, Israel "will mount up with wings like eagles" as they return through "the wilderness" (Is. 40:3) to the land in a new exodus from Babylon. G. Beale, *The Book of Revelation*, p. 669. Also E. Corsini, *The Apocalypse* (Wilmington, DE: Michael Glazier, 1983), p. 217; J. Ford, *Revelation*, p. 201.

[146] W. Harrington, *Revelation* (Collegeville: Liturgical Press, 1993), p. 131; G. Beale, *The Book of Revelation*, p. 670; R. Brown, *Mary in the New Testament*, p. 231; cf. R. Mounce, *The Book of Revelation*, p. 234.

[147] "It is more probable that the phrase refers to believers in general as distinguished from the male child of vv. 5 and 13. They are the brothers and sisters of Christ (cf. Rom 8:29; Heb 2:11). The faithful are described as those who 'obey God's commandments and hold to the testimony of Jesus.'" R. Mounce, *The Book of Revelation*, p. 242. Similarly, Ladd: "The woman has other children against whom Satan now directs his wrath. These are actual Christians who constitute the empirical church on earth." G. Ladd, *A Commentary on the Revelation of John*, p. 174. Beale argues that Rev. 12:17 "portrays the suffering individuals who compose the whole church, in distinction from Christ as the woman's firstborn seed in vv 1-5 and vv 10-12." G. Beale, *The Book of Revelation*, p. 676. He goes on to argue that the offspring described as "those who keep the commandments of God and bear testimony to Jesus" probably point to the entire Church (Jew and Gentile), facing the devil's attacks, especially in persecution (p. 679).

[148] R. Brown, *Mary in the New Testament*, pp. 233–34. "The author first assures the reader that as a consequence of the birth of the Messiah, the dragon already has been defeated in heaven. . . . But such a victory in heaven does not destroy the dragon; rather it leads to a continued struggle on earth—an insight that came from the Christian experience of ongoing combat with satanic forces (Eph 6:12; 2 Thess 2:9)."

[149] See U. Vanni, "La Decodificazione 'Del Grande Segno' in Apocalisse 12,1-6," *Marianum* 40 (1978): 151. "Un'esegesi scientifica non può applicare la figura della donna a Maria." McHugh reports a few scholars who do hold to an exclusively Marian position. For a list and bibliography, see J. McHugh, *The Mother of Jesus*, p. 406. For an extensive bibliography on those who have discussed this issue, see A. Feuillet, *Apocalypse*, pp. 112–15.

[150] Beasley-Murray makes this point in his commentary on Revelation in order to show the shortcomings of the Mariological view: "This use of the [woman] figure seems clearly to depend on the prophetic symbolism of Jerusalem (= Zion) as the mother of the people of God." G. Beasley-Murray, *The Book of Revelation*, p. 198.

[151] A. Feuillet, *The Apocalypse*, p. 115.

[152] J. Roloff, *Revelation*, p. 151: "With her rescue the same thing befalls the woman as befell the salvation community of Israel, which had been led by God as 'on eagles

wings' out of Egypt into the wilderness (Exod. 19:4; Deut. 32:11). As Israel has been miraculously fed then with manna, so also will the church be nourished and kept alive by God." A. Johnson, *Revelation*, pp. 13–14: The devil described as having "pursued" the woman in 12:13 refers to the early Christians' being persecuted. "The word 'pursue' was no doubt carefully chosen by John because it is also the New Testament word used for 'persecute' (Mt. 5:10, et. al.)."

[153] G. Beale, *The Book of Revelation*, p. 629.

[154] For example, J. Roloff, *The Revelation of John*, p. 145. "The heavenly woman . . . is an image of the end-time salvation community, a symbol of the church. She is the heir of the promises of the Old Testament people of God; pointing to this is the reference to the twelve stars (cf. Gen. 37:9), which symbolize the holy twelve tribes in their end-time fullness and perfection (cf. 7:4-8; 14:1)." As for the woman's flight into the desert and her protection from the dragon's attacks, Roloff argues that the exodus imagery in this scene shows how the New Testament Church symbolized by the woman will be delivered from her persecutors like Israel was saved from their enemies in the Old Testament (p. 151). Along similar lines, Johnson identifies the woman as "the believing covenant-messianic community" that began with the followers of John the Baptist and then later merged into the community of Jesus' disciples and became the church. A. Johnson, *Revelation*, p. 119.

[155] I. Gebara and M. Bingemer, *Mary: Mother of God, Mother of the Poor* (Maryknoll, NY: Orbis Books, 1989), p. 83. Cf. J. Ford, *Revelation*, p. 188: "In Revelation 'woman' or 'women' occurs nineteen times . . . It might be said therefore, that the woman symbol is almost as important as the Lamb. This woman and the new Jerusalem are the antithesis of the harlot."

[156] A. Collins, *The Combat Myth in the Book of Revelation* (Missoula, MT: Scholars Press, 1976), p. 106: "In what sense then can it be said that the Church gives birth to Christ? Unless the interpreter resorts to an artificial allegorization of the child, the interpretation of the woman as the Church is untenable." B. Le Frois, "The Woman Clothed with the Sun," p. 171: "The Church may well be depicted as the mother of Christians, the members of Christ, but never of the personal Christ." Similarly, J. Court, *Myth and History in the Book of Revelation*, p. 118; J. McHugh, *The Mother of Jesus*, p. 407.

[157] J. McHugh, *The Mother of Jesus*, p. 407: "To identify the woman with the Christian Church while excluding both Mary and the people of Israel before the birth of the Messiah, is to do violence to the plain meaning of the text." McHugh also asks how the Christian Church can be in torment until it brought forth the Messiah (12:2), since the New Testament Church originates with the Messiah. Similarly, Le Frois quips, "Would anyone ever think of calling the United States of America the mother of George Washington? Likewise it is incorrect to call the Church the Mother of Jesus." B. Le Frois, "The Woman Clothed with the Sun," *AER*, p. 171.

[158] For examples of this view, see J. Court, *Myth and History in the Book of Revelation*, pp. 106–21; C. Giblin, *The Book of Revelation* (Collegeville: Liturgical Press. 1991), pp. 123–30.

[159] G. Beale, *The Book of Revelation*, p. 677; D. Aune, *Revelation 6–16*, p. 688.

[160] "The equation of singular 'male' with plural 'children' and collective 'seed,' all alluding to the same offspring from Zion, is virtually identical to the phenomenon in Revelation 12 of the Jerusalemite woman bearing a male and also having plural seed." G. Beale, *The Book of Revelation*, p. 677. Beale also notes how the targumic tradition has viewed the male offspring of Isaiah 66:7 as Zion's "king" and the sons of Isaiah 66:8 as "people." Fekkes makes a similar observation, noting the messianic interpretation in early Christian sources as well: "An individual messianic interpretation of Isa. 66.7 can be found in both Jewish and Christian sources: *Targ. Isa.* 66.7; *Gen. R.* 85; *Lev. R.* 14.9; Justin *Dial.* 85.8-10; Iren. *Dem.* 54. 1QH 3.9 also appears to allude to 66.7, but it is debated whether an individual or collective sense is in view." J. Fekkes, *Isaiah and Prophetic Traditions*, p. 185 n. 30.

[161] J. Roloff, *The Revelation of John*, p. 145: "Against the possibility that the heavenly woman refers to the people of God of the old covenant, out of which the Messiah was born, is both the continuation of the story (vv. 13–17) and quite generally the fact that nowhere in Revelation is the question of the relationship of Israel to the church treated as a theological theme." B. Le Frois, "The Woman Clothed with the Sun," p. 170: "If John had Israel in mind, his emphasis upon the Woman after the birth of the child (vv. 13-17) is meaningless. To imagine that it refers to a special protection of God for the unbelieving Jewish people in the Christian era does not fit into the picture." Also A. Johnson, *Revelation*, p. 119; cf. A. Feuillet, *Jesus and His Mother*, p. 27.

[162] G. Beale, *The Book of Revelation*, p. 631.

[163] For example, the authors of *Mary in the New Testament* conclude that the woman in Revelation 12 in one sense personifies God's covenant people of the Old Testament, but after giving birth to the messianic male child in Revelation 12:5 she becomes a symbol for God's covenant people of the New Testament, the Church. R. Brown, *Mary in the New Testament*, p. 232. I. De La Potterie, *Mary in the Mystery of the Covenant*, p. 246: "This 'Woman' is, first, a symbol of Israel, of the people of God, who has given birth to the Messiah. . . . But in the New Testament the Woman Zion becomes the Church." R. Brown, *Introduction to the New Testament*, p. 791 n. 35: "The coming of the Messiah through the sufferings of Israel is run together with the sufferings of the church that will lead to the second coming of the Messiah, for the church must remain in the wilderness after the Messiah is taken up to God, until he returns again. It is debated whether this woman is also the bride of the Lamb (Rev 19:7) and the New Jerusalem (21:2, 9). The plasticity of apocalyptic symbols could allow a figure who is both mother and bride, and both on earth and coming down from heaven." G. Beale, *The Book of Revelation*, p. 631: "Vv 2-6 reveal that this woman is a picture of the faithful community, which existed both before and after the coming of Christ." McHugh argues that this view of the woman as representing "the people of God on earth, the Church of the Old and New Testaments" provides a coherent explanation of Revelation 12 (though he argues for a Marian view as well). J. McHugh, *The Mother of Jesus in the New Testament*, p. 421. See also A. Feuillet, "The Messiah and His Mother," p. 280; F. Murphy, *Fallen is Babylon: The Revelation of John* (Harrisburg, PA: Trinity Press, 1998), p. 283; R. Mounce, *The*

Book of Revelation, p. 232; G. Beasely-Murray, *Revelation*, p. 198; W. Harrington, *Understanding the Apocalypse*, p. 169.

[164] R. Brown, *Mary in the New Testament*, p. 232.

[165] J. Collins, *The Apocalyptic Imagination* (New York: Crossroad, 1984), p. 13. "The tendency of much historical scholarship has been to specify the referents of apocalyptic imagery in as unambiguous a manner as possible. . . . Yet Paul Ricoeur has rightly protested against the tendency to identify apocalyptic symbols in too univocal a way. This tendency misses the element of mystery and indeterminacy which constitutes much of the 'atmosphere' of apocalyptic literature." The authors of *Mary in the New Testament* similarly note that in apocalyptic literature, "characteristically there is an exuberant use of symbolic images . . . the same set of events or characters may be described over again or recapitulated under a succession of different images. This warns us against assuming logical sequences from one scene to another and too quickly assigning unique significance when we turn to the symbolism of Revelation 12." R. Brown, *Mary in the New Testament*, p. 220. For more on the interpretation of apocalyptic symbols, see G. Beale, *The Book of Revelation*, pp. 50–69.

[166] R. Brown, *Introduction to the New Testament*, p. 779.

[167] Ibid., p. 779.

[168] R. Mounce, *The Book of Revelation*, p. 232. Similarly, A. Feuillet, "The Messiah and His Mother," p. 280: "Thus, after having given Christ to men, the people of God of the old Covenant has become the Christian Church. The author of the Apocalypse, like all the authors of the New Testament writings, is persuaded that the clear separation of the two economies of the old and new Testaments does not at all prevent the one from being a continuation of the other, since they are both the progressive fulfillment of a simple divine plan." See also R. Brown, *Mary in the New Testament*, p. 234. The authors of this work suggest that much of the Old Testament imagery is employed to depict the New Testament community reliving key moments of Israel's history. "The idea that the woman represents both Israel and the Church is less troublesome if we see that in the author's mind the Church is reliving aspects of Israel's career."

[169] R. Brown, *Mary in the New Testament*, pp. 239, 292. "Whether there is also a secondary reference to Mary as the Mother of the Messiah *in the intention of the author* is a question the answer to which depends in large measure on what view one takes of the relation between the Book of Revelation and the Fourth Gospel" (p. 292).

[170] For surveys on this issue, see: D. Aune, *Revelation 1–5* (Waco: Word Books, 1997), pp. xlvii–lvi; R. Mounce, *The Book of Revelation*, pp. 8–15; R. Brown, *Introduction to the New Testament*, pp. 802–5; A. Feuillet, *Apocalypse*, pp. 95–108; S. Fiorenza, "The Quest for the Johannine School: The Book of Revelation and the Fourth Gospel," *NTS* 23 (1976–77) as reprinted in S. Fiorenza, *The Book of Revelation: Justice and Judgment* (Philadelphia: Fortress, 1985), pp. 85–113.

[171] There are some scholars who do maintain that both books were written by a common author, John the apostle. For a list of those holding this view, see J. Robinson, *Redating the New Testament*, p. 255; A. Wainwright, *Mysterious*

Apocalypse: Interpreting the Book of Revelation (Nashville: Abingdon Press, 1993), p. 117 n. 51. While not necessarily arguing for common authorship, the following suggest that such a view cannot be ruled out: B. Wescott, *The Gospel According to St. John* (Grand Rapids: Eerdmans, 1950), p. lxxxvi; G. Caird, *The Revelation of St. John*, p. 4; C. Pate, *Four Views on the Book of Revelation* (Grand Rapids: Zondervan, 1998), p. 14; R. Mounce, *The Book of Revelation*, p. 15.

[172] Internal and external evidence have led some interpreters to conclude that there is no significant relationship between the Book of Revelation and the Gospel of John. Internally, it has been argued that the differences between these two books in terms of vocabulary, style and theological outlook greatly outweigh the similarities and point to not only two separate authors but two distinct traditions/communities. For example, Aune concludes "though Revelation has been linked with the other Johannine writings in the NT, there are in fact very few features that suggest that this author was part of the Johannine community in any meaningful sense." D. Aune, *Revelation 1–5*, p. lvi. While Roloff recognizes that there are some similarities between the two writings, he maintains that "the similarities are no closer than those between Revelation and other New Testament writings." J. Roloff, *The Revelation of John*, p. 12. For an extensive treatment on the similarities and differences in vocabulary, grammar and style between Revelation and the Fourth Gospel, see H. Swete, *The Apocalypse of St. John* (London: MacMillan, 1906), pp. cxv-cxxv. In terms of external evidence, there has been much discussion on Dionysius' argument for the two books having separate authors and on Eusebius' account of writings attributed to Papias that may suggest there were two different persons with the name John, John the Apostle and John the Elder. For more on these and other issues surrounding the external evidence, see D. Aune, *Revelation 1–5*, pp. l–liii.

[173] Some maintain that the similarities between the two books suggest Revelation was written substantially by John the Apostle, while the Fourth Gospel was written by someone in the Johannine community discipled by John: W. Harrington, *Understanding the Apocalypse*, pp. 4–5; G. Ladd, *A Commentary on the Revelation of John*, p. 8; S. Smalley, "John's Revelation and John's Community," *Bulletin of the John Rylands University Library* 69 (1986–87): 549–71 (especially pp. 568–70); J. Bernard, *The Gospel According to St. John*, vol. 1 (New York: Charles Scribner's Sons, 1929), pp. lxiv–lxvii; M. Boismard, "The Apocalypse," in *Introduction to the New Testament*, eds. A. Robert & A. Feuillet (New York: Desclee Company, 1965), p. 721. Harrington and Boismard suggest this view, but are also open to seeing things the other way around with John the Apostle as the author of the Fourth Gospel and a disciple of his as the author of Revelation. More common is the view that the authors of Revelation and the Fourth Gospel were different members of the same Johannine school or circle. C. Barrett, *The Gospel According to St. John* (London: SPCK, 1955), p. 113; G. Beasley-Murray, *The Book of Revelation*, p. 36; R. Brown, *The Gospel of John*, p. cii; C. Pate, *Four Views on the Book of Revelation*, p. 14; O. Cullmann, *The Johannine Circle* (Philadelphia: Westminister, 1975), p. 54; L. Johnson, *The Writings of the New Testament* (Philadelphia: Fortress, 1986), pp. 518–20; M. Hengel, *The Johannine Question* (London: SCM Press, 1989), pp. 126–27; Cf. R. Brown, *1 John* (Garden City, NY: Doubleday, 1982), pp. 56–57 n. 131. Along similar lines, Feuillet explains, "It is legitimate . . . to relate the Apocalypse to the Johannine tradition. Whatever position one may adopt with

regard to the unity of the authorship of the fourth Gospel, of the Apocalypse and of the so-called Johannine Epistles, there is no doubt that these writings are of the same school, and that it is correct to explain one of them by the others." A. Feuillet, "The Messiah and His Mother," pp. 285–86. After evaluating the vocabulary, style and theology of both books, Swete concludes that the evidence points to "a strong presumption of affinity between the Fourth Gospel and the Apocalypse." H. Swete, *Apocalypse of John*, p. cxxx. Corsini, Beale and Johnson explain that the differences in vocabulary, style and theology are probably based not on different authors, but more likely on the fact that the Book of Revelation employs a literary genre (apocalyptic) that is very different from the genre of the Fourth Gospel. E. Corsini, *The Apocalypse*, pp. 59–60; G. Beale, *The Book of Revelation*, pp. 34–35; L. Johnson, *Writings of the New Testament*, p. 519. Taking a different approach, Schussler Fiorenza argues that the author of Revelation was part of a prophetic-apocalyptic school who had much familiarity with Pauline traditions, but also had access to Johannine traditions as well. E. Schussler Fiorenza, *The Book of Revelation: Justice and Judgment* (Philadelphia: Fortress, 1985), p. 107. In his more recent work, Brown argues that one should posit "some contact between the seer and the Johannine traditions or writings." He suggests that the author of Revelation likely had some points of contact with members of the Johannine community which was shaped in the area of Palestine and later moved to the area of Ephesus—a career path similar to that which was likely followed by the author of Revelation. R. Brown, *Introduction to the New Testament*, p. 804.

[174] See A. Feuillet, "The Messiah and His Mother," pp. 285–91; R. Brown, *The Gospel According to John*, p. 926; I. De La Potterie, *Mary in the Mystery of the Covenant*, pp. 259–62; A. Valentini, "Il 'Grande Segno,'" pp. 56-62; F. Molina, "La Mujer en Apocalipsis 12," *EphMar* 43 (1993): 385–89; J. Fenton, *The Gospel According to John* (Oxford: Clarendon Press, 1970), p. 196; W. Harrington, *Understanding the Apocalypse*, pp. 174–75; A. Sera, "Bibbia," p. 270; S. De Fiores, *Maria, Madre di Gesu*, pp. 102–3; I. Gebara and M. Bingemer, *Mary*, pp. 85–86.

[175] Feuillet notes "the insistence with which the Mother of Jesus is called 'woman' [in Jn. 19:25-27]. This coincidence between the two scenes of Cana and of Calvary betrays an intent of the author which must be of the doctrinal order. . . . These same characteristics do apply to the Mother of the Messiah in the Apocalypse. She is called Woman." A. Feuillet, "The Messiah and His Mother," p. 286. Also A. Valentini, "Il 'Grande Segno,'" p. 58; R. Brown, *The Gospel According to John*, pp. 108, 925; R. Brown, *Mary in the New Testament*, p. 237; B. Buby, *Mary of Galilee*, pp. 156–57.

[176] "The scene at the foot of the cross has these details in common with xvi 21: the use of the words 'woman' and 'hour'; the theme of maternity; and the theme of Jesus' death." R. Brown, *The Gospel According to John*, p. 925. "The various literary points of contact between these two passages allow us to suppose that the evangelist, in writing the text of Jn 16:21 had in mind the Hour of Jesus and the 'Woman' whom he gave as 'mother' to his disciple." I. De La Potterie, *Mary in the Mystery of the Covenant*, p. 222. See also R. Lightfoot, *St. John's Gospel* (London: Oxford University Press, 1956), p. 317; A. Feuillet, *Jesus and His Mother*, p. 119; A. Feuillet, "The Messiah and His Mother," pp. 287–88; A. Valentini "Il 'Grande Segno' di Apocalisse 12," pp. 58–59; R. Brown, *Mary in the New Testament*, p. 237.

[177] "How can one fail to take into account also the similarity between Apoc. 12:2,5 and the text of Jn. 16:21-22 which throws so much light on the Marian scenes of Cana and Calvary?" A. Feuillet, *Jesus and His Mother*, p. 23. "La portata del brano emerge non solo dal confronto con la scena di Cana, ma anche con Gv 16,21, che inizia proprio con il termine γυνὴ presenta la passione-risurrezione di Gesù come una maternità che avviene nel dolore, ma cui segue la gioia grande per la nascita di un figlio. Questo testo sia dal punto di vista letterario che del contenuto può servire da ponte di congiunzione tra Ap 12 e Gv 19, 25-27. Anche in 16,21 si parla di: *donna, maternità, ora*." A. Valentini, "Il 'Grande Segno,'" p. 58. De la Potterie notes that Revelation 12 has significant points of contact with John 19: "For, in Revelation 12, there is also question—and in a messianic context—of a woman in the pains of childbirth." I. De La Potterie, *Mary in the Mystery of the Covenant*, p. 222. Also I. Gebara and M. Bingemer, *Mary*, pp. 84–86; B. Buby, *Mary of Galilee*, pp. 149, 162; W. Harrington, *Understanding the Apocalypse*, p. 175; R. Brown, *Mary in the New Testament*, pp. 237, 216 n. 480; R. Brown, *The Gospel According to John*, pp. 731–32, 926; cf. J. Ford, *Revelation*, p. 189. The links between John 19 and Revelation 12 can be drawn even clearer if Revelation 12:5 is seen primarily as a metaphorical birth describing Christ's death (the birth pains) and resurrection (the actual birth) in similar fashion to the parable in John 16:20–21 studied above. It has been pointed out that the New Testament often uses birth imagery to describe the resurrection (1 Cor. 15:20, 36; Col. 1:18; Acts 13:33; Jn. 12:24, 16:20–21), including the Book of Revelation's use of "first born of the dead" (Rev. 1:5), while birth pang imagery is associated with Christ's sufferings on Calvary (Jn. 16:20–21; cf. Acts 2:24). And since the word describing the woman "in anguish" (*basanizomene*) in Revelation 12:2 is never used in the LXX or New Testament to describe actual physical birth pains (only referring to torment or great sorrow in general), this may also indicate the passage is describing something different from the ordinary physical sufferings of natural childbirth. For more on this view, see G. Beale, *The Book of Revelation*, p. 640; A. Feuillet, "The Messiah and His Mother," pp. 258–67; J. McHugh, *The Mother of Jesus in the New Testament*, pp. 410–12; I. De La Potterie, *Mary in the Mystery of the Covenant*, pp. 252–53; A. Serra, "Bibbia," pp. 266–67; R. Brown, *Mary in the New Testament*, pp. 236–37; cf. J. Ford, *Revelation*, p. 190. We have already seen how the child-birth imagery from the parable of the woman's sufferings in labor (Jn. 16:20–21) stands in the background of the scene of Mary at the Cross in John 19:25–27. Therefore, if Revelation 12:5 is a metaphorical birth describing Christ's death and Resurrection, we would have yet another clear link between Revelation 12 and John 19. As Gebara and Bingemer explain: "The scene described in Revelation 12:4-5 can be read in light of John 16:21-3, where the passion and resurrection of Jesus are depicted in terms of the sorrow and joy of the birth process; and that same scene in Revelation can also be read in light of John 19:25-27, where the emphasis is on the extension of the community of faithful followers of Jesus. What John describes in a historico-interpretive fashion, Revelation describes in terms of a symbolic vision." I. Gebara and M. Bingemer, *Mary*, p. 85.

[178] R. Brown, *Mary in the New Testament*, p. 237; B. Buby, *Mary of Galilee*, p. 138; R. Brown, *The Gospel According to John*, pp. 925–26.

[179] "The scene in Apocalypse XII:9-12, with the defeat of Satan, his fall to earth and the heavenly voice heard to celebrate the victory of God and of Christ recalls closely that of [John 12:28-32] (a heavenly voice linked to the defeat of the devil and the glorification of Jesus)"—which comes to fulfillment in John 19. A. Feuillet, "The Messiah and His Mother," p. 286. "The symbolism of the Fourth Gospel has a certain resemblance to that of Rev xii 5, 17 where a woman gives birth to the Messiah in the presence of the Satanic dragon or ancient serpent of Genesis." R. Brown, *The Gospel According to John*, p. 926. R. Brown, *Mary in the New Testament*, p. 237.

[180] There has been much debate surrounding the nature of this maternal relationship. Those following a literal, historical interpretation conclude that the scene is primarily about Jesus arranging care for His mother. C. Barrett, *The Gospel According to St. John*, p. 459; L. Morris, *The Gospel According to John* (Grand Rapids: Eerdmans, 1995), pp. 717–18; D. Carson, *The Gospel According to John* (Leicester: InterVarsity Press, 1991), pp. 616–18; G. Beasley-Murray, *John* (Waco: Word, 1987), pp. 349–50 (though he is open to the possibility of an added symbolic meaning of this passage, following Schnackenburg's interpretation, considered below); cf. F. Neirynck, "ΕΙΣ ΤΑ ΙΔΙΑ: Jn 19,27 (et 16,21)," in *Evangelica*, ed. F. Van Segbroeck (Leuven University Press, 1982), pp. 456–64. A variety of approaches are found among those who hold a symbolic interpretation. Bultmann viewed Mary as a symbol for Jewish Christianity. R. Bultmann, *The Gospel of John* (Oxford: Basil Blackwell, 1971), p. 673. Schnackenburg saw the woman as representing those seeking salvation. R. Schnackenburg, *The Gospel According to John*, vol. 3 (New York: Crossroad, 1982), pp. 278–79. Brodie interprets her as symbolizing those Jews who are responsive to the Gospel. T. Brodie, *The Gospel According to John* (New York: Oxford University Press, 1993), pp. 174–75, 549–50. Brown sees the woman as representing the Church in light of the Daughter Zion and New Eve themes which he argues are likely in the background of John 19:25–27. R. Brown, *The Gospel According to John*, pp. 107–9, 923–27. Brown recognizes that John 19 is more than an account about Jesus taking care of his mother before he dies. "The action of Jesus in relation to his mother and the Beloved Disciple completes the work that the Father has given Jesus to do and fulfills the Scripture [Jn. 19:28-30]. . . . All this implies something more profound than filial care" (p. 923). In addition to affirming a symbolic discipleship interpretation of John 19:25–27 in which Mary becomes part of Christ's eschatological family and the beloved disciple becomes a true brother of Jesus [see R. Brown, *The Community of the Beloved Disciple* (New York: Paulist Press, 1979), pp. 196–97], Brown also argues that the mother of Jesus is a symbol of the church in this passage. He discusses how the Fourth Gospel depicts Mary becoming the mother of the Beloved Disciple in ways which evoke the themes of Daughter Zion giving birth to the messianic people (Jn. 16:20–21; Is. 27:17–18; Is. 66:7–14): "In becoming the mother of the Beloved Disciple, Mary is symbolically evocative of Lady Zion who, after the birth pangs, brings forth a new people in joy (John xvi 21; Isa xlix 20-22, liv 1, lxvi 7-11)" (R. Brown, *The Gospel According to John*, p. 925). In light of this Daughter Zion imagery and possible Eve allusions, Brown concludes that Mary is a symbol of the collective people of God, the Church: "Jesus' mother and the Beloved Disciple are being established in a new relationship representative of that which will bind the Church and the Christian" (p. 926). De La Potterie argues that this passage presents Mary's spiritual maternity toward the

Church and all Christians. I. De La Potterie, *Mary in the Mystery of the Covenant*, pp. 211–35. Whatever view one may hold about the nature of Mary's maternity in this passage, for our purposes, it is at this point important simply to note that Mary is presented as the mother not only of Jesus but also mother of the beloved disciple, who represents the ideal follower of Christ (see below).

[181] In the Fourth Gospel, the "beloved disciple" figure is the one who shared a close intimacy with Jesus, remained with Jesus during His crucifixion and was the first to believe in the risen Lord and continued to bear testimony to Jesus (Jn. 13:23, 19:26, 20:8, 21:7, 20, 24). For more on the Beloved Disciple's role in John's Gospel, see C. Koester, *Symbolism in the Fourth Gospel* (Minneapolis: Fortress, 1995), pp. 217–18; R. Brown, *The Gospel According to John*, p. 924: "There is little doubt that in Johannine thought the Beloved Disciple can symbolize the Christian." For a treatment on the identity of the beloved disciple, see ibid., pp. xcii–xcviii.

[182] R. Brown, *The Gospel According to John*, p. 926. This connection between John 19 and Revelation 12 seems even more likely if one considers the Daughter Zion background to John 19:25–27. Considering the parable of the woman's labor pains and her joy after delivery in John 16:20–21 (which we looked at above), Feuillet and Brown have noted how the birth imagery in John 16:21 describing the apostle's trials during Christ's death and Resurrection ("When a woman is in travail she has sorrow, because her hour has come, but when she is delivered of the child, she no longer remembers the anguish, for joy that a child is born into the world") has its roots in Isaiah 26, which describes Zion as a woman crying out in labor pains, suffering God's wrath only for "a little while," but then rejoicing in a new era which is depicted with resurrection imagery of the dead rising (Is. 26:17–21). Similarly, Isaiah 66 is likely in the background, for it speaks of Zion's labor pains, her bringing forth children and then her rejoicing (Is. 66:7–10). The likelihood of this second allusion to Lady Zion in John 16:21 is strengthened by the fact that the following verse also cites Isaiah 66. Feuillet and Brown have shown how John 16:22 ("I shall see you again and your hearts will rejoice") is taken almost verbatim from the LXX version of Isaiah 66:14. A. Feuillet, "The Messiah and His Mother," p. 264; R. Brown, *The Gospel According to John*, p. 731. Finally, since John 16:21 is related to the scene at Calvary (as discussed above), this theme of Zion giving birth to the messianic people may serve as a background to John 19:25–7, thus shedding light on Mary's motherhood over the Beloved Disciple, who represents the messianic people as the ideal Christian disciple. All this is significant because, as the authors of *Mary in the New Testament* have discussed, this background might allow us to see Mary's motherhood toward the Beloved Disciple (who represents the ideal Christian) in light of the Old Testament theme of Israel/Daughter Zion, giving birth in pain to the messianic people (Jn. 16:21–22; Is. 26:17; Is. 66:6–7). They explain that such a view would place the Johannine scene at the cross in close similarity with the scene in Revelation 12. Like John 19, where we find Mary not only is the mother of Jesus but also is symbolically representing Israel/Zion's maternity toward the messianic people represented by the Beloved Disciple (Jn. 19:25–27), "Revelation 12 . . . seems to employ the symbolism of a woman described like Israel who is the mother of the Messiah and the mother of Christian disciples." R. Brown, *Mary in the New Testament*, p. 217. See also R. Brown, *The Gospel According to John*, pp. 925–26; I. Gebara and M. Bingemer, *Mary*, pp. 84–85; A. Valentini, "Il 'Grande Segno,'" p. 59; W. Harrington, *Understanding*

the Apocalypse, p. 175; A. Feuillet, "The Messiah and His Mother," p. 286; cf. I. De La Potterie, *Mary in the Mystery of the Covenant*, p. 260.

[183] After treating the various parallels between John 19 and Revelation 12, De La Potterie concludes, "It is the text of John 19:25-27 which has made possible the Marian interpretation of Rev. 12." I. De La Potterie, *Mary in the Mystery of the Covenant*, p. 263. Similarly, A. Serra, "Bibbia," p. 270: "La presenza di Maria accanto al Crocifisso rende possibile l'estensione mariologica alla 'donna' dell'Apocalisse, in lotta col dragone." See also A. Serra, "Maria nell'Apocalisse," in *Maria, Madre di Dio* (Florence: SS. Annunziata, 1991), p. 214. Feuillet sees the prophetic image of the messianic birth pains that stands behind Revelation 12 and John 19 (via Jn. 16:20–21) as clearly uniting the "woman" at the Cross and the "woman clothed with the sun": "Even if it is true that this passage [Rev. 12] has in view principally [the] people of God personified, it now seems to us to be all but impossible that the author should not have thought of Mary, since the fourth Gospel affirms that already at Cana, and above all at Calvary, John saw in Mary the Woman whose wonderful childbirth the prophetic oracles had foretold, (i.e., the ideal Sion of the messianic era)." A. Feuillet, "The Messiah and His Mother," p. 288. Also pp. 285, 291. Also supporting a Marian view of Revelation 12 in light of John 19 are the following: M. Thurian, *Mary: Mother of All Christians* (New York: Herder, 1964), pp. 179–83; E. Hoskyns, *The Fourth Gospel* (London: Faber and Faber, 1947), p. 530; B. Forte, *Maria, La Donna Icona del Mistero* (Milan: Edizioni Paoline, 1989), p. 102; J. McHugh, *The Mother of Jesus in the New Testament*, pp. 130–32; P. Gaffney, "Mary in the Book of Revelation," *Queen of All Hearts* (July–August, 1998), p. 15; R. Laurentin, "Mary in the Old Testament," in *Mary in Faith and Life in the New Age of the Church* (Ndola, Zambia: Franciscan Mission Press, 1983), p. 101; F. Braun, *Mother of God's People* (Staten Island: Alba House, 1967), pp. 149–50, 168; B. Buby, *Mary of Galilee*, pp. 156–57; S. De Fiores, *Maria Madre di Gesu*, pp. 102–3; F. Molina, "La Mujer en Apocalipsis 12," pp. 389–91; A. Valentini, "Il 'Grande Segno,'" pp. 62–63; P. Kearney, "Gen. 3:15 and Johannine Theology," p. 105. Some authors defend the possibility of a Marian view, without holding to its necessity. For example, Harrington discusses the parallels between John 19 and Revelation 12 and concludes "it would seem not unreasonable to suppose that the author of Ap. does have Mary in mind when he speaks of the mother of the Messiah." W. Harrington, *Understanding the Apocalypse*, p. 175. Holding a similar view: M. Boismard, "The Apocalypse," p. 718. The authors of *Mary in the New Testament* conclude that affirming a secondary Marian interpretation is possible, but it depends in large part on establishing a relationship between Revelation and the Fourth Gospel. R. Brown, *Mary in the New Testament*, p. 292. Other authors who recognize the possibility of the woman referring to Mary: J. Court, *Myth and History in the Book of Revelation*, p. 115; G. Beale, *The Book of Revelation*, p. 628; F. Murphy, *Fallen Is Babylon*, p. 283; H. Boer, *The Book of Revelation* (Grand Rapids: Eerdmans, 1979), p. 89; J. Guimond, *The Silencing of Babylon* (New York: Paulist, 1991), p. 57; J. Grassi, *Mary, Mother and Disciple* (Wilmington, DE: Michael Glazier, 1988), p. 96.

[184] For more on the canonical approach to Scripture, see PBC, *Interpreting the Bible in the Church*, I, C, 1; R. Brown, *Introduction to the New Testament*, pp. 24–25, 42–44; R. Brown, *Mary in the New Testament*, pp. 30–31.

[185] R. Brown, *Mary in the New Testament*, p. 293.

[186] Ibid., p. 239. Similarly, see I. Gebara and M. Bingemer, *Mary*, p. 83.

[187] Collins and Aune see the astral symbols of sun, moon, and twelve stars as paralleling not only Old Testament figures of speech, but also the description of pagan goddesses portrayed as "cosmic queen" figures. A. Collins, *Combat Myth*, pp. 71–76; D. Aune, *Revelation 6–16*, p. 680.

[188] "In Hellenistic Greek the term στέφανος could be used to express royalty, a use that appears to have been more common among Jewish authors. The translators of the LXX and Josephus consistently use στέφανος rather than διάδημα to identify the golden Israelite crown. . . . [I]t demonstrates that in the minds of some later Israelites στέφανος was considered an acceptable term for describing a royal crown." G. Stevenson, "Conceptual Background to Golden Crown Imagery in the Apocalypse of John (4:4,10; 14:14)," *JBL* 114 (1995): p. 260.

[189] U. Vanni, "La Decodificazione 'Del Grande Segno' in Apocalisse 12,1–6," p. 131; I. Gebara and M. Bingemer, *Mary*, p. 83; F. Molina, "La Mujer en Apocalipsis 12," p. 374.

[190] "The crown on the woman's head is best defined from within the Apocalypse itself. Other references to crowns . . . show that here the crown connotes the saints' share in Christ's kingship and the reward that the true people of God throughout the ages receive for their victory over opposition to their faith." G. Beale, *The Book of Revelation*, p. 627. "She shared fully by anticipation in the victory of Christ over the forces of evil, a victory which foreshadows the triumph of the Church at the end of time (the twelve tribes of the new Israel) and therefore foreshadows the last chapters of the Apocalypse." A. Feuillet, *Jesus and His Mother*, pp. 32, 129. Also A. Serra, "Bibbia," p. 265.

[191] G. Ladd, *A Commentary on the Revelation of John*, p. 168; R. Mounce, *The Book of Revelation*, p. 232.

[192] R. Mounce, *The Book of Revelation*, p. 232 n. 5.

[193] U. Vanni, "La Decodificazione 'Del Grande Segno,'" p. 129. See also D. Chilton, *The Days of Vengeance* (Fort Worth: Dominion Press, 1987), pp. 297–98.

[194] "The moon beneath her feet (perhaps a footstool) speaks of dominion." R. Mounce, *The Book of Revelation*, p. 232. Since the moon was important for time (Genesis 1:14–19 and the Jewish lunar calendar), this image may symbolize dominion over the temporal realm. See A. Serra, "Bibbia," p. 265: "Se la luna sta sotto i piedi della 'donna,' vuol dire che la 'donna' esercita un dominio sul tempo, ne è padrona (cf Sal 110,1; Gs 10,24)." Also A. Serra, "Regina," pp. 1079–80; D. Chilton, *The Days of Vengeance*, pp. 297–98. Cf. I. De La Potterie, *Mary in the Mystery of the Covenant*, p. 248; F. Molina, "La Mujer en Apocalipsis 12," p. 373.

[195] A. Feuillet, "The Messiah and His Mother," pp. 272–76; I. De La Potterie, *Mary in the Mystery of the Covenant*, pp. 247–48; B. Buby, *Mary of Galilee*, p. 147.

[196] Cf. R. Brown, *Mary in the New Testament*, p. 230; R. Brown, *Introduction to the New Testament*, p. 791; G. Ladd, *A Commentary on the Revelation of John*, p. 168;

J. Roloff, *The Revelation of John*, p. 145; J. Court, *Myth and History in the Book of Revelation*, p. 108.

[197] "É una regina senza dirlo," P. Farkas, *La Donna di Apocalisse 12*, p. 211. Also A. Collins, *The Combat Myth*, p. 71; A. Collins, *The Apocalypse*, p. 85; B. Le Frois, "The Woman Clothed with the Sun," p. 167.

[198] A. Luis, *La Realeza de Maria*, p. 31.

[199] O. Lukefahr, *Christ's Mother and Ours*, pp. 40–42; H. Cazelles, "Note D'Exegese Sur Apocalypse 12," p. 133; P. Farkas, *La Donna di Apocalisse 12*, pp. 210–12; D. Bertetto, *Maria La Serva del Signore* (Napels: Edizioni Dehoniane, 1988), p. 440; G. Kirwin, *Nature of the Queenship*, pp. 296–97; T. Gray, "God's Word and Mary's Royal Office," 386–87; P. Kearney, "Gen. 3:15 and Johannine Theology," p. 105.

[200] "Supponendo che l'autore si era ispirato all'immagine anticotestamentaria della donna partoriente (il popolo), rimane sempre la difficoltà: la donna di Ap 12 è descritta come una regina e l'immagine della regina partoriente il Messia totalmente manca nell'AT." P. Farkas, *La Donna di Apocalisse 12*, p. 210.

[201] P. Farkas, *La Donna di Apocalisse 12*, p. 211.

[202] G. Kirwin, *Nature of the Queenship*, p. 297.

[203] J. Ford, *Revelation*, p. 195: "A text which is peculiarly pertinent is Isa 7:10-17. Here the Lord asks Ahaz to request a sign, be it 'deep as Sheol or high as heaven' (RSV). The sign is a young woman who will conceive, bear a son, name him 'God with us,' Heb. *Immanuel*. It is a confirmation that the Davdic dynasty will continue; cf. II Sam 7:12-16. Our sign appears to be something similar, especially as the woman brings forth a male child who will rule." See also: D. Aune, *Revelation 6-16*, p. 688; A. Feuillet, "The Messiah and His Mother," p. 284; J. Roloff, *The Revelation of John*, pp. 146–47; D. Chilton, *Days of Vengeance*, pp. 298–99; J. Grassi, *Mary, Mother and Disciple*, p. 93. G. Beale, *The Book of Revelation*, p. 631. Cf., J. Fekkes, *Isaiah and Prophetic Traditions in the Book of Revelation*, p. 181.

[204] For a more extensive treatment on the Isaiah 7:14 background to Revelation 12, including verbal parallels between Isaiah 7:10, 14 and Revelation 12:1–2, see G. Beale, *The Book of Revelation*, pp. 630–31: "The language of 12:1-2 may be patterned partly after the typological prophecy of the mother and child in Isa. 7:10, 14" (p. 630). Furthermore, we saw earlier how the woman in Genesis 3:15 could be seen as a proto-typical queen-mother figure giving birth to a royal offspring in Davidic dynasty imagery. Since Revelation 12 is narrated as the Christian fulfillment of Genesis 3:15 with the woman associated with Eve, the possible queen-mother allusion in Genesis 3 may contribute to an interpretation of the woman of Revelation 12 as a queen mother.

Chapter Four

[1] See R. Laurentin, *The Question of Mary*, p. 106: "One must, therefore, be on one's guard against the unhappy notion which has been current in mariology since the sixteenth century, that Scripture is silent on the subject of Mary. . . . The inverse error which would *per fas et nefas* find everything explicitly in Scripture must be avoided as much." Laurentin notes how the doctrines of the Immaculate Conception and the Assumption have a basis in Scripture, but are not formally indicated. Also, R. Brown, *Biblical Exegesis and Church Doctrine* (New York: Paulist, 1985), pp. 96–97: "The very wrong question (the one unfortunately almost unfailingly posed by the very literal-minded and conservative) is: Are the Marain doctrines found in the NT?" Brown notes how an ecumenical Mariology must instead ask whether the lines of development leading to Marian doctrines proceed from the Scriptures.

[2] S. De Fiores, *Maria Presenza Viva nel Popolo di Dio*, p. 58.

[3] S. De Fiores, "Regina," pp. 1077–78.

[4] C. González, *Mariologia: Maria Madre e Discepola* (Alessandria: Edizioni Piemme, 1988), p. 240; G. Kirwin, *Nature of the Queenship*, pp. 182–83.

[5] Pius XII, *Exercise of the Royalty of Mary*, in *Papal Teachings: Our Lady* (Boston: St. Paul Editions, 1961), p. 410 (*AAS* 46 [1954] 662). He continues: "True, the marvels of heaven can be represented only through the ever imperfect words and expressions of human language; but this does not mean that, in order to honor Mary, one must adhere to a determined form of government or a particular political structure. Mary's Queenship is a supernal reality which at the same time penetrates men's innermost hearts and touches all that is spiritual and immortal in their very essence."

[6] Rene Laurentin explained already in 1970 how the idea of queenship itself has lost its meaning for much of the modern world. "La nozione stessa di regalità ha perduto il suo fascino, a vantaggio delle idee democratiche. Parallelamente ci si allontana sempre più dai modelli politici, sociologici, iconografici del passato." Laurentin goes on to stress the need to begin with a biblical theology of Mary's queenship. R. Laurentin, "Attuali Indirizzi di Teologia Mariana," *Settimana del Clero* (December 20, 1970): 4, as cited in S. De Fiores, *Maria Presenza Viva nel Popolo di Dio*, p. 58. Also, S. De Fiores, "Regina," pp. 1081.

Mary's queenship is viewed by some as a "segno di un prestigio tramontato e di un privilegio individualistico, quando non è addirittura la sacralizzazione istituzionale di un rapporto di subordinazione, vassallaggio, servilismo. La cultura odierna, radicalmente democratica e gelosa della libertà personale, deve ripensare la regalità di Maria ed esprimerla in termini consoni all'antropologia che la sorregge." S. De Fiores, "Regina," p. 1081. Furthermore, some have argued that this title is contrary to the Gospel message which emphasizes the salvation God brings to those who are humble and poor. For example, see M. Warner, *Alone of All Her Sex: The Myth and the Cult of the Virgin Mary* (New York: Alfred Knopf, 1976), pp. 104, 117: "It would be difficult to concoct a greater perversion of the Sermon on the Mount than the sovereignty of Mary and its cult . . . and equally difficult to imagine a greater distortion of Christ's idealism than this identification of the rich and powerful with the good" (p. 117). Gebera and Bingemer discuss how Mary's Assumption (and queenship) "could seem to respond more to a triumphalistic ecclesiology than to the desires and intuitions of the poorest and humblest folk." Commenting on the queenship in relationship to the Assumption, Gebara and Bingemer raise the concern: "As a dogma that sets Mary in the bosom of God's glory, making her Queen and Our Lady, might it not also distance her from the poor woman of Nazareth, with whom the humblest people can identify?" They however go on to show how the doctrine, when properly understood, actually offers great hope for the poor and the lowly (see below). I. Gebara and M. Bingemer, *Mary,* p. 120. Cf. J. Macquarrie, *Mother of All Christians* (Grand Rapids: Eerdmans, 1990), pp. 94–95.

[7] It has been noted that for some, Mary's queenship has been reduced to an honorific title not meant to suggest that she has a real unique royal role in Christ's kingdom. Cf. H. Schulz, L. Scheffczyk, G. Voss, "Beata Vergine Maria Regina," in *Il Culto di Maria Oggi* (Rome: Edizioni Paoline, 1978), p. 223; S. De Fiores, "Regina," p. 1077.

[8] S. De Fiores, *Maria Presenza Viva nel Popolo di Dio,* p. 58.

[9] S. De Fiores, "Regina," p. 1078.

[10] S. De Fiores, "Regina," p. 1078. See also S. De Fiores, *Maria Presenza Viva nel Popolo di Dio,* p. 58. De Fiores speaks of "un approfondimento teologico-pastorale, che non rinneghi i contenuti tradizionali della regalità di Maria, ma li ripresenti in una visione più ampia e più significativa per i cristiani del nostro tempo."

[11] C. González, *Mariologia,* p. 240.

[12] C. González, *Mariologia,* p. 240. "Maria è Regina solo in relazione a Gesù, in quanto sua Madre. Ma Gesù rifiutò ogni regno di questo mondo (Gv 18,36). E l'unica corona che accettò fu quella di spine, segno della sua donazione totale per noi; e l'unico titolo regale, quello della croce (Gv 19,19). Cristo regna dal legno, con una regalità che, per la sua risurrezione, non avrà più fine."

[13] E. Touron, "De María Reina a María Liberadora," *EphMar* 46 (1996): 469–70. "Pretende ser el reino y el rey escatológico *no por vía de dominación y de imposición político-económico-militar* sobre los demás hombres y pueblos, sino *por el servicio amoroso y desprendido hasta la muerte por todos,* y en especial por los pobres y hermanos pequeños del mundo: 'no he venido a ser servido sino a servir y a dar la vida en rescate por muchos' (Mc. 10,45)."

[14] A. Serra, "Regina," p. 1076.

[15] S. De Fiores, *Maria nel Mistero di Cristo e della Chiesa* (Rome: Edizioni Monfortane, 1984), p. 89.

[16] A. Serra, "Regina," p. 1076.

[17] D. Bertetto, *Maria La Serva del Signore,* p. 443: "Inoltre, come ai misteri dolorosi di Gesù è seguita l'esaltazione alla regalità universale su tutte le creature del cielo e della terra da parte del Padre (cf Fil 2,8-9), così anche alla compassione salvifica di Maria ed alla sua partecipazione all'obbedienza e alle umiliazioni del Figlio, è seguita l'esaltazione della incoronazione gloriosa, come regina dell'universo." See also: S. De Fiores, *Maria nel Mistero di Cristo,* pp. 88–90; A. Serra, "Regina," p. 1076; C. O'Donnell, *At Worship with Mary* (Wilmington, DE: Michael Glazier, 1988), pp. 153–54.

[18] "It is worth remarking that the great hymn of redemption in Philippians 2:5-11 finds echoes in the first chapter of St. Luke's gospel. Jesus took the form of a slave (Greek *doulos*, Phil. 2:7), Mary describes herself as a slave (Greek *doule*; Luke 1:38). Jesus humbled himself (Phil. 2:8), Mary describes her state as one of humiliation (Luke 1:48). God exalted Jesus (Phil. 2:9); the humble are exalted (Luke 1:52). Every knee shall bend . . . confess Jesus is Lord (Phil. 2:11); all generations will call Mary blessed (Luke 1:48). The similarity of Greek expressions throughout seems to suggest deliberate borrowing by Luke to illustrate the mystery of poverty being exalted in both Son and mother." C. O'Donnell, *Life in the Spirit and Mary* (Wilmington, DE: Michael Glazier, 1981), p. 45. Cf. C. O'Donnell, *At Worship with Mary*, pp. 153–54.

[19] In this passage, Mary is portrayed as "the spokeswoman of a theme of reversal" in which the poor and lowly become exalted. R. Brown, *Mary in the New Testament*, pp. 141–42.

[20] S. De Fiores, *Maria nel Mistero di Cristo*, p. 89.

[21] Ibid., p. 88. See also S. De Fiores, "Regina," p. 1079. "Maria partecipa al dominio di Cristo sui nemici dell'uomo, poiché—come i padri hanno convenuto in armonia con i dati evangelici—ella non ha mai conosciuto peccato (fin dall'inizio della sua esistenza, preciserà il magistero), cioè il suo io non è stato mai cattivo, alienato da Dio, schiavo dell'egoismo. . . . Con la sua assunzione la Vergine partecipa al dominio di Cristo sull'ultima nemica, la morte (1 Cor 15,26), e per mezzo del suo corpo 'spirituale' è libera perfino dalle leggi spazio-temporali (1 Cor 15,42-49)."

[22] "Like her divine Son, Mary is not a 'queen' of this world, but in the Kingdom of God, which, developing here below as an ecclesial reality, will come to completion in the heavenly Jerusalem. For this reason, the 'kingdom' of Mary, like Christ's, is not one of those shortlived [sic] powers, not rarely based on injustice and oppression, but it is—as St. Paul says—a kingdom of 'justice, peace and joy in the Holy Spirit' (Rm. 14;17)." Pope John Paul II, "Mary, Queen of the Universe, Shows the Way to Unity," in *Marian Reflections: The Angelus Messages of Pope John Paul II*, ed. D. Brown (Washington, NJ: AMI Press, 1990), p. 124. H. Schulz, et. al., "Beata Vergine Maria Regina," in *Il Culto di Maria Oggi*, p. 226. Also, p. 224: "Questo carattere regale non risulta da una pretesa di dominio a lei spettante e a lei concessa, bensì dal carattere di servizio perfetto ínsito nella sua vita. Si tratta di quella forma regale fondata sulle qualità interiori, cui la liturgia pensa anche altrove, quando afferma che 'servire Dio' equivale a 'regnare' e che la grandezza spirituale e interiore dell'uomo nasce appunto dalla sua sottomissione e dal suo servizio."

[23] A. Serra, "Regina," p. 1075: "Nella s. Vergine si adempiono a meraviglia le condizioni per aver parte attiva alla regalità di Cristo. Dall'annunciazione alla pentecoste, ella ha sposato il disegno divino sulla propria esistenza, ha prestato ascolto alla parola del Figlio, l'ha seguito nelle prove fino all'ora suprema dell'immolazione. Adesso, pertanto, in comunione con tutta la chiesa, consegue il premio di tanta fedeltà. Volendo ricorrere all'immagine dell'Apocalisse, diremmo che Cristo fa sedere la madre accanto a sè, sul suo trono (Ap 3,21), la rende compartecipe di quel divino potere che egli ha di sottomettere a sé tutte le cose (cf Fil 3,21)." Also, S. De Fiores,

Maria Presenza Viva nel Popolo di Dio, pp. 59–60. In contrast to some queen mothers of the Old Testament who used their influential position for wrongdoing (e.g., 2 Kg. 11:1–3; 2 Chron. 22:3), we see that Mary, as the new queen mother, used her unique position *for service of the kingdom.* Cf. B. Buby, *Mary of Galilee*, p. 118.

[24] *AAS* 79 (1987): 417. For more on Mary's queenship being based on her being a humble and obedient "servant of the Lord," see J. Galot, *Maria: La Donna Nell'Opera di Salveza* (Roma: Universitá Gregoriana Editrice, 1984), p. 373; B. Buby, *Mary of Galilee*, pp. 117–18; C. O'Donnell, *At Worship with Mary*, pp. 154–55; B. Fernandez, "Maria, Reina Perspectiva Escatológica," *EphMar* 46 (1996): 461; E. Touron, "De María Reina a María Liberadora," p. 479.

[25] A. Serra, "Regina," pp. 1074–75.

[26] Ibid.

[27] P. Bearsley, "Mary, The Perfect Disciple," pp. 461–504; R. Brown, *Mary in the New Testament*, pp. 125–26, 135–37, 142, 151, 157, 162, 168, 171, 174. Cf. G. Paredes, *Mary and the Kingdom of God*, pp. 206–7: "She submitted herself to the criterion for belonging to the Kingdom, which was to listen to and carry out the Word even though it could lead to something like the wound produced by a sharp sword."

[28] C. O'Donnell, *At Worship with Mary*, p. 155.

[29] S. De Fiores, *Maria Presenza Viva nel Popolo di Dio*, p. 58.

[30] ". . . non è una figura isolata ed estranea, ma colei che in comunione con tutti i cristiani partecipa alla stessa regalità di Cristo." S. De Fiores, *Maria Presenza Viva nel Popolo di Dio*, p. 59. Mary's association with the biblical symbol of the crown also illustrates this point. As we saw in chapter three, Mary may be seen in Revelation 12 in the woman crowned with twelve stars. In the New Testament, the crown serves as a symbol that expresses the eschatological gift God gives to *all* believers for their faith and perseverance (1 Pet. 5:4; James 1:12; Rev. 2:10; 2 Tim. 4:7–8). Consequently, Mary's crown should not be viewed apart from the eschatological crowning of all faithful disciples of the Lord. See S. De Fiores, "Regina," pp. 1079–80: ". . . esso non deve né allontanare Maria dalla storia degli uomini, né velare di oblio la sua realtà ugualmente biblica di serva del Signore e pellegrina nella fede" (p. 1080). A. Serra, "Bibbia," p. 265: "La corona è simbolo di trionfo, di vittoria, come si può vedere dall'impiego metaforico di questo vocabolo nel NT in genere e nell'Apocalisse in specie."

[31] M. Masciarelli, "Laici," in S. De Fiores and S. Meo, eds., *Nuovo Dizionario di Mariologia* (Milan: Edizioni San Paolo, 1986), p. 659.

[32] I. Gebara and M. Bingemer, *Mary*, p. 118. See also A. Bernard, "Simbolismo," in S. De Fiores and S. Meo, eds., *Nuovo Dizionario di Mariologia*, (Milan: Edizioni San Paolo, 1986), p. 1170. Mary is the "prima creatura a partecipare alla gloria del Cristo risorto ed esaltato alla destra di Dio, primizia della chiesa chiamata anch'essa alla gloria eterna, e tipo di ogni cristiano."

[33] S. De Fiores, *Maria Presenza Viva nel Popolo di Dio*, pp. 61–62.

[34] Ibid., p. 62.

[35] Pope John Paul II, "To Serve is to Reign," Angelus Message at Castel Gandolfo (August 23, 1981) in *L'Osservatore Romano*, English edition, 35, no. 699 (August 31, 1981): 3.

[36] M. O'Driscoll, "Mary in the Christian Life," in E. De Cea, ed., *Compendium of Spirituality*, vol. 1 (New York: Alba House, 1992), p. 116.

[37] R. Laurentin, *The Question of Mary*, p. 134.

[38] Ibid., p. 134.

[39] Ibid., pp. 133–36.

[40] Ibid., p. 133; John Paul II, *Ut Unum Sint*, no. 79 (*AAS* 87 [July–December 1995]: 968)

[41] J. Moltmann, "Editorial," in H. Kung and J. Moltmann, eds., *Mary in the Churches*, (Edinburgh: T&T Clark, 1983), pp. xiv–xv; G. Maron, "Mary in Protestant Theology," in *Mary in the Churches*, p. 46; K. Borresen, "Mary in Catholic Theology," *Mary in the Churches*, p. 55; S. De Fiores, "Mary in Postconciliar Theology," in R. Latourelle, ed., *Vatican II Assesment and Perspectives*, vol. 1 (New York: Paulist, 1988), pp. 490–92; F. Jelly, *Madonna*, p. 202; cf. F. Jelly, "Ecumenical Aspects of *Redemptoris Mater*," *Marian Studies* 39 (1988): 122.

Bibliography

Magisterial Teachings
Catechism of the Catholic Church. Rome: Urbi et Orbi
   Communications, 1994.

Conciliar Documents
Flannery, A., ed. *Vatican Council II: The Conciliar and Post
   Conciliar Documents.* Collegeville: Liturgical Press, 1992.

Papal Teaching
Benedict XIV. Bull *Gloriosae Dominae* (September 27, 1748).
   In Benedictine Monks of Solesmes, ed., *Papal Teachings:
   Our Lady*, pp. 25–29. Boston: St. Paul Editions, 1961.
Pius IX. Bull *Ineffabilis Deus* (December 8, 1854). In
   Benedictine Monks of Solesmes, ed., *Papal Teachings:
   Our Lady.* Boston: St. Paul Editions, 1961.
Pius X. Encyclical Letter *Ad Diem Illum* (February 2, 1904).
   AAS 36 (1903–1904): 449–62.
Pius XI. Encyclical Letter *Rerum Ecclesiae*
   (February 28, 1926). *AAS* 18 (1926): 5–83.
———. Encyclical Letter *Lux Veritatis* (December 25, 1931).
   AAS 23 (1931): 493–517.
Pius XII. Encyclical Letter *Mystici Corporis* (June 29, 1943).
   AAS 42 (1950): 193–248.
———. Bull *Munificentissimus Deus* (November 1, 1950).
   AAS 42 (1950): 754–71.
———. Encyclical Letter *Ad Caeli Reginam* (October, 11,
   1954). *AAS* 46 (1954): 625–40.

————. Allocution to the faithful assembled at St. Peter's (November 1, 1954). *AAS* 46 (1954): 662–66.

Paul VI. Apostolic Exhortation *Marialis Cultus* (February 2, 1974). *AAS* 66 (1974): 113–68.

John Paul II. Angelus Message at Castel Gandolfo "To Serve Is to Reign" (August 23, 1981). *L'Osservatore Romano* 35, no. 699, August 31, 1981, English edition.

————. Angelus Message at Bari "Mary, Queen of the Universe, Shows the Way to Unity" (February 26, 1984). In D. Brown, ed., *Marian Reflections: The Angelus Messages of Pope John Paul II*. Washington, NJ: AMI Press, 1990.

————. Encyclical Letter *Redemptoris Mater* (March 25, 1987). *AAS* 79 (1987): 361–433.

————. Encyclical Letter *Ut Unum Sint* (May 25, 1995). *AAS* (July–December 1995): 921–82.

Roman Congregation Documents

Pontifical Biblical Commission. *Bible and Christology* (1984). In J. Fitzmyer, *Scripture and Christology: A Statement of the Biblical Commission with a Commentary*. New York: Paulist Press, 1986.

————. *The Interpretation of the Bible in the Church* (1993). In J. Fitzmyer, *The Biblical Commission's Document "The Interpretation of the Bible in the Church": Text and Commentary*. Rome: Editrice Pontificio Istituto Biblico, 1995.

Books

Aalders, G. *Genesis*. Grand Rapids: Zondervan, 1981.

Allen, L. *The Books of Joel, Obadiah, Jonah, and Micah*. Grand Rapids: Eerdmans, 1976.

Auer, J. *The Church: The Universal Sacrament of Salvation*. Washington, D.C.: Catholic University of America Press, 1993.

Aune, D. *Revelation 1–5*. Dallas: Word, 1997.

———. *Revelation 6–16*. Nashville: Thomas Nelson, 1998.

Barrett, C. *The Gospel According to St. John*. London: SPCK, 1955.

Beale, G. *The Book of Revelation*. Grand Rapids: Eerdmans, 1999.

Beasley-Murray, G. *The Book of Revelation*. Grand Rapids: Eerdmans, 1974.

———. *John*. Waco: Word, 1987.

Benko, S. *The Virgin Goddess: Studies in Pagan and Christian Roots of Mariology*. Leiden: E. J. Brill, 1993.

Bernard, J. *The Gospel According to St. John*. New York: Charles Scribner's Sons, 1929.

Bertetto, D. *Maria la Serva del Signore*. Napoli: Edizioni Dehoniane, 1988.

Bock, D. *Proclamation from Prophecy and Pattern: Lukan Old Testament Christology* (JSNTSup 12). Sheffield Academic Press, 1987.

Boer, H. *The Book of Revelation*. Grand Rapids: Eerdmans, 1979.

Boismard, M. *St. John's Prologue*. Westminister: Newman Press, 1957.

Braun, F. *Mother of God's People*. Staten Island: Alba House, 1967.

Brodie, T. *The Gospel According to John*. New York: Oxford University Press, 1993.

Brown, R. *The Gospel According to John*. Garden City, NY: Doubleday, 1970.

———. *Biblical Reflections on Crises Facing the Church*. New York: Paulist Press, 1975.

———. *The Community of the Beloved Disciple*. New York: Paulist Press, 1979.

———. *1 John*. Garden City, NY: Doubleday, 1982.

————. *Biblical Exegesis and Church Doctrine.* New York: Paulist Press, 1985.

————. *The Birth of the Messiah.* New York: Doubleday, 1993.

————. *The Death of the Messiah.* New York: Doubleday, 1994.

————. *An Introduction to the New Testament.* New York: Doubleday, 1997.

Brown, R., et. al. *Mary in the New Testament.* Philadelphia: Fortress Press, 1978.

Buber, M. *The Prophetic Faith.* New York: Harper, 1949.

Buby, B. *Mary of Galilee.* Vol. 2. New York: Alba House, 1995.

Bultmann, R. *The Gospel of John.* Oxford: Basil Blackwell, 1971.

Caird, G. *Commentary on the Revelation of St. John the Divine.* London: A & C Black, 1984.

Cantinant, J. *Mary in the Bible.* Westminister: Newman, 1965.

Carroll, E. *Understanding the Mother of Jesus.* Wilmington, DE: Michael Glazier, 1979.

Carson, D. *The Gospel According to John.* Leicester: InterVarsity Press, 1991.

Cassuto, U. *A Commentary on the Book of Genesis.* Jerusalem: Magnes Press, 1961.

Chilton, D. *The Days of Vengeance.* Fort Worth: Dominion Press, 1987.

Clements, R. *Prophecy and Covenant.* Naperville, IL: Alec R. Alleson, 1965.

————. *Abraham and David.* London: SCM Press, 1967.

Collins, A. *The Combat Myth in the Book of Revelation.* Missoula, MT: Scholars Press, 1976.

————. *The Apocalypse.* Wilmington, DE: Michael Glazier, 1979.

Collins, J. *The Apocalyptic Imagination.* New York: Crossroad, 1984.

Corsini, E. *The Apocalypse.* Wilmington, DE: Michael Glazier, 1983.

Court, J. *Myth and History in the Book of Revelation.* London: SPCK, 1979.

Cuellar, M. *María, Madre del Redentor y Madre de la Iglesia.* Barcelona: Editorial Herder, 1990.

Cullmann, O. *The Johannine Circle.* Philadelphia: Westminister, 1975.

Danker, F. *Jesus and the New Age.* Philadelphia: Fortress, 1988.

De Fiores, S. *Maria Presenza Viva nel Popolo di Dio.* Rome: Edizioni Monfortane, 1980.

———. *Maria nel Mistero di Cristo e della Chiesa.* Rome: Edizioni Monfortane, 1984.

———. *Maria Madre di Gesù.* Bologna: Edizioni Dehoniane, 1993.

De Fraine, J. *Adam and the Family of Man.* New York: Alba House, 1965.

De Gruyter, L. *De Beata Maria Regina: Disquisitio Positivo-Speculativa.* Turin: Marietti, 1934.

Deiss, L. *Mary: Daughter of Zion.* Collegeville: Liturgical Press, 1972.

De La Potterie, I. *Mary in the Mystery of the Covenant.* New York: Alba House, 1992.

De Vaux, R. *Ancient Israel.* New York: McGraw-Hill, 1961.

Ellis, E. *The Gospel of Luke.* London: Nelson, 1966.

Ellis, P. *The Yahwist: The Bible's First Theologian.* Collegeville: Liturgical Press, 1968.

Evans, C. *Saint Luke.* London: SCM Press, 1990.

Farkas, P. *La 'Donna' di Apocalisse 12: Storia, Bilancio, Nuove Prospettive.* Tesi Gregoriana: Serie Teologia 25. Roma: Editrice Pontificia Università Gregoriana, 1997.

Fearghail, F. *The Introduction to Luke-Acts: A Study of the Role of Lk 1,1-4,44 in the Composition of Luke's Two-Volume Work*. Rome: Editrice Pontificio Istituto Biblico, 1991.

Fekkes, J. *Isaiah and Prophetic Traditions in the Book of Revelation* (JSNTSup 93). Sheffield Academic Press, 1994.

Fenton, J. *The Gospel According to John*. Oxford: Clarendon Press, 1970.

Feuillet, A. *The Apocalypse*. Staten Island, NY: Alba House, 1965.

————. *Jesus and His Mother*. Still River, MA: St. Bede's, 1984.

Fitzmyer, J. *The Gospel According to Luke*. Garden City, NY: Doubleday, 1981.

Ford, J. *Revelation*. Garden City, NY: Doubleday, 1975.

Forte, B. *Maria, La Donna Icona del Mistero*. Milan: Edizioni Paoline, 1989.

Freedman, H. *Jeremiah*. London: Soncino Press, 1950.

Galot, J. *Maria: La Donna Nell'Opera di Salveza*. Roma: Universitá Gregoriana Editrice, 1984.

Gaventa, B. *Mary: Glimpses of the Mother of Jesus*. Columbia, South Carolina: University of South Carolina Press, 1995.

Gebara, I. and M. Bingemer. *Mary: Mother of God, Mother of the Poor*. Maryknoll, NY: Orbis Books, 1989.

Giblin, C. *The Book of Revelation*. Collegeville: Liturgical Press, 1991.

González, C. *Mariologia: Maria Madre e Discepola*. Alessandria: Edizioni Piemme, 1988.

Goppelt, L. *Typos*. Grand Rapids: Eerdmans, 1982.

Gordon, C. *Ugaritic Literature*. Rome: Pontificium Istitutum Biblicum, 1949.

Gowan, D. *From Eden to Babel*. Grand Rapids: Eerdmans, 1988.

Grassi, J. *Mary, Mother and Disciple.* Wilmington, DE: Michael Glazier, 1988.

Green, J. *The Gospel of Luke.* Grand Rapids: Eerdmans, 1997.

Guimond, J. *The Silencing of Babylon: A Spiritual Commentary on the Revelation of John.* New York: Paulist Press, 1991.

Hagner, D. *Matthew 1–13.* Dallas: Word, 1993.

Hamilton, V. *The Book of Genesis.* Grand Rapids: Eerdmans, 1990.

Harrington, W. *Understanding the Apocalypse.* Washington: Corpus Books, 1969.

———. *Revelation.* Collegeville: Liturgical Press, 1993.

Hengel, M. *The Johannine Question.* London: SCM Press, 1989.

Hoskyns, E. *The Fourth Gospel.* London: Faber and Faber, 1947.

Howell, K. *Mary of Nazareth: Sign and Instrument of Christian Unity.* Santa Barbara, CA: Queenship Publishing, 1998.

Ibánez, J. and F. Mendoza. *La Madre del Redentor.* Madrid: Ediciones Palabra, 1988.

Iglesias, A. *Reina y Madre.* Madrid: PS Editorial, 1988.

Jelly, F. *Madonna: Mary in the Catholic Tradition.* Huntington, IN: Our Sunday Visitor, 1986.

Jensen, J. *Isaiah.* Wilmington, DE: Michael Glazier, 1986.

Johnson, A. *Revelation.* Grand Rapids: Zondervan, 1983.

Johnson, L. *The Writings of the New Testament.* Philadelphia: Fortress, 1986.

———. *Luke.* Collegeville: Liturgical Press, 1991.

Johnson, M. *The Purpose of the Biblical Genealogies, with Special Reference to the Setting of the Genealogies of Jesus.* Cambridge University, 1969.

Kaiser, O. *Isaiah 1–12.* Philadelphia: Westminister Press, 1983.

Kaiser, W. *The Messiah in the Old Testament*. Grand Rapids: Zondervan, 1995.

Kingsbury, J. *Matthew: Structure, Christology, Kingdom*. Philadelphia: Fortress, 1975.

———. *Matthew as Story*. Minneapolis: Fortress, 1988.

Kirwin, G. *The Nature of the Queenship of Mary*. Ann Arbor, MI: UMI Dissertation Services, 1973.

Kline, M. *Images of the Spirit*. Grand Rapids: Baker, 1980.

Koester, C. *Symbolism in the Fourth Gospel*. Minneapolis: Fortress, 1995.

Ladd, G. *A Commentary on the Revelation of John*. Grand Rapids: Eerdmans, 1972.

Lampe, G. and K. Woollcombe. *Essays on Typology*. London: SCM Press, 1957.

Laurentin, R. *The Question of Mary*. Techny, IL: Divine Word Publications, 1964.

———. *The Truth of Christmas*. Petersham, MA: St. Bede's, 1986.

———. *A Short Treatise on the Virgin Mary*. Washington, NJ: AMI Press, 1991.

Le Frois, B. *The Woman Clothed with the Sun: Individual or Collective*. Rome: Orbis Catholicus, 1954.

Lightfoot, R. *St. John's Gospel*. London: Oxford University Press, 1956.

Lukefahr, O. *Christ's Mother and Ours*. Liguori, MO: Liguori, 1998.

Luis, A. *La Realeza de Maria*. Madrid: Editorial El Perpetuo Socorro, 1942.

Macquarrie, J. *Mother of All Christians*. Grand Rapids: Eerdmans, 1990.

Maher, M. *Genesis*. Wilmington, DE: Michael Glazier, 1982.

Manelli, S. *Mariologia Biblica*. Frigento: Casa Mariana Editrice, 1989.

Marshall, I. *The Gospel of Luke*. Grand Rapids: Eerdmans, 1978.

Mays, J. *Micah*. Philadelphia: Westminister, 1976.

McHugh, J. *The Mother of Jesus in the New Testament*. London: Darton, Longman & Todd, 1975.

Meier, J. *Matthew*. Wilmington, DE: Michael Glazier, 1980.

Menninger, R. *Israel and the Church in the Gospel of Matthew*. New York: Peter Lang, 1994.

Meo, G. *La Donna che ci Salva in Cristo e nella Chiesa*. Roma: Edizioni Teologico 'Don Orione,' 1975.

Miguens, M. *Mary, 'The Servant of the Lord': An Ecumenical Proposal*. Boston: St. Paul Editions, 1978.

Miravalle, M. *Mary: Coredemptrix, Mediatrix, Advocate*. Santa Barbara, CA: Queenship Publishing, 1993.

Moloney, F. *The Gospel of John*. Collegeville: Liturgical Press, 1998.

Montague, G. *Companion God: A Cross-Cultural Commentary on the Gospel of Matthew*. New York: Paulist Press, 1989.

———. *Our Father, Our Mother: Mary and the Faces of God*. Steubenville, OH: Franciscan University Press, 1990.

Montgomery, J. *Daniel*. Edinburgh: T&T Clark, 1964.

Morris, L. *The Gospel According to John*. Grand Rapids: Eerdmans, 1995.

Mounce, R. *The Book of Revelation*. Grand Rapids: Eerdmans, 1998.

Mowinckel, S. *He That Cometh*. New York: Abingdon, 1954.

Murphy, F. *Fallen Is Babylon: The Revelation of John*. Harrisburg, PA: Trinity Press, 1998.

Nichols, A. *The Shape of Catholic Theology*. Edinburgh: T&T Clark, 1991.

Nolan, B. *The Royal Son of God*. Orbis Biblicus et Orientalis 23. Gottingen: Vandenhoeck & Rupprecht, 1979.

Nolland, J. *Luke 1–9:20*. Dallas: Word, 1989.

O'Donnell, C. *Life in the Spirit and Mary*. Wilmington, DE: Michael Glazier, 1981.

————. *At Worship With Mary: A Pastoral and Theological Study*. Wilmington, DE: Michael Glazier, 1988.

Oswalt, J. *The Book of Isaiah*. Grand Rapids: Eerdmans, 1986.

Paredes, J. *Mary and the Kingdom of God*. Middlegreen: St. Paul Publications, 1991.

Pate, C. *Four Views on the Book of Revelation*. Grand Rapids: Zondervan, 1998.

Pelikan, J. *Mary through the Centuries*. New Haven: Yale University Press, 1996.

Perkins, P. *Mary, Woman of Nazareth*. New York: Paulist Press, 1989.

Pfeiffer, R., ed. *State Letters of Assyria*. New York: Krause, 1967.

Pritchard, J., ed. *Ancient Near Eastern Texts Relating to the Old Testament*. Princeton University Press, 1955.

Rahner, K. *Mary: Mother of the Lord*. New York: Herder and Herder, 1963.

Ratzinger, J. *Daughter Zion*. San Francisco: Ignatius Press, 1983.

————. *Principles of Catholic Theology*. San Francisco: Ignatius Press, 1987.

Robert, A. and A. Feuillet. *An Introduction to the Old Testament*. New York: Desclee Company, 1968.

Robinson, H. *Corporate Personality in Ancient Israel*. Philadelphia: Fortress Press, 1964.

Robinson, J. *Redating the New Testament*. Philadelphia: Westminister, 1976.

Roloff, J. *Revelation*. Minneapolis: Fortress Press, 1993.

Rossier, F. *L'intercession entre les hommes dans la Bible hébraique* Orbis Biblicus et Orientalis, 152. Gottingen: Vandenhoeck & Ruprecht, 1996.

Rowland, C. *Revelation*. London: Epworth Press, 1993.

Sailhamer, J. *The Pentateuch as Narrative.* Grand Rapids: Zondervan, 1992.

Schaeffer, F. *Genesis in Space and Time.* Downers Grove: InterVarsity Press, 1972.

Schillebeeckx, E. *Mary, Mother of the Redemption.* New York: Sheed and Ward, 1964.

Schnackenburg, R. *The Gospel According to John.* New York: Crossroad, 1982.

Schussler Fiorenza, E. *The Book of Revelation: Justice and Judgment.* Philadelphia: Fortress, 1985.

Semmelroth, O. *Mary, Archtype of the Church.* New York: Sheed and Ward, 1963.

Shaw, C. *The Speeches of Micah: A Rhetorical-Historical Analysis* (JSOTSup 145). Sheffield Academic Press, 1998.

Sloyan, G. *John.* Atlanta: John Knox, 1988.

Smith, R. *Micah-Malachi.* Waco: Word, 1984.

Spires, D. "Yahwist Patterns: Genesis 2:4b-25:11." Ann Arbor: UMI Dissertation Services, 1978.

Strauss, M. *The Davidic Messiah in Luke-Acts: The Promise and Its Fulfillment in Lukan Christology* (JSNTSup 110). Sheffield Academic Press, 1995.

Stigers, H. *A Commentary on Genesis.* Grand Rapids: Zondervan, 1976.

Swete, H. *The Apocalypse of St. John.* London: MacMillan, 1906.

Tannehill, R. *The Narrative Unity of Luke-Acts.* Philadelphia: Fortress, 1986.

———. *Luke.* Nashville: Abingdon Press, 1996.

Thompson, L. *Revelation.* Nashville: Abingdon Press, 1998.

Thompson, W. *The Struggle for Theology's Soul.* New York: Crossroad Herder, 1996.

Thurian, M. *Mary: Mother of All Christians.* New York: Herder, 1964.

Vawter, B. *The Conscience of Israel.* New York: Sheed and Ward, 1961.

———. *On Genesis.* Garden City, NY: Doubleday, 1977.

Von Rad, G. *Genesis.* London: SCM Press, 1972.

Wainwright, A. *Mysterious Apocalypse: Interpreting the Book of Revelation.* Nashville: Abingdon Press, 1993.

Wainwright, E. *Towards a Feminist Critical Reading of the Gospel According to Matthew.* Berlin: Walter de Gruyter, 1991.

Warner, M. *Alone of All Her Sex: The Myth and the Cult of the Virgin Mary.* New York: Alfred Knopf, 1976.

Watts, J. *Isaiah 1-33.* Waco: Word, 1985.

———. *Word Biblical Themes: Isaiah.* Dallas: Word, 1989.

Wenham, G. *Genesis 1-15.* Waco: Word, 1987.

Wescott, B. *The Gospel According to St. John.* Grand Rapids: Eerdmans, 1950.

Westermann, C. *Genesis: A Practical Commentary.* Grand Rapids: Eerdmans, 1987.

Wildberger, H. *Isaiah 1-12.* Minneapolis: Fortress, 1991.

Wolff, H. *Micah: A Commentary.* Minneapolis: Ausburg, 1990.

Wright, C. *Knowing Jesus Through the Old Testament.* Downers Grove, IL: InterVarsity Press, 1992.

Wright, N. *The New Testament and the People of God.* Minneapolis: Fortress, 1992.

———. *Jesus and the Victory of God.* Minneapolis: Fortress, 1996.

Young, E. *The Book of Isaiah.* Vol. 1. Grand Rapids: Eerdmans, 1965.

Articles

Ackerman, S. "The Queen Mother and the Cult in the Ancient Near East." In K. King, ed., *Women and Goddess Traditions*, pp. 179–209. Minneapolis: Fortress, 1997.

Ahern, B. "The Mother of the Messiah." *Marian Studies* 12 (1961): 27–48.

Andreasen, N. "The Role of the Queen Mother in Israelite Society." *CBQ* 45 (1983): 179–94.

Aragon, R. "La Madre con el Niño en la Casa: Un Estudio Narratologico." *EphMar* 43 (1993): 47–60.

Bastero de Eleizalde, J. "Fundamentos Cristológicos de la Realeza de María." *EstMar* 51 (1986): 201–11.

Bauer, D. "Son of David." In J. Green, et. al., eds., *Dictionary of Jesus and the Gospels*, pp. 766–69. Downers Grove, IL: InterVarsity Press, 1992.

Bearsley, P. "Mary the Perfect Disciple: A Paradigm for Mariology." *TS* 41 (1980): 461–504.

Ben-Barak, Z. "The Status and Right of the *Gebira*." *JBL* 110 (1991): 23–34.

Besutti, G. "Litanie." In S. De Fiores and S. Meo, eds., *Nuovo Dizionario di Mariologia*, pp. 682–90. Milano: Edizioni San Paolo, 1996.

Blanco, S. "Sola Scriptura o Hermeneutica Biblica." *EphMar* 44 (1994): 393–411.

Boismard, M. "The Apocalypse." In A. Robert and A. Feuillet, eds., *Introduction to the New Testament*, pp. 691–722. New York: Desclee Company, 1965.

Borresen, K. "Mary in Catholic Theology." In H. Kung and J. Moltmann, eds., *Mary in the Churches*, pp. 48–58. Edinburgh: T&T Clark, 1983.

Branick, V. "Mary in the Christologies of the New Testament." *Marian Studies* 32 (1981): 27–50.

Brown, R. "Hermeneutics." In R. Brown, et al., eds., *The Jerome Biblical Commentary*, pp. 605–23. London: Geoffrey Chapman, 1968.

———. "The Annunciation to Mary, the Visitation, and the Magnificat (Luke 1:26-56)." *Worship* 62 (1988): 249–59.

———. "God's Future Plans for His People: The Messiah." In R. Brown, et. al., eds., *The New Jerome Biblical Commentary*, pp. 1310–15. London: Geoffrey Chapman, 1989.

———. "Hermeneutics." In R. Brown, et. al., eds., *The New Jerome Biblical Commentary*. Englewood Cliffs, New Jersey: Prentice Hall, 1990: 1146–65.

Brueggemann, W. "David and His Theologian." *CBQ* 30 (1968): 156–81.

———. "Kingship and Chaos: A Study in Tenth Century Theology." *CBQ* 33 (1971): 317–32.

———. "From Dust to Kinship." *ZAW* 84 (1972): 1–18.

———. "Weariness, Exile and Chaos: A Motif in Royal Authority." *CBQ* 34 (1972): 19–38.

Cahill, J. "Hermeneutical Implications of Typology." *CBQ* 44 (1982): 266–81.

Carmignac, J. "La Sainte Vierge par Rapport à la Royauté, au Règne et au Royaume de Dieu." *EtMar* 41 (1984): 49–59.

Carroll, E. "Our Lady's Queenship in the Magisterium of the Church." *Marian Studies* 4 (1953): 29–81.

Cazelles, H. "La Mere du Roi-Messie dans L'Ancien Testament." In *Mater et Ecclesia*. Vol. 5, pp. 39–56. Congressus Mariologicus Lourdes, 1958.

———. "Note d'exegese sur Apocalypse 12." In *Mater Fidei et Fidelium Marian Library Studies*. Vol. 17–23 (1985–1991): 131–34.

De Boer, P. "The Counselor." VTSup 3, pp. 42–71. Leiden: Brill, 1955.

De Fiores, S. "Mary in Postconciliar Theology." In R. Latourelle, ed., *Vatican II Assessment and Perspectives*, Vol. 1, pp. 469–539. New York: Paulist, 1988.

———. "Regina: Approfondimento Teologico Attualizzato." In S. De Fiores and S. Meo, eds., *Nuovo Dizionario di Mariologia*, pp. 1077–82. Milan: Edizioni San Paolo, 1996.

De La Potterie, I. "The Spiritual Sense of Scripture." *Communio* 23 (1996): 738–56.

Del Moral, A. "La Realeza de Maria Segun La S. Escritura." *EphMar* 12 (1962): 161–82.

———. "Santa Maria, La Guebiráh Mesiánica." *Communio* (Spanish edition) 13 (1980): 3–70.

Donnelly, M. "The Queenship of Mary During the Patristic Period." *Marian Studies* 4 (1953): 82–108.

Egan, J. "The Unique Character of Mary's Queenship." *Thomist* (1962): 293–306.

Feinberg, C. "The Virgin Birth in the Old Testament." *BS* 119 (1962): 251–58.

Fenton, J. "Our Lady's Queenship and the New Testament Teachings." In *Alma Socia Christi*, pp. 68–86. Rome: Academia Mariana, 1950.

Fernandez, B. "Maria, Reina Perspectiva Escatológica." *EphMar* 46 (1996): 453–62.

Feuillet, A. "The Messiah and His Mother According to Apocalypse XII." In *Johannine Studies*, pp. 257–92. Staten Island, NY: Alba House, 1964.

———. "L'heure de la Femme (Jn 16,21) et l'heure de la Mère de Jesus (Jn 19,25-27)." *Biblica* 47 (1966): 169–84, 361–80.

Gaffney, P. "Mary in the Book of Revelation." *Queen of All Hearts* (July–August, 1998): 14–15.

Gambero, L. "La Regalità di Maria nel Pensiero dei Padri." *EphMar* 46 (1996): 433–52.

Gaventa, B. "Glimpses of Mary." *BibRev* (April 1996): 17, 48.

Gray, T. "God's Word and Mary's Royal Office." *MI* 13 (1995): 372–88.

Guinan, M. "Davidic Covenant." In D. Freedman, ed., *The Anchor Bible Dictionary*. Vol. 2. pp. 69–72. New York: Doubleday, 1992.

Hahn, S. "Prima Scriptura: Magisterial Perspectives on the Primacy of Scripture for Catholic Theology and Catechetics." In *The Church and the Universal Catechism: Proceedings from the 15th Convention of the Fellowship of Catholic Scholars*, pp. 83–116. Steubenville, OH: Franciscan University Press, 1992.

Harrison, R. "Queen Mother." In G. Bromiley, ed., *The International Standard Bible Encyclopedia*, pp. 7–8. Grand Rapids: Eerdmans, 1988.

Hill, W. "Our Lady's Queenship in the Middle Ages and Modern Times." *Marian Studies* 4 (1953): 134–69.

Hurtado, L. "Christ. " In J. Green, et. al., eds., *Dictionary of Jesus and the Gospels*, pp. 106–17. Downers Grove, IL: InterVarsity Press, 1992.

Jelly, F. "Ecumenical Aspects of *Redemptoris Mater*." *Marian Studies* 39 (1988): 115–29.

———. "Roman Catholic Ecumenical Response to the Theme ('Ut Unum Sint,' PT. 3)." *Marian Studies* 48 (1997): 129–37.

Jensen, J. "The Age of Immanuel." *CBQ* 41 (1979): 220–39.

———. "Isaiah 1–39." In R. Brown, et. al., eds., *The New Jerome Biblical Commentary*, pp. 229–44. London: Geoffrey Chapman, 1989.

Jones, J. "Subverting the Textuality of Davidic Messianism: Matthew's Presentation of the Genealogy of the Davidic Title." *CBQ* 56 (1994): 256–72.

Kearney, P. "Gen. 3:15 and Johannine Theology." *Marian Studies* 27 (1976): 99–109.

Kirwin, G. "Mary's Salvific Role Compared with That of the Church." *Marian Studies* 25 (1974): 29–43.

Klassen-Wiebe, S. "Matthew 1:18-25." *Interpretation* 46 (1992): 392–95.

Kosmala, H. "*gabhar*." In G. Botterweck and H. Ringgren, eds., *Theological Dictionary of the Old Testament*, pp. 367–82. Grand Rapids: Eerdmans, 1975.

Kugelman, R. "Mariology and Recent Biblical Literature." *Marian Studies* 18 (1967): 122–34.

Kuper, H. "Kinship Among the Swazi." In A. Radcliffe-Brown and D. Forde, eds., *African Systems of Kinship and Marriage*, pp. 86–110. London: Oxford University, 1950.

Laberge, L. "Micah." In R. Brown, et. al, eds., *The New Jerome Biblical Commentary*, pp. 249–54. London: Geoffrey Chapman, 1989.

Lamirande, E. "The Universal Queenship of Mary." *Marianum* 16 (1954): 481–507.

La Sor, W. "Prophecy, Inspiration and *Sensus Plenior*." *TynBul* 29 (1978): 49–60.

Le Frois, B. "The Woman Clothed with the Sun." *AER* 76 (1952): 161–80.

Lodi, E. "Preghiera Mariana." In S. De Fiores and S. Meo, eds., *Nuovo Dizionario di Mariologia*, pp. 1023–31. Milano: Edizioni San Paolo, 1996.

Luis, A. "La Realeza de María en los Últimos Veinte Años." *EstMar* 11 (1951): 221–51.

Maggioni, B. "La Madre del Mio Signore: Esegesi di Lc 1,39-45." *Theotokos* 5 (1997): 11–24.

Manicardi, E. "L'annuncio a Maria. Lc 1,26-38 nel Contesto di Lc 1,5-80." *Theotokos* 4 (1996): 297–331.

Maron, G. "Mary in Protestant Theology." In H. Kung and J. Moltmann, eds., *Mary in the Churches*, pp. 40–47. Edinburgh: T&T Clark, 1983.

Martin, R. "The Earliest Messianic Interpretation of Genesis 3:15." *JBL* 84 (1965): 425–27.

Masciarelli, M. "Laici." In S. De Fiores and S. Meo, eds., *Nuovo Dizionario di Mariologia*, pp. 644–61. Milan: Edizioni San Paolo, 1996.

May, E. "Mary in the Old Testament." In J. Carol, ed., *Mariology.* Vol. 1. pp. 56–62. Milwaukee: Bruce, 1955.

———. "The Problems of a Biblical Mariology." *Marian Studies* 11 (1960): 21–59.

McKane, W. "The Interpretation of Isaiah VII 14-25." *VT* 17 (1967): 208–19.

McKenzie, J. "The Literary Characteristics of Genesis 1-3." *TS* 15 (1954): 541–72.

———. "Royal Messianism." *CBQ* 19 (1957): 25–52.

———. "The Mother of Jesus in the New Testament." In H. Kung and J. Moltmann, eds., *Mary in the Churches*, pp. 3–11. Edinburgh: T&T Clark, 1983.

Merrill, E. "Covenant and the Kingdom: Genesis 1-3 as Foundation for Biblical Theology." *CTR* (1987) 1.2: 295–308.

Molina, F. "La Mujer en Apocalipsis 12." *EphMar* 43 (1993): 367–92.

Moltmann, J. "Editorial." In H. Kung and J. Moltmann, eds., *Mary in the Churches*, pp. xii–xv. Edinburgh: T&T Clark, 1983.

Moore, K. "The Queenship of the Blessed Virgin in the Liturgy of the Church." *Marian Studies* 3 (1952): 218–27.

Moriarty, F. "Isaiah 1–39." In R. Brown, et. al., eds., *The Jerome Biblical Commentary*, pp. 265–82. Englewood Cliffs, NJ: Prentice Hall, 1968.

Most, W. "The Queenship of Mary." In S. Matthews, ed., *Queen of the Universe*, pp. 176–86. Saint Meinrad, IN: Grail Publications, 1957.

Mullaney, T. "Queen of Mercy—Part I." *AER* 126 (1951): 412–19.

———. "Queen of Mercy—Part II." *AER* 127 (1952): 31–35.

———. "Queen of Mercy—Part III." *AER* 127 (1952): 117–22.

Neirynck, F. "ΕΙΣ ΤΑ ΙΔΙΑ: Jn 19,27 (et 16,21)." In F. Van Segbroeck, ed., *Evangelica*, pp. 356–65. Leuven University Press, 1982.

Nelson, R. "David: A Model for Mary in Luke?" *BTB* 18 (1988): 138–42.

Nicolas, M. "La Vierge-Reine." *RevThom* 45 (1939): 1–29, 207–31.

———. "Nature de la Souverainete de Marie." In *Mater et Ecclesia*. Vol. 5, pp. 191–99. Congressus Mariologicus Lourdes 1958.

North, C. "Immanuel." In G. Buttrick, et. al., eds., *The Interpreter's Dictionary of the Bible*. Vol. 2. pp. 685–88. New York: Abingdon, 1962.

O'Connor, J. *"Maria Regina: Presidential Address." Marian Studies* 39 (1988): 52–59.

O'Driscoll, M. "Mary in the Christian Life." In E. De Cea, *Compendium of Spirituality*. Vol. 1. pp. 105–17. New York: Alba House, 1992.

Peinador, R. "Propedeutica a la Enciclica 'Ad Caeli Reginam.'" *EphMar* 5 (1955): 291–316.

———. "Fundamentos Escriturísticos de la Realeza de María." *EstMar* 17 (1956): 27–48.

Peirce, F. "The Protevangelium," *CBQ* 13 (1951): 239–52.

Peña, N. "La Encíclica 'Ad Caeli Reginam' y su influjo en el magisterio posterior." *EphMar* 46 (1996): 485–501.

Perez, G. "La Visitacion: El Arca Nuevamente en Camino." *EphMar* 43 (1993): 189–211.

Perkins, P. "Mary in the Gospels: A Question of Focus." *Theology Today* 56 (1999): 297–306.

Pikaza, X. "La Madre de mi Señor (Lc 1,43)." *EphMar* 46 (1996): 395–432.

Pozo, C. "La Regalità di Maria in una Prospettiva Biblica." *Mater Ecclesiae* 9 (1973): 134–37.

Preuss, H. "*zera'.* " In G. Botterweck and H. Ringgren, eds., *Theological Dictionary of the Old Testament.* Vol. 4. pp. 143–62. Grand Rapids: Eerdmanns, 1980.

Reist, T. "Mary, Queen and Mediatrix." *Miles Immaculatae* 22 (1986): 269–83.

Rigaux, B. "The Woman and Her Seed in Genesis 3:14–15." *Theology Digest* 6 (1958): 25–31.

Roschini, G. "Breve commento all'Enciclica 'Ad Caeli Reginam.'" *Marianum* 16 (1954): 409–32.

Rowe, S. "An Exegetical Approach to Gen. 3:15." *Marian Studies* 12 (1961): 49–79.

Ruger, H. "On Some Versions of Genesis 3:15, Ancient and Modern." *The Biblical Translator* 27 (1976): 105–10.

Salgado, J. "La Royauté ou Souveraineté Universelle de la Très Sainte Vierge Marie." *Divinitas* 33 (1989): 173–88, 286–309.

Schearing, L. "Queen." In D. Freedman, ed., *The Anchor Bible Dictionary.* Vol. 5, pp. 583–88. New York: Doubleday, 1992.

Schmidt, F. "The Universal Queenship of Mary." In J. Carol, ed., *Mariology.* Vol. 2, pp. 493–549. Milwaukee: Bruce Publishing Company, 1957.

Schulz, H., L. Scheffczyk, and G. Voss, "Beata Vergine Maria Regina." In W. Beinert, ed., *Il Culto di Maria Oggi,* pp. 222–26. Rome: Edizioni Paoline, 1978.

Scullion, J. "An Approach to the Understanding of Isaiah 7:10–17." *JBL* 87 (1968): 288–300.

Segalla, G. "Il Bambino con Maria sua Madre in Matteo 2." *Theotokos* 4 (1996): 15–27.

Senior, D. "Matthew 2:1–12." *Interpretation* 46 (1992): 395–99.

Serra, A. "Maria, nell'Apocalisse." In L. Crociani, ed., *Maria, Madre di Dio*, pp. 197–218. Florence: Ss. Annunziata, 1991.

———. "Bibbia." In S. De Fiores and S. Meo, eds., *Nuovo Dizionario di Mariologia*, pp. 209–80. Milan: Edizioni San Paolo, 1996.

———. "Regina: Ulteriore Elaborazione Biblica sulla Regalità di Maria." In S. De Fiores and S. Meo, eds., *Nuovo Dizionario di Mariologia*, pp. 1073–77. Milan: Edizioni San Paolo, 1996.

Smalley, S. "John's Revelation and John's Community." *Bulletin of the John Rylands University Library* 69 (1986–1987): 549–71.

Smith, E. "The Scriptural Basis for Mary's Queenship." *Marian Studies* 4 (1953): 109–17.

Spanier, K. "The Queen Mother in the Judean Royal Court: Maacah—A Case Study." In A. Brenner, *A Feminist Companion to Samuel and Kings*, pp. 186–95. Sheffield Press, 1994.

Stanley, D. "The Mother of My Lord." *Worship* 34 (1960): 330–32.

Stendahl, K. "Quis et Und?" In G. Stanton, ed., *The Interpretation of Matthew*, pp. 69–80. Edinburgh: T&T Clark, 1995.

Stevenson, G. "Conceptual Background to Golden Crown Imagery in the Apocalypse of John (4:4, 10; 14:14)." *JBL* 114 (1995): 257–72.

Stuhlmueller, C. "The Mother of Emmanuel (Is. 7:14)." *Marian Studies* 12 (1961): 165–204.

Touron, E. "De María Reina a María Liberadora." *EphMar* 46 (1996): 465–82.

Unger, D. "The Use of Sacred Scripture in Mariology." *Marian Studies* 1 (1950): 67–116.

Valentini, A. "Editoriale: L'Annuncio a Maria." *Theotokos* 4 (1996): 281–95.

———. "Lc 1,39-45: Primi Inizi di Venerazione della Madre del Signore." *Marianum* 58 (1996): 329–52.

———. "Il 'Grande Segno' di Apocalisse 12: Una Chiesa ad Immagine della Madre di Gesu." *Marianum* 59 (1997): 31–63.

Vandry, F. "The Nature of Mary's Universal Queenship." *Marian Studies* 4 (1953): 13–28.

———. "The Nature of Mary's Universal Queenship." *Laval Thèologique et Philosophique* 10 (1954): 54–66.

Vanni, U. "La Decodificazione 'Del Grande Segno' in Apocalisse 12,1-6." *Marianum* 40 (1978): 121–52.

Viviano, B. "The Gospel According to Matthew." In R. Brown, et. al, eds., *The New Jerome Biblical Commentary*, pp. 630–74. London: Geoffrey Chapman, 1989.

Weinfield, M. "*berith*." In G. Botterweck and H. Ringgren, eds., *Theological Dictionary of the Old Testament*, pp. 253–79. Vol. 2. Grand Rapids: Eerdmanns, 1980.

Witfall, W. "The Breath of His Nostrils." *CBQ* 36 (1974): 237–40.

———. "Gen. 3:15—A Protevangelium?" *CBQ* 36 (1974): 361–65.

Witherington, B. "Lord." In J. Green, et. al, eds., *Dictionary of Jesus and the Gospels*, pp. 484–92. Downers Grove, IL: InterVarsity Press, 1992.

Wolff, H. "The Kerygma of the Yahwist." *Interpretation* 20 (1966): 131–58.

———. "A Solution to the Immanuel Prophecy in Isaiah 7:14–8:22." *JBL* 91 (1972): 444–56.